MICK WALKER

CROWOOD

First published in 2004 by
The Crowood Press Ltd
Ramsbury, Marlborough
Wiltshire SN8 2HR

www.crowood.com

British Library Cataloguing-in-Publication Data
A catalogue record for this book is available from the British Library.

ISBN 1 86126 708 8

Typeface used: Bembo.

Typeset and designed by
D & N Publishing, Hungerford, Berkshire.

Printed and bound in Great Britain by CPI Bath.

Contents

Acknowledgements

The name 'Matchless' was for many years the hallmark of what was the very best in British motorcycle manufacturing regarding performance, the quality of its innovative designs and its value for money. The Collier family was responsible for both the creation and the success of the marque; though sadly, when the Colliers passed on, so did the fortunes of this once great name. Even during the immediate post-war era following the end of hostilities in 1945, Matchless continued to mean the very best in British craftsmanship. The decline really began after the last of the Colliers, Charlie, died in August 1954, the business increasingly suffering from, as one commentator so aptly put it, 'the substitution of Engineers, Craftsmen, Motorcyclists and Businessmen by snobs, bookkeepers, whiz kids and paper for work'. What this meant was that in little over a decade, the Plumstead works went from being a shining star of the British motorcycle industry, to liquidation in 1966. There was a short period during which everyone thought that Manganese Bronze and Dennis Poore would continue with the Matchless (and AJS) name, but this didn't happen, and gloom once more descended upon Plumstead. And soon the once great hive of industry became derelict, and was then simply demolished, the site eventually becoming yet another suburban housing estate with not a single feature that was recognizable or remembered of the company that the Colliers and their loyal workforce had striven so hard to build up in the first half of the twentieth century.

So I feel my task in compiling *Matchless – The Complete Story* has been to celebrate just what this great marque achieved during its lifetime. A truly vast number of good people have also in some way contributed to the finished product, by way of photographs, memories or information. This list includes Tony Henderson and Steven Whitebread of The Arrow and Hawk Owners Group; John and Rose Rourke who compiled their memories in a booklet published in November 1987; Barry and John Pook, for helping with several old brochures; Eric Green for wartime pictures; Les Harris for inviting me to the launch of the reborn G80 in 1987; and ex-AMC raceshop man Tom Mortimer, a good friend of many years. Others in no particular order of merit are Colin Seeley, Tony Charnock, Bill Little, Andy Ward, George Ward (no relation), Billy Woodnough, Peter Tester, Malcolm Wheeler, Alan Shepherd, John Surtees, Eric Downey, Mick Hemmings, Don and Derek Rickman, Graham Boothby, Nick Nicholls, John Cooper, Cheffins auctioneers of Cambridge, and Richard Walker.

Mick Walker, February 2004

1 The Colliers

The Collier family was behind the Matchless marque, and like several others, the Colliers came to motorcycles via pedal cycles. During the late nineteenth century Henry Albert Collier, together with his wife Louisa and their two young sons Harry and Charlie, were living in rented accommodation in Plumstead, south-east London, right next to the Royal Arsenal in Woolwich; in fact, Henry Collier was employed as an engineer in the gun shop of the Royal Arsenal. His first foray into cycle manufacture was made in his spare time whilst he was still working for the Royal Arsenal, and it was to these early pedal cycles that Collier senior first applied the Matchless name. However, confusingly, during the early 1880s Nahum Soloman, owner of the Bicycle & Tricycle Supply Association of Holburn Viaduct, East London, had registered the Matchless name. Soloman continued to market Matchless cycles until the mid-1880s, when the manufacturing rights and Matchless name were acquired by the Coventry-based Singer concern. But the Matchless trademark was not re-registered after 1889 and thus lapsed by default.

'Henry Collier & Sons, Cycle Manufacturers'

Henry Collier now joined forces with John Watson, who had built up a business designing and manufacturing machinery for steam laundry. The idea behind the Watson & Collier partnership was to manufacture bicycles. Henry Collier suggested using the Matchless name, but Watson was worried about the rights to the name; however, after an enquiry at the national Patent Office they discovered that Singer's right to the name had lapsed, and so in July 1891 'Watson & Collier' applied for its use and were subsequently able to officially register the name and trademark. This trademark – No. 157,538 Class 2, 1891 – comprised a gear wheel being held in one hand, whilst being measured with a caliper in the other. The Watson & Collier partnership did not last long, however, and in 1892 John Watson had decided that two wheels were not for him, and that he wanted to concentrate on his laundry business. So Henry Collier became the sole proprietor and owner of the new trademark. At first he retained the trading title of Watson & Collier, though moved his cycle business to St James' Place (now Burrage Place) in Plumstead – and the firm prospered, thanks to his hard work. By now he was manufacturing pedal cycles in reasonable numbers, besides carrying out general engineering work, including subcontract work for his former employer the Royal Arsenal. During the next few years the business continued to expand, and by 1899 Henry Collier's financial position was such that he was able to purchase a freehold house for his family, as well as a business premises in Herbert Street, Plumstead, having moved out of the St James' Place location.

Eldest son Harry joined his father in the business as soon as he reached fifteen years of age; Charlie, now fourteen, was still at school, but wanted to do the same thing. Both sons were super-keen cyclists, and spent every spare hour either cycling or helping their father in his business. As a mark of his appreciation, Henry Collier commissioned a local signwriter to remove the 'Watson & Collier' sign and replace it with a new one that read 'Henry Collier & Sons, Cycle Manufacturers'.

The year 1899 was also significant for several other reasons. First, Charlie Collier made his debut in competitions, and won his very first race riding one of his father's machines; later that same year he was victorious in the Woolwich Cycling Club's 10 Mile Championship. Most significant of all was that Harry Collier had read an article in *The English Machinist* that gave drawings and details of a powered version of a pedal cycle, pioneered by the French Werner brothers. So Harry and Charlie decided to make their own engine based on the information provided in the article. But as Peter Hartley revealed in his *Matchless* history published in 1981: 'When the machine was ready and they came to try it on local roads, … they met with the same difficulties encountered by the Werner brothers on their machine.'

These problems centred upon what pioneer motorcyclists referred to as 'side slip'. This was due to the combination of poor road surfaces (often simply dirt) and the high centre of gravity associated with having the engine located over the front wheel. So the question was asked, where should one mount the engine for maximum stability and within the mechanical constraints of a production motorcycle? So, together with the efforts of others throughout Europe, the Colliers spent the next few months carrying out experiments of all possible engine positions.

The Early Years of Matchless Motorcycles

The first of what could be termed a Matchless racing motorcycle arrived in 1901, when Charlie Collier took part on one of the firm's prototype machines. This was followed in 1902 by the very first production Matchless motorcycle: it used a 2¾hp aiv (automatic inlet valve) MMC (based on the French de Dion) power unit, fitted centrally within the frame tubes of a conventional Matchless pedal cycle; the specification included a Linguemare spray-type carburettor, whilst the ignition was by battery/coil. The price was £45. (MMC stood for 'Motor Manufacturing Company', owned by Harry J. Lawson.)

By 1903, motorcycle racing was being held at tracks all over Great Britain – mainly existing cycle venues. Local ones for the Colliers were Canning Town, Crystal Palace and Herne Hill, and by now both Harry and Charlie Collier were taking part on a regular basis.

The 1904 Matchless motorcycle range was displayed by Henry Collier & Sons at the National Cycle & Motor Cycle Show at Crystal Palace during the final week of November 1903. Two models were displayed: the 2¾hp MMC-engined machine described earlier, together with a larger, 3½hp (85 × 85mm) engine (again manufactured

The very first Matchless motorcycle built by brothers Harry and Charlie Collier in 1899, using information gleaned from an article in The English Machinist.

by MMC). Also on display was the new Matchless forecar, available to order with either an MMC or de Dion engine. The forecar was basically a three-wheeler built around the Matchless motorcycle, but with twin front wheels and a single rear wheel; the cost was £65. Henry Collier & Sons still manufactured Matchless pedal cycles during this era, and also acted as south-east London distributors for Rudge Whitworth bicycles.

By 1904 Matchless was able to boast a smart works racing team of riders, the two Collier brothers having been joined by Bert Colver. This squad proceeded to accumulate an impressive number of victories and lap records at venues such as Canning Town and Crystal Palace. Each of the three riders played a vital role, with Charlie proving the best rider, Harry the design genius, and Bert Colver the engine tuner. In their search for improvements, during 1905 the Colliers contacted JAP (John A. Prestwich) of Tottenham, north London, and began using this company's V-twin engines for both production and racing machines. Also during 1905 Charlie Collier made the first of many successful attempts on the British 1-Hour motorcycle speed record.

In 1906, the series-production range of Matchless motorcycles increased to five models. Two of these were 3½hp (500cc) singles, one powered by a 427cc (80 × 85mm) White & Poppe engine with the famous T-shape head, the other by a 482cc (85 × 85mm) Belgian Antoine power unit; this used side valves and weighed only 140lb (63.5kg) fully equipped. Next was a new 2½hp (350cc) Matchless Ladies' Model, powered by a 316cc aiv JAP unit; and the remaining two models were both v-twins – a 5hp 745cc (77 × 80mm) Antoine side-valve, and the top-of-the-range 6hp 731cc aiv JAP.

Early Racing Successes

On Tuesday 28 May 1907 the first ever Isle of Man TT (Tourist Trophy) race was held; it was divided into two classes, for singles and twins. Both Harry and Charlie Collier entered the race on 432cc (85 × 76mm) JAP ohv singles, and although Harry Collier set the fastest lap at 41.81mph (67.27km/h), his younger brother won the event in 4hr 8min 8.2sec, an average speed of 38.33mph (61.67km/h). This was despite suffering broken front forks!

Charlie Collier with an early V-twin Matchless, c. 1907.

Throughout 1907 Matchless machines continued in this successful vein, both in pure racing events and record breaking. And as a fitting conclusion to the season – by far the best in the history of the fledgling marque to date – on 6 September 1907 Henry Collier's wife Louisa gave birth to their third son, christened Herbert William Collier. Almost from the moment he was born the latest addition to the family was referred to as 'Young Bert'.

Only a few weeks after that historic TT victory another event of great importance took place: the official opening on the 17 June 1907 of the newly constructed Brooklands circuit near Weybridge in Surrey. Although a car meeting was held shortly after the opening, the first motorcycle affair did not take place until 20 April 1908. Amongst the twenty-one entrants for this were the two Collier brothers, Charlie and Harry. Even though neither won, Charlie still managed to come home third, riding a machine with an engine that was half the size of the 984cc NLG Peugeot of race winner Will Cook.

Charlie Collier pictured in 1909 with one of his JAP-engined V-twin racers.

Harry Collier put himself in the record book when over the 5 and 6 May 1909, riding an 862cc (76 × 95mm) JAP-engined Matchless V-twin, he succeeded in breaking the 24-hour motorcycle speed record (despite numerous problems) by covering 775 miles 1,340yd (1,248km 225m) at an average speed of 32.32mph (52km/h). Considering this included a stop of no less than 1hr 32min 42sec due to 'fatigue', one can only be amazed at the endurance of both man and machine in those far-off days. Later, those taking part in such feats of endurance used a team of several riders, rather than a single competitor.

Then in the autumn, on 23 September 1909 to be exact, Matchless scored their second TT victory: this time it was Harry Collier's turn. Riding a 738cc (85 × 65mm) JAP-engined V-twin, Harry won in 3hr 13min 37sec, at a new race record speed of 49mph (78.8km/h).

The various racing and record-breaking successes helped the Matchless marque establish itself as one of the premier British motorcycle brands. And so sales of the series-production models forged ahead as the first decade of the twentieth century came to an end.

It was Charlie Collier's turn to taste a TT victory in 1910. The event staged on Thursday 26 May had attracted a record entry, with no fewer than eighty-three riders gathered at the start of St John's. The race was a triumph for the Plumstead factory, with Charlie Collier winning in 2hr

48min 23sec at an average speed of 60.63mph (97.55km/h), brother Harry finishing runner-up, and the third member of the team, Bert Colver, coming in tenth.

At the end of November 1910, H. Collier & Sons displayed what *The Motor Cycle* described as a 'full range of models' at London's Olympia Show. By now the entire range sported JAP power units, both singles and V-twins, built by over fifty employees now working at the works in Herbert Road, Plumstead.

In 1911 the American Indian rider Jake de Rosier crossed the Atlantic to do battle with the British on their home ground. In point of fact it turned out to be a contest between de Rosier and Matchless-mounted Charlie Collier. The two first met in the Isle of Man, where the American came out on top: first Charlie Collier ran out of petrol, and then he was disqualified. Subsequently came a series of highly promoted 'Match Races', with Charlie Collier's 998cc Matchless-JAP and de Rosier's 994cc Indian fighting it out around the Brooklands speed bowl. These races resulted in a 2-1 victory for America – but Collier and Matchless had the final laugh, as the combination set new flying kilometre records at over 91mph (146km/h).

Above-Average Motorcycles for the Marketplace

Against this backcloth of competition came intensive development, in which Matchless forged ahead, building what was described by Richard Rosenthal in the February 2004 issue of *The Classic Motor Cycle* as:

> A range of above-average motorcycles for the market place, including singles and V-twins with side or overhead valves, and by 1912, a six-speed variable gear system intended for sport but also available on roadsters.

During this period the Colliers and JAP co-operated on engine design, including in 1912 a 496cc ohv V-twin weighing a mere 46lb (21kg). At the same time Matchless built, albeit on JAP lines, their first engine, a 488cc (85.5 × 85mm) single. Other notable Matchless models of the same year included the Model S V-twin side-valve with a choice of either 771cc or 965cc JAP V-twin power units. Another was the Model 7B, another JAP V-twin, with choice of engine sizes.

The variable gear mentioned earlier, which had been such a successful feature of the 1911 Matchless race effort, was introduced as a production component on two Matchless models in the 1912 range. This gear, which was in fact a modified version of the well-known Gradua gear invented by Freddie Barnes, was manufactured by the Colliers under licence from Zenith, and was fitted to the Matchless Model SG and Model 6. The Matchless series production of the Gradua variable gear featured two levers in a quadrant on the side of the fuel tank, as on the Matchless works racing bikes, not the 'coffee-mill' control handle layout employed in the Zenith-Gradua models.

As far as competitive events were concerned, in 1912 Matchless gained successes in trials, rather than road racing, with awards in such events as the ACU's Spring One Day Trial and the ACU Six Days Trial (the forerunner of the ISDT).

A New Factory

By the end of 1912 the production facilities of Herbert Road, Plumstead, had reached a point where they were restricting further growth, and so, at the beginning of 1913, H. Collier & Sons moved to a new, larger facility in Burrage Grove, Plumstead, within a stone's throw of Woolwich Arsenal Railway Station. The move was completed in a few weeks early in the new year, whilst new offices, together with a showroom, were opened in Plumstead Road.

By now the company was emerging as a leading player, and the board of directors was as follows: Henry Collier, managing director; Harry Collier, works manager; Charlie Collier, manager of the Finishing Department; A. Walker, sales manager/company secretary; S.H. Turner, stores department manager. Unlike the situation of the British motorcycle industry years' later in the 1950s and 1960s, being a director meant that you were very much a practical man who was deeply

LEFT: Postcard showing the five members of the board of directors in 1913: H.H. Collier managing director and founder, C.R. Collier, H.A. Collier, A. Walker and S.H. Turner.

BELOW: 1915 Matchless 8B with 7hp 993cc (82 × 94mm) ohiv MAG-engined V-twin. The overhead inlet valves were each operated by enclosed pushrod and rocker, and for the first time on a motorcycle Renold 'silent chain' primary drive; the Model 8B had made its debut in 1914.

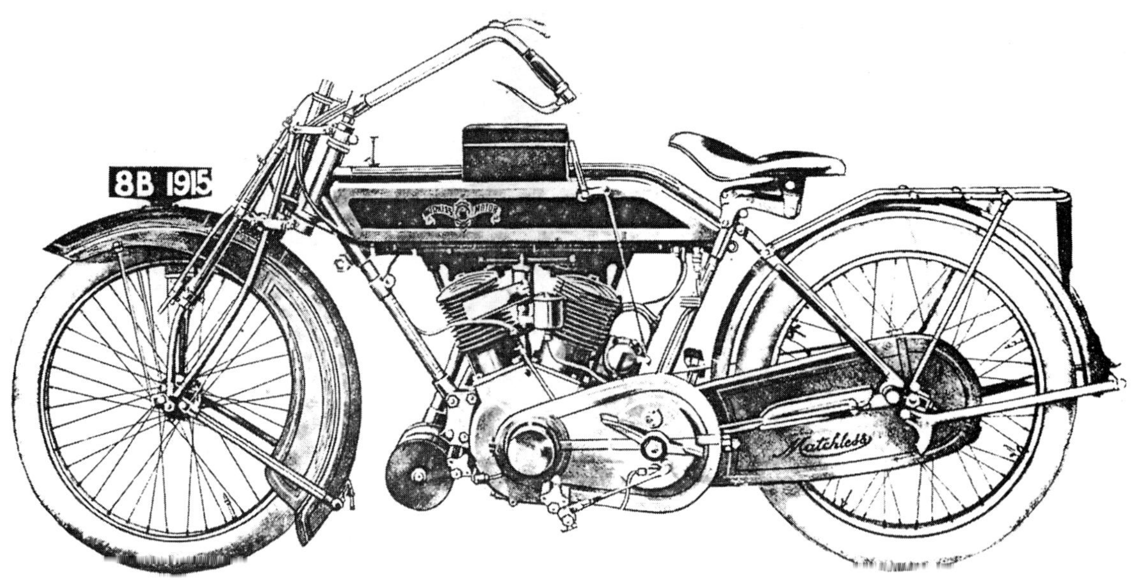

involved in the everyday running of the company you represented. Certainly there was no room for what today would be described as a non-executive director. In the pioneering days at the beginning of the twentieth century you actually toiled at the coalface!

In the months prior to the outbreak of World War I on the 4 August 1914, Matchless ceased production of their smaller-engined models to concentrate on a range of three 8hp V-twins, including the Model 8B with a Swiss-made MAG 10e engine. This bike featured enclosed chain drive, three-speed countershaft gearbox, kick-starter, and internal expanding drum rear brake. The 8B/2 also featured interchangeable wheels. But despite listing a military model, Matchless

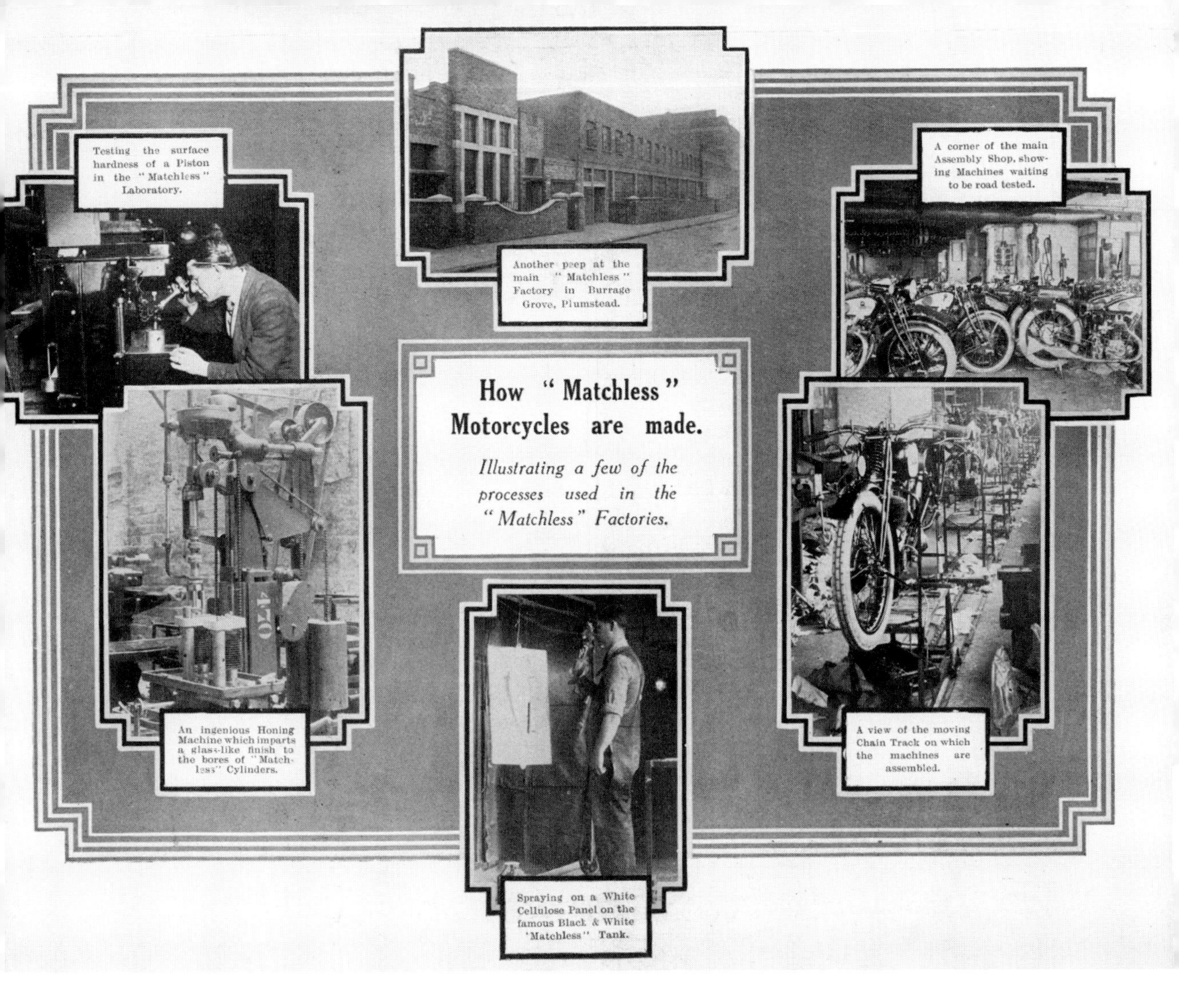

ABOVE: Various illustrations from the 1920s, showing some of the processes used at the Matchless works during the production cycle.

RIGHT: A 1960 advertisement showing the latest G50 496cc racer, together with Charlie Collier, TT winner in 1907 and 1910, reminding everyone of the marque's great history.

received no significant orders, and the Plumstead works, noted for its fine engineering quality, was instead largely put over to munitions and aircraft components when the British authorities ended all civilian motorcycle manufacture in 1916.

As for the Colliers, in typical fashion they threw their entire energies into this new task of helping the war effort, in readiness for the day when, with the conflict over, peacetime and thus motorcycle production would resume.

2 Inter-War Singles

Returning to civilian motorcycle production in 1919, the Colliers continued with a range of big V-twins (*see* Chapter 3) including the 8B/2 (renamed the Victory) and the Model H outfit, a revised 8B/2 with swinging-arm frame and electric lighting. Then in 1923 the Matchless badge reappeared on a single, the L2, with a 348cc (71 × 85mm) Blackburne side-valve engine and three-speed Sturmey-Archer gearbox. This engine sported outside flywheels and a detachable cylinder head. Its most significant feature, however, was the fitment of a saddle fuel tank (the first ever on a Matchless) over the top frame tube. Harry Collier had also been working on a new three-fifty overhead camshaft single, which it was hoped would be ready for production for 1924.

Marque Models in the Early 1920s

In the autumn of 1923 Matchless launched its 1924 range of models; one of these was the 348cc side-valve single fitted with a Matchless 'own make' engine with the revised designation of L/3, available with or without a sidecar. There was also the production version of the experimental overhead cam single, known as the L/R Super Sports 350. This had long stroke dimensions of 69 × 93mm.

The L/R had its inclined overhead valves positioned transversely across the cylinder as opposed to the traditional fore and aft arrangement on other single-cylinder motorcycle engines. The single overhead camshaft was driven by a vertical shaft and bevel gears at the rear of the cylinder head. A single exhaust port on the nearside (left) matched the inlet port on the offside (right). The reasoning behind Harry Collier's decision for the unusual location of the camshaft drive was to provide optimum cooling for the cylinder head, particularly in the area of the exhaust valve. The camshaft was carried on roller bearings in an aluminium casing, supported above the detachable head. Other features of the sporting L/R included a three-speed gearbox and mechanical duplex oil pump.

Another of the 1924 Matchless range to use one of the company's own engines was the Model M. This featured a 591cc low compression, single-cylinder, side-valve 'slogger' of an engine. Intended mainly for sidecar work, it featured a mechanical oil pump and three-speed gearbox. In solo trim the Model M cost £67 10s; with a factory-supplied sidecar fitted, the price rose to £85.

At the beginning of November 1924 Matchless announced the range of motorcycles for the 1925 model year. The 348cc side-valve single had been re-designated L/4, restyled, and offered in three variants: the standard solo; the solo with engine enclosure; and with a sidecar. Matchless considered this to be its mainstream model for the masses. The models M and L/R continued largely unchanged, except that now the M could be supplied in any one of four sidecar choices, as well as a solo machine. The sidecar options were single seat, double seat, commercial box and airmail box.

One sad occasion in 1925 was the death of the company's founder and managing director Henry Herbert Collier; however, his three sons Harry, Charlie and Herbert Junior (Bert) had already shown that they were well capable of continuing in their father's footsteps.

New Bikes for 1926

The big news for 1926 was the introduction of a two-fifty. Known as the Model R, this was a side-valve with a displacement of 246cc (62.5 × 80mm). Costing £34 13s, it was very competitive on price and, with its smart black enamel and gold lining, became a popular choice. Other features included a magneto mounted at the front of the crankcase and chain-driven from the engine shaft; a rigid frame; girder front forks with shock absorbers; a mechanical oil pump bolted directly on to the timing case, and with no outside delivery pipe; fully adjustable handlebars; and an internal expanding rear brake.

The larger-engined 348cc side-valve single, the L/4, was unchanged, except for the provision of improved brakes.

There was a new single for 1926: this was the L/S. This featured an identical chassis and cycle parts to the L/4, but was fitted with a 498cc side-valve engine, again with mechanical pump lubrication.

The 348cc overhead-cam L/R sporting single was also considerably updated for the 1926 season. The camshaft now featured double row bearings at either end, whilst the rockers were mounted on roller bearings. The entire valve operating mechanism, including the casings, had not only been shortened, but also strengthened, thus improving both reliability and service life. Although a potent-looking affair, the earlier version of this power unit had not always proved robust enough when ridden on the limit; hence the changes for 1926.

The engine of the L/R had also been modified because Matchless had decided to contest the 1926 Isle of Man TT; their rider on this occasion was Reg Barber who worked in the firm's experimental department. But neither he nor two private owners, Norman Scott and E.A. Todd, were destined to have much success. All three machines were essentially standard production examples, the only real change being the fitment of separate oil tanks under the saddles – plus, of course, more minor modifications to make them suitable for racing, such as exhaust, gearing, and the removal of road-going equipment. But a mixture of crashes and mechanical glitches affected all three riders throughout practice and the race, and none of them managed to finish.

In 1926 Matchless also took part in trials; for example, nineteen-year-old Bert Collier, the youngest of the Collier brothers, rode one of eleven Matchless models in the famous London to Edinburgh, gaining a gold medal. In fact this event was a great success for the marque, with Matchless riders winning no fewer than nine golds! And in August that year an official Matchless team took part in the International Six Days Trial. The three riders, all mounted on 348cc overhead cam L/R singles, were Freddie Neill, H. Quilter and the Australian rider, Roy Charman, and all won gold medals; Freddie Neill was also a member of the Great Britain B team in the International Trophy, thereby gaining more glory for Matchless because the team finished runners-up.

Marque Models for the Late 1920s

When the 1927 model range was announced in the autumn of 1926, the Model R two-fifty side-valve had been singled out for special attention as it had proved a huge sales success that year. So the development team at Plumstead had carried out a couple of useful modifications and also widened the choice for buyers. One of the technical changes was that the magneto now ran at half engine speed from the crankshaft by way of a totally enclosed and automatically lubricated drive chain. In addition to the standard model, a de luxe Model R was made available, featuring a Lycelt Aero spring saddle, magneto shield, brakes on both wheels, and 2.75 x 25 Dunlop Cord tyres in place of the standard models 2½ × 24 rubber. The de luxe version cost an additional £3 10s.

The larger side-valve singles, the 348cc L/4 and 498cc L/S, were replaced for 1927 by what was known as the new T series: the three-fifty was the T/2, whilst the five-hundred was simply the Model T. Apart from the engine sizes, the two newcomers were identical except for gearing, carburettor jetting and the like. Compared with the outgoing L/4 and L/5 SV singles, the new

T/2 and T machines were much more compact and modern-looking. Furthermore the new frame, together with the increased width and strength of the front forks, meant that the handling and roadholding, both for solo or when a sidecar was attached, was much improved. Not only this, but wider section tyres (and matching mudguards) gave the newcomers an altogether more sturdy, cobby appearance.

The engine unit fitted to the T-series machines was considerably improved, with increased finning area, particularly on the cylinder head; this was to improve the cooling, particularly in the area of the exhaust port. Other features of the T-series included a roller-bearing big end; a rear-mounted magneto; an aluminium alloy piston; a pilgrim mechanical oil pump; and the automatic lubrication of the magneto drive chain. There was also a new type of Sturmey Archer clutch, with six springs instead of the earlier single spring. This new clutch (featuring a shock absorber) was a significant improvement both in terms of operating and in reliability, being much lighter to handle. The T/2 and T also employed a Sturmey Archer three-speed hand-change gearbox.

The Pilgrim mechanical oil pump featured a sight feed glass incorporated directly on the timing cover. In practice this meant that only a single oil pipe was required, the feed pipe that ran from the oil tank to the suction side of the pump, the lubricant being supplied to the engine direct from the pump via a port drilled through the timing cover into the crankcase. There was also an automatic lubrication supply direct to the magneto drive chain: as on the Model R two-fifty side-valve single, this was totally enclosed, thanks to an extension of the primary chaincase.

De luxe versions of both the new three-fifty and the five-hundred side-valve models were available at an additional cost of £4 10s 0d each.

The Model V

The most exciting newcomer to the Matchless catalogue for 1927 was without doubt the Model V. A pre-production prototype of this machine had been campaigned by the young Bert Collier at the annual MCC (Motor Cycling Club) High Speed Trials in September 1926. Designed by older brother Harry Collier, this sportster employed a new 495cc (85.135 × 85.5mm) overhead valve engine.

The valves of the Model V were operated by long duralmin pushrods and overhead rockers. Roller-ended cam levers were used in the timing gear in conjunction with high-lift cams, while the rockers were carried on roller bearings. The entire rocker gear and pushrods were totally enclosed, and grease nipples were provided for lubrication purposes. In addition these received oil mist from the crankcase, thanks to the Pilgrim pump.

Other features included an aluminium piston with floating gudgeon pin, a special steel connecting rod (machined and polished all over), roller big-end bearing, polished inlet and exhaust ports, and heavy-duty flywheels. Running on a compression ratio of 6.6:1, maximum power was 22.5bhp at 4,800rpm. A Model V was speed-tested by ISDT star Freddie Neill, and achieved a speed of 75mph (120km/h) over the flying-start quarter-mile in late 1926. Because of its performance, the Model V featured a close-ratio Sturmey Archer three-speed gearbox with ratios of 4.9:1; 6.5:1 and 10.7:1; the spring-girder forks were from the Model M/3S V-twin sports model, whilst 7in (178mm) drum brakes were specified for each wheel.

The first half of 1927 saw Harry Collier working tirelessly to provide the following year's model range, including the singles, with an entirely new look. The first time the public could judge his work, at least in the metal so to speak, came at the annual London Show at Olympia in November 1927. As Peter Hartley said:

> One of the most significant features of the new range was the adoption of black enamelling on the cycle parts, 'saddle type' welded-steel petrol tanks with white enamelled side panels, and diamond-pattern frames on all models except the Model M 591cc ohv and Model R 246cc side-valve machines.

It is worth noting that these last two models remained unaltered for 1928, with the exception of a new-type silencer.

Other Models for 1928

A new Matchless machine for the 1928 season was the Model T/S. Offered as a 'sports' bike, this featured a twin-exhaust port, ohv, single-cylinder engine with a mechanically operated oil pump. Sharing the same 348cc (69 × 93mm) dimensions as the overhead-cam Model L/R2 (previously L/R) which continued in production, its power was transmitted to the rear wheel via a three-speed Sturmey Archer gearbox. Retailing at £46 10s 10d solo, or £61 for a factory-fitted sidecar, potential buyers had the option of either conventional rider's footrests or footboards.

Another newcomer was the Model R/S, which employed a 246cc (62.5 × 80mm) side-valve engine. Its general specification, except for engine size, was identical to that of the new Model T/S 348cc overhead valve sports bike. Meanwhile the Model V had been replaced by the Model V/2, the 495cc ohv engine now featuring a fashionable twin-port cylinder head, which had become popular; otherwise it was largely unchanged. A technical feature of the 1928 Models T/S, L/R2 and V/2 was that they now came with graphite-filled grooves in their valve guides, this being aimed at providing improved lubrication.

Matchless Motorcycles (Colliers Ltd)

The combination of their father's death in 1925, and the continuing expansion of the Matchless concern, led the three Collier brothers to take the decision to become a public limited company.

The 1929 L/R2

Engine:	Air-cooled sohc vertical single, detachable cylinder head; cam driven by bevel gears; single port
Bore:	69mm
Stroke:	93mm
Displacement:	347cc
Compression ratio:	6.04:1; high compression 9.7:1 to special order
Lubrication:	Twin gear oil pumps
Ignition:	Lucas magneto
Carburettor:	Amal two-lever type
Primary drive:	Chain
Final drive:	Chain
Gearbox:	Three-speed hand-change, close ratio
Frame:	All-steel tubular construction
Front suspension:	Matchless girder forks
Rear suspension:	Rigid, unsprung
Front brake:	Drum, 8in
Rear brake:	Drum, 8in
Tyres:	Palmer Flexicord 3.25 × 26 front and rear

General Specifications

Wheelbase:	54in (1,372mm)
Ground clearance:	4in (102mm)
Seat height:	26½in (673mm)
Fuel tank capacity:	2gal (9ltr)
Dry weight:	287lb (130kg)
Maximum power:	16.5bhp @ 5,000rpm (with standard CR)
Top speed:	75mph (120km/h)

For the 1929 model year, all Matchless models were given a saddle tank, including the side-valve R/S two-fifty.

1928 Matchless T/3 (347cc) and T/4 (498cc) side-valve singles were popular and reasonably priced.

The 1929 V/S

Engine:	Air-cooled sv vertical single; enclosed valve gear; aluminium piston; roller bearing big end
Bore:	85.5mm
Stroke:	101.6mm
Displacement:	583cc
Compression ratio:	4.8:1
Lubrication:	Pilgrim mechanical oil pump; with incorporated sight-feed glass
Ignition:	Lucas magneto
Carburettor:	Amal
Primary drive:	Chain
Final drive:	Chain
Gearbox:	Three-speed, hand-change, Sturmey-Archer
Frame:	All-steel tubular construction
Front suspension:	Matchless girder forks
Rear suspension:	Rigid
Front brake:	Drum, 8in
Rear brake:	Drum, 8in
Tyres:	3.25 × 26 front and rear

General Specifications

Wheelbase:	54in (1,372mm)
Ground clearance:	5in (227mm)
Seat height:	26½in (673mm)
Fuel tank capacity:	2gal (9ltr)
Dry weight:	406lb (184kg)
Maximum power:	N/A
Top speed:	60mph (97km/h)

V/2 engine: note the webbed crankcase and heavily finned exhaust port.

The L/R2 Super Sports with overhead camshaft engine.

The 1929 Matchless 347cc (69 × 93mm) Sports model. Coded T/S and T/R, the latter could be supplied at additional cost with modified engine, including a direct oil feed to the big-end bearing and the V/2 (racing)-type timing gear.

The V/2 (495cc ohv) and L/R2 (347cc ohc) were identical except for the engine unit. This is the former, which had a guaranteed speed of 85mph (137km/h) – but with tuning could achieve over 100mph (160km/h).

And so on the 13 November 1928, the firm was registered on the London Stock Exchange under the name Matchless Motorcycles (Colliers) Ltd.

Earlier the same month Matchless had displayed their range for the 1929 model year. Essentially there were ten basic models, eight of which were singles:

- R/S 246cc sv;
- R/3 246cc ohv two-port;
- T/4 347cc sv;
- T/3 498cc sv;
- T/S 347cc ohv two-port;
- L/R2 347cc ohc;
- V/2 495cc ohv two-port;
- V/5 586cc sv.

Racing versions of the Model T/R 347cc ohv twin-port, and Model V/2 495cc ohv twin-port, were available for an additional £5 on the price of the standard version. At least one V/2 was bored out to 598cc for competition use.

Models for the Early 1930s

The 1930 Matchless model line-up saw the introduction of the narrow-angle V-twin Silver Arrow four-hundred (*see* Chapter 4). Compared with this, the singles seem far less exciting, although they actually comprised much of the marque's sales during the 1930s. They consisted of:

- R/4 246cc sv;
- R/6 246cc ohv two-port;
- T/5 498cc sv;
- T/S2 347cc ohv two-port;
- V/3 495cc ohv two-port;
- V/3 495cc Special Super Sports;
- V/6 586cc sv.

For the 1930 model year all the side-valve singles models (except the 347cc model) featured detachable cylinder heads with enclosed valves, and in common with the ohv singles, dry sump lubrication.

The lubrication system found on the latest single-cylinder Matchless models was an industry leader for both design and efficiency in a motorcycling world that had been brought up on inefficient total loss lubrication. At the offside (right) of the crankcase a longitudinally positioned oil pump was to be found at the base of the timing case. This consisted of a double-ended steel plunger, featuring both reciprocating and rotary action, achieved thanks to a worm on the crank mainshaft, and a stationary guide-stud mating with a specially shaped 'slot cut', as *The Motor Cycle* described it, in the circumference of the plunger – the plunger cylinder having been machined in aluminium. One end of this plunger forced oil from the tank via the worm gear, through the mainshaft to the crankpin and the big-end assemblies.

Lubricating oil was also circulated via the camshaft bearing to an annular passage situated between the cylinder base and the vertically split crankcase. From there it passed through a trio of 1/16in (1.5mm) holes to the cylinder walls and piston, and in a third direction via a restricted passage to the timing case. When the oil reached a certain level on the timing case, it overflowed into the crankcase. The function at the other end of the plunger was to retrieve the oil that had built up in the crankcase up through a pipe, the mouth of which was situated just below the bottom of the flywheel circumference. In this way it was not possible for the oil in the crankcase to rise above this level. It was then forced back through a filter into the oil tank.

Other features of the 1930 model range included redesigned cylinder heads on ohv engines; modified fuel tanks with quickly detachable 'Griptight' filler caps; revised silencers; new handlebars; brake diameter of 6in (152mm) front and 8in (203mm) rear on all models except 246cc; increased cams and camshaft pinion width; and a series of channels inside the primary chaincase, resulting in reduced mechanical noise and longer chain life. Also during 1930, inclined cylinders (often referred to as 'slopers') had been introduced by several rival manufacturers to their single-cylinder ranges – most notably the Ariel marque. This had proved a sales success, so for the 1931 season Matchless followed suit.

The 1931 Matchless single-cylinder line-up was as follows:

- R/7 246cc sv (62.5 × 80mm);
- D 347cc sv (69 × 93mm);
- D/S 246cc ohv (62.5 × 80mm);
- C 586cc sv (85.5 × 101.6mm);
- C/S 495cc ohv (85.5 × 85.5mm).

The most inexpensive model was the 246cc R/7 side-valve with vertical cylinder. With electric lighting equipment it weighed in at under 224lb (102kg), thus enabling it to take advantage of the £1 10s taxation limit for motorcycles of that weight or under – this legislation having been reintroduced in July 1930 after pressure from the motorcycle industry. It should be remembered that by now the British economy was beginning to feel the first effect of the financial meltdown caused by the Wall Street crash of October 1929.

At the other end of the single-cylinder range was the C/S, powered by a 495cc ohv engine with an inclined cylinder and twin-port head. It was also noteworthy in having a four-speed Sturmey-Archer gearbox.

The majority of the 1931 Matchless range were available in either standard or de luxe guises; the latter had electric lighting, speedometer, a handlebar-mounted instrument panel and sometimes wider-section tyres in addition to the usual fitments. Also notable in 1931 was the introduction of the big 'M' logo for the fuel tanks, whilst on all models – except the budget-priced R/7 – the tanks were chrome-plated with white side panels, on to which were attached the chrome-plated 'M' badges.

Early in 1931 Matchless acquired the Wolverhampton-based A. J. Stevens & Co. Ltd, the manufacturers of the famous AJS brand name after it went into liquidation. And so began a new chapter in the history of both Matchless and AJS, the latter outside the scope of this book, except to say that certainly in the post-war years, as time went by the two brands became ever closer in the products they offered, until the words 'badge engineering' meant precisely what it said. But in the early 1930s these days were long into the future: suffice it to say that AJS production was moved to Plumstead, thus marking the beginning of an ever-closer association between these two great marques.

A view from the other side of the fence, so to speak, of the AJS takeover was provided by Gregor Grant in his 1969 book *AJS: The History of a Great Motorcycle*:

> The Wolverhampton factory was closed down and AJS moved to the home of its new masters, H. Collier & Sons Ltd, at Plumstead, near Woolwich – surely the most unsuitable site for a motorcycle factory it would be possible to find. Located just off one of the busiest roads in the London area, deliveries by road from the Midlands' component makers were usually delayed.

A New Light Five-Hundred

With the economic gloom becoming ever greater, at the very height of the depression Matchless announced the 1932 range in September 1931. As *The Motor Cycle* commented, 'Value for money, as was announced last week, is the most striking feature of the new Matchless range' – and no more so than the new light five-hundred single, the D/S. Powered by a 498cc inclined cylinder side-valve engine, this machine not only cost a mere £35, but also came into the £1 10s taxation category, due to its overall weight of only 222½lb (101kg), complete with electric lighting.

Many asked how such a machine was possible, but as *The Motor Cycle* said: 'The answer is to be found in the machine itself – in its design. From stem to stern the new "Light 500" has been designed for low-cost production and low weight.' But there was certainly no drop in quality, as was exemplified by the frame: this was of the duplex loop type, and for lightness and strength it was constructed from aircraft-quality buffed tubing.

Lubrication was of the previously described Matchless dry-sump system, with a 3pt (1.7ltr) oil tank mounted on the seat pillar tube. The system, which was exactly the same throughout the 1932 range, incorporated a simple fabric filter through which all the oil had to pass after being pumped out of the engine. Another feature of the 1932 range was the use of both Burman and Sturmey-Archer gearboxes, whilst a face-cam type of engine shock absorber had been standardized on all the single-cylinder models except the two-fifty side-valve. Yet another was the use of Invastrut pistons: these were specified in preference to a less expensive piston of conventional design, their advantage being that close clearances could be employed without fear of seizing, which meant far less piston slap.

The 1933 Range

As *The Motor Cycle* reported in their 29 September 1932 issue: 'Although the Matchless range of machines for 1933 remains substantially the same as for last year, all models have undergone a thorough revision, which has not only resulted in several mechanical improvements, but has also caused the machines to assume a subtle air of distinction.' This was particularly true of the smaller-

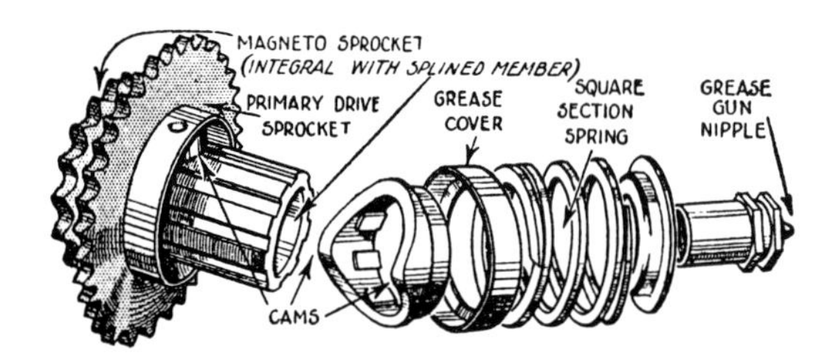

Engine shock absorber standardized on all 1932 singles, except the two-fifty side-valve.

capacity models, since the imminent lifting of the tax-by-weight regulations had resulted in the use of more substantial components: wider and sturdier front brakes, larger section handlebars, larger tyres and deeper finning on the cylinder barrels. Most noticeable to the casual observer, and applicable to all models, was the alteration in the design and finish of the fuel tanks, the chromium tank with its white panels replaced by a businesslike, gold-lined black finish with an embossed chromium 'M' at the forward end.

For 1933 all the single cylinders had their engines inclined in the frame, but except for minor details the engines themselves were unaltered in design, with the exception of an improved big-end bearing.

Other features throughout the range included 'clean' handlebars with Bowden fittings, including ring-type switches, and Lucas magdyno lighting equipment with a flush-fitting instrument panel on all but the two-fifty side-valve model, which had a Maglita set.

The D Series

The D series of singles included the two-fifty sv, the two-fifty ohv twin port, the three-fifty single and twin port, plus the five-hundred sv, and these were the backbone of Matchless sales. All, with the exception of the smallest engine size, featured 6½in ribbed-section chromidium brakes of a new design (with chrome-plated water shields) and oil-bath primary chaincases featuring a detachable chromium jointing strip.

Another distinctive feature was the fitment of a plated and rustless (or so it was claimed!) strip to the domed mudguards.

On ohv models four-speed gearboxes were now standard, with foot control optional – without extra charge. The machines could also be supplied with upswept exhaust pipes and tubular silencers instead of the usual low pipes/fishtail silencers. There was also a new oil-bath chaincase, the two halves being bound together by an aluminium band, with packing material between the band and the outer lips of the chaincase portions.

The 1933 Single-Cylinder Range and Prices

D 347cc sv £35 (lighting and horn £5 7s 6d extra)
D/6 347cc ohv single port £38 (lighting and horn £5 7s 6d extra)
D/5 Light 500 497cc sv £36 (lighting and horn £5 7s 6d extra)
33/D7 246cc sv £34 (lighting £5 5s extra)
33/D7 246cc de luxe sv £42 10s (fully equipped)
33/D2 246cc ohv twin-port £40 10s (lighting £5 10s extra)
33/D2 246cc de luxe twin-port £49 (fully equipped)
33/D3 347cc twin-port £41 10s (lighting £5 10s extra)
33/D3 347cc de luxe twin-port £50 (fully equipped)
33/D6 347cc single port £40 10s (lighting £5 10s extra)
33/D6 347cc de luxe single port £49 (fully equipped)
33/D5 497cc sv £38 10s (lighting £5 10s)
33/D5 497cc sv de luxe £47 (fully equipped)
33/CS 491cc ohv twin-port £49 10s (lighting £5 10s extra)
33/CS 491cc ohv de luxe twin-port £58 10s (fully equipped)
33/C 586cc sv £17 10s (lighting £5 10s)
33/C 586cc sv de luxe £56 10s (fully equipped)

The de luxe specification consisted of tank instrument panel, electric lighting, speedometer, electric horn, oil indicator, air filter and ignition switch. There was also a range of no fewer than six sidecars available, known under the following numbers: 1, 3, 8, 8A, 13 and 16.

In mid-March 1933 *The Motor Cycle* reported the arrival of a new, light five-hundred ohv Matchless, with the designation 33/D80 Sports:

> Inexpensive speed is the aim of the Matchless designers in a new, light, compact ohv five-hundred which is about to be placed on the market. For the £43 15s demanded, the purchaser obtains, it is claimed, a mount that is not only really lively as regards acceleration, but capable of 80mph [130km/h].

Complete with Lucas magdyno electric lighting (£5 10s extra) and horn, the new Matchless weighed 300lb (136kg). This was an unusually low figure for a twin-port five-hundred with full equipment, and as a consequence the bike had a notably high power-to-weight ratio. A foot-change, four-speed Burman gearbox (ratios of 4.86, 6.23, 7.3 and 12.9:1), a 2gal (9ltr) fuel tank, 7in brakes on both wheels, and a duplex frame, were just part of the specification. When road-tested by *The Motor Cycle*, the new lightweight five-hundred received an excellent report in their 6 April 1933 issue; the tester obtained a maximum speed of 82mph (132km/h) and said:

> The latest product of the Plumstead factory, the sports 498cc ohv Matchless, is a motor cycle of which its designer can be justly proud. In appearance, with its black and chromium finish, it looks most businesslike – and in performance it is even more businesslike. In fact the only real criticism is that carburettion at low engine speeds resulted in a rather uncertain tickover, and made starting difficult in spite of the decompressor. The trouble was somewhat accentuated by unsuitable gearing of the kickstarter pedal in relation to the engine.

The 1934 Model 34/F Sports

Engine:	Air-cooled, ohv vertical single; enclosed valve gear; 'Lo-Ex' alloy piston; roller-bearing big end
Bore:	62.5mm
Stroke:	80mm
Displacement:	246cc
Compression ratio:	6:1
Lubrication:	Dry sump, duplex horizontal reciprocating rotary plunger pump
Ignition:	Magneto
Carburettor:	Amal two-lever, semi-automatic with horizontal mixing chamber
Primary drive:	Chain
Final drive:	Chain
Gearbox:	Three-speed, hand-change
Frame:	Duplex cradle, with twin front down-tubes
Front suspension:	Girder forks
Rear suspension:	Rigid
Front brake:	Internal expanding drum type
Rear brake:	Internal expanding drum type
Tyres:	Firestone Cord 3.25 × 26 front and rear

General specifications

Wheelbase:	N/A
Ground clearance:	N/A
Seat height:	N/A
Fuel tank capacity:	N/A
Dry weight:	N/A
Maximum power:	14bhp
Top speed:	68mph (109km/h)

New Two-Fifties for 1934

Following the introduction of the high performance, lightweight D80 five-hundred in spring 1933, on the eve of the Olympic Show in November 1933 two new Matchless 246cc models were launched: the side-valve 34/F7, and the overhead valve 34/F Sports. Both shared bore and stroke dimensions of 62.5 × 80mm. The factory claimed '50–60mph' (80–100km/h) for the side-valve, and '65–70 mph' (105–115km/h) for the ohv sportster. Both shared many features and were of particularly modern appearance – although both had hand- instead of foot-change gearboxes. Otherwise the 1934 model range, announced a few weeks earlier at the beginning of October 1933, saw detail improvements rather than any notable major change.

New Sports 250 model (34/F) introduced for the 1934 season.

Matchless Models for the Mid-Thirties

The Matchless programme for 1935 was announced at the end of September 1934. All machines were now sold equipped with electric lighting as standard, otherwise most of the alterations were to be found in the D-series of singles; these included a 498cc side-valve and 498cc ohv twin-port machine in Sports and Super Sports guises. In design these models departed completely from usual Matchless practice, in that the front fork girders were built from round-section tubing, and also had a considerably greater range of movement, the spring having been increased in length and the links strengthened, whilst hand-operated shock dampers were now incorporated in the lower fork links. The front brake had also been improved.

On both the side-valve and overhead-valve engines the decompressor had been abandoned in favour of an exhaust valve lifter. The flywheel assembly had been beefed up considerably, and a larger diameter, two-row roller big-end bearing with an aluminium cage was employed. Also the diameter of the main shaft had been increased to 1¼in (30mm), and now ran in three rows of caged rollers.

On both the ohv five-hundreds there was a direct oil feed to the pushrods, oil being forced under pressure from the rocker box through jets that projected it on to the sides of the rocker ends, thereafter trickling down the pushrod cups.

On all 1935 Matchless models (with the exception of the four-cylinder Silver Hawk) Lo-Ex 'interrupted' skirt aluminium pistons were employed.

The Clubman Range

For the 1936 season there were two distinct Matchless ranges of single-cylinder models: 'Clubman' and 'Tourist'. The Clubmans were high-performance, ohv machines of 250, 350 and 500cc, all with the engine set vertically in the frame; the Tourists were of 250 and 350cc only (plus a 990 V-twin).

The 1936 Model 36/G2 overhead-valve single, with four-speed gearbox. For a small additional cost, positive stop foot-change could be supplied to order for this 246cc (62.5 × 80mm) bike. There was coil ignition, whilst the 30-watt dynamo for the lighting was rigidly mounted on engine plates and driven by a chain enclosed in the main oil-bath chaincase.

The 1936 350 'Clubman' 36/G3 347cc (69 × 93mm) with single-port head and hi-level exhaust.

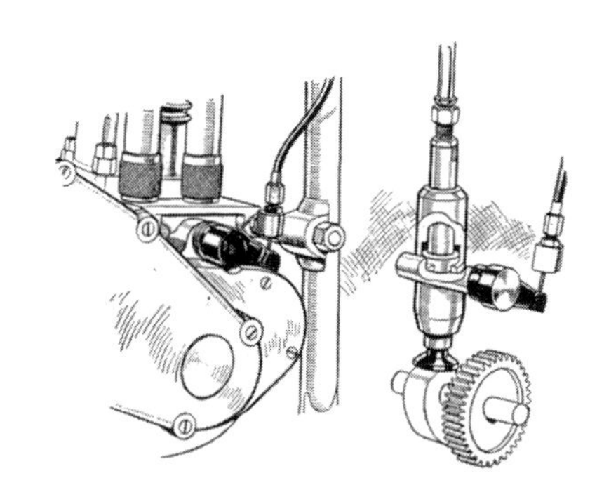

Drawing showing exhaust valve lifter on the single-cylinder Matchless engines of the late 1930s. The rocking lever engaged a collar formed on the exhaust-valve tappet, so that the mechanism was totally enclosed and there was a reliable operation.

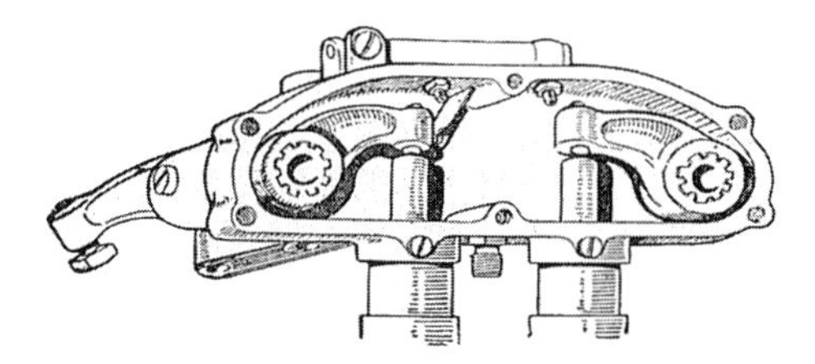

On the 500 'Clubmans' there was a direct feed of oil from the main oil pump to the overhead rocker gear. Oil was supplied to the rocker-shaft bearings, and by means of small jets, which can be seen in the drawing; oil was projected on to the ball ends of the pushrods, the oil being fed just where it was needed.

The Clubman range was new except for the 350. At the lower end of the engine size was the 246cc ohv Clubman selling at £39 10s. One journalist of the day described it as a 'good-looking, full-sized two-fifty', the latter attribute probably helped by the fact that all the Clubman models had a 3gal (14ltr) fuel tank. In addition the smallest Clubman model had Miller coil ignition and lighting and a low-level exhaust. A new design of frame was fitted, of the duplex type, with twin, straight front down-tubes. The engine was of 'straightforward design' – *The Motor Cycle* – with enclosed pushrods and rocker gear, coil valve springs, and the contact breakers housed in the timing cover. A four-speed Burman gearbox was provided, but foot change was available at extra cost. With the latter fitted, either a low- or a high-level exhaust could be used.

The three-fifty Clubman models had in fact been introduced a few months earlier 'to test the market', as one company spokesman put it when questioned at the Olympia Show in November 1935. There were two three-fifties: the standard Clubman and the Clubman Special. Like the two-fifty, a single exhaust port was used, together with a

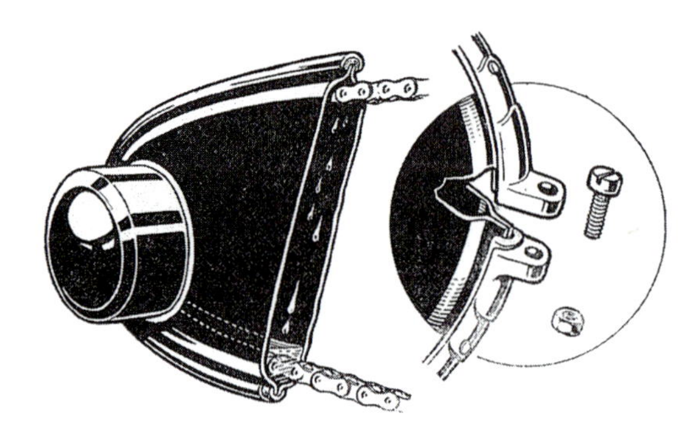

Details of the oil-bath chaincase.

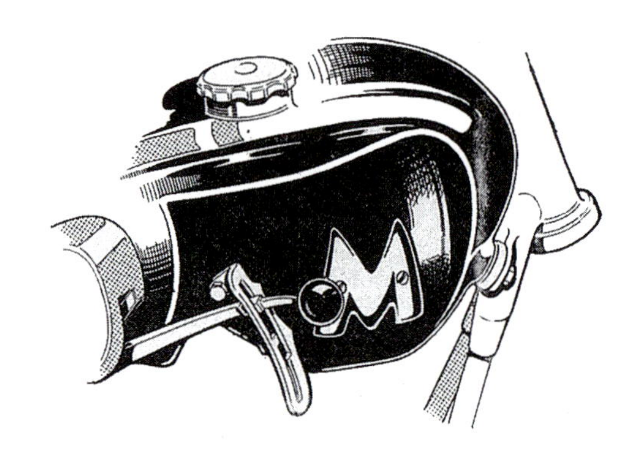

All Matchless fuel tanks of the late 1930s were distinguished by the embossed chromium 'M' badge that was carried on either side of the tank.

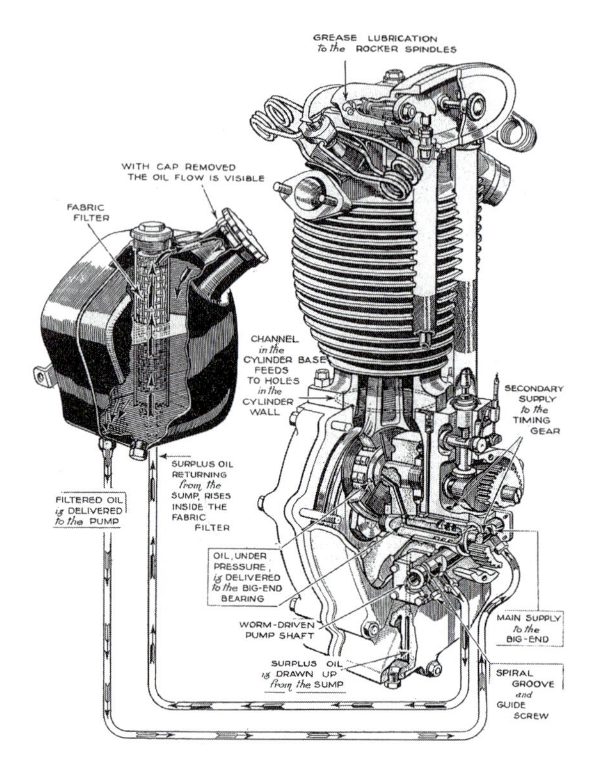

Drawing showing construction of the 1936 three-fifty 'Clubman' engine, and describing the operation of the dry-sump lubrication system. The rotary reciprocating plunger pump, which was driven by a worm from the crankshaft, drew oil from the oil tank and forced it to all working parts of the engine.

vertical cylinder, but hairpin rather than coil valve springs were fitted. There was magneto ignition with a separate dynamo for the lighting, both of Lucas manufacture.

There were a number of differences on the 347cc Clubman Special. First, it cost £57 10s, as compared to the standard model at £52 10s. Then, in the words of the company, 'The Special has been designed specifically to appeal to the trials enthusiast'; the most noticeable changes were to the mudguards, tyres and front forks, the latter being factory changes to suit off-road use. Other changes were twin toolboxes in place of only a single component on the standard bike; modified stands (main and side); not having the rubber-mounted handlebars of the standard Clubman; and fully adjustable controls. The gear ratios were also different: 6.09, 9.25, 12.5, 19.5:1 (against 5.73, 7.4, 8.7 and 15.4:1 for the standard Clubman).

There were no fewer than four 500 Clubman models. All came with ohv twin-port engines similar to those of the D/80, but with a new cylinder head and hairpin valve springs. Modifications to the head consisted of a new inlet port angle and a wider angle between the exhaust ports. There were two standard and two trials models, the differences between the two models in each pair being with regard to engine state of tune. The 500 Clubman at £55 and the 500

Super Clubman at £60 were identical, except that the latter had a specially tuned engine with high compression piston, 14mm spark plug and polished components such as flywheels, connecting rod and ports. There were similar differences in the case of the 500 Clubman Special (£60) and the 500 Super Clubman Special (£65), these last two being trials bikes and having the differences to their specifications already outlined for their 350 brother as regards gearing, tyres and the like.

The Tourist Range

First of the Tourist range was the coil-ignition 246cc side-valve at £35 14s. This was similar to the 1935 two-fifty, but fitted with a four-speed Burman gearbox. The engine was of the non-detachable-head type and had valve springs enclosed, and was accessible by way of a bolted-on cover.

The 497cc side-valve Tourist followed much of its Clubman counterpart, but instead there was an inclined detachable-head engine mounted in the duplex frame. It also featured the same 3gal (14ltr) fuel tank and large oil tank as its ohv Clubman brother. The price of the five-hundred Tourist, complete with Lucas magdyno lighting, was £51.

Except for the 246cc side-valve, any model in the 1936 range could be supplied to order (ex-factory) with a red and chromium finish for an additional £2 10s.

The 1936 36/G80 500 Clubman

Engine:	Air-cooled ohv twin-port vertical single, iron head and barrel, exposed hairpin valve springs, roller big end
Bore:	82.5mm
Stroke:	93mm
Displacement:	498cc
Compression ratio:	6.2:1 (Super Clubman (36/G90) version with 7.5:1 compression ratio, specially tuned engine, 90mph/145km/h)
Lubrication:	Dry sump, duplex horizontal reciprocating rotary plunger oil pump
Ignition:	Lucas magneto
Carburettor:	Amal 1in
Primary drive:	Chain
Final drive:	Chain
Gearbox:	Four-speed foot-change
Frame:	All-steel tubular construction
Front suspension:	Girder forks
Rear suspension:	Rigid
Front brake:	Drum
Rear brake:	Drum
Tyres:	3.25 × 26 front and rear

General specifications

Wheelbase:	N/A
Ground clearance:	N/A
Seat height:	N/A
Fuel tank capacity:	3gal (14ltr)
Dry weight:	N/A
Maximum power:	26bhp
Top speed:	80mph (130km/h)

Side-valve 500 'Tourist' Model 36/D5. For 1936 there was also a two-fifty version coded 36/F7, which was generally similar but with coil instead of magneto ignition.

Changes for the Late 1930s

There were more changes for the 1937 model year, although the basic titles of Tourist and Clubman remained. These were as follows:

Side-valve:
- 246 and 497cc engines now vertically mounted;
- cylinders of new design with 'dwarf' tappet chests;
- strengthened frame for 246cc model.

Overhead-valve:
- redesigned cylinder heads and barrels, with improved finning;
- rocker gear now lubricated direct from main oil pump;
- 250 and 350 models came into line with 500 by having adjustable oil feed to inlet valve guide;
- new 250 de luxe model with magneto ignition;
- 250 and 350 models strengthened frame;
- new big-end bearing for 350 and 500 engines, using a three-row roller bearing (in place of the original two-row type).

Common to both engine types:
- constant voltage control dynamos;
- foot-change standardized (hand change could not be fitted);
- new duplex fork damper;
- improved brake hubs, with brakes transferred to nearside (left).

The purchase of the Sunbeam marque in August 1937 was followed in October 1937 by Matchless Motorcycles (Colliers) Ltd being changed to Associated Motor Cycles Ltd (AMC for short). The full story of this new organization is covered in Chapter 7. In mid-September 1937 the 1938 Matchless range was announced; this included what *The Motor Cycle* referred to as 'Improved Clubman and Tourist Models'. But the really big news related to a new engine to be fitted to the 350 and 500 Super models, and which was to form the basis for Matchless ohv singles for the next three decades

1937 Prices and Models

Tourist:

37/G7 246cc sv (coil ignition) £39 15s
37/G5 497cc sv (coil ignition) £50

Clubman:

37/G2 246cc ohv single-port (coil ignition) £41 10s
37/G2M 246cc ohv single-port de luxe (magneto) £45 5s
37/G2MC 246cc ohv single-port competition (magneto) £50 5s
37/G3 347cc ohv single-port (magneto) £54
37/G3C 347cc ohv single-port competition (magneto) £59
37/G80 498cc ohv twin-port (magneto) £57
37/G80C 498cc ohv single-port competition (magneto) £62
37/G90 498cc ohv twin-port Super (magneto) £62
37/G90 498cc ohv single-port Super competition (magneto) £67

A New Engine

The outstanding feature of the new engine was an entirely new cylinder-head design in which the valves and valve gear, including the hairpin valve springs, were totally enclosed. Compared to the other singles produced by the company at the time, this head casting was massive, with extensive finning. The cylinder head, rocker box and valve spring chambers were all formed in a single casting. A pair of springs was used for each valve, but instead of the springs being located in the valve collars at the top end on their respective sides, they were crossed over and located on the opposite sides. Thus the full length of the arms of the springs was retained, whilst the coils lay close to the valve stems.

Access to each valve was obtained via detachable covers, whilst tappet adjustment was the same as on the standard Clubman models – at the top of the pushrods – and access was gained through a detachable plate. In the new head casting the cylinder fins were unbroken on the offside (right), and the pushrods passed through

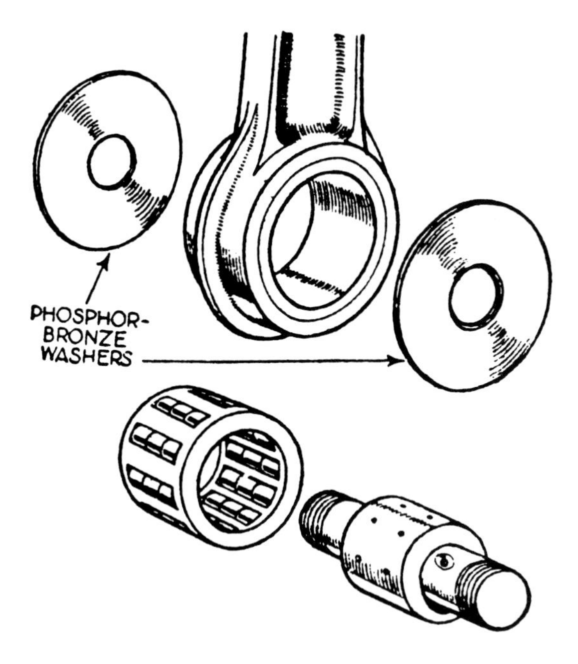

A three-row roller bearing on a two-piece crankpin, fitted to the 1937 model; this replaced the earlier two-row bearing.

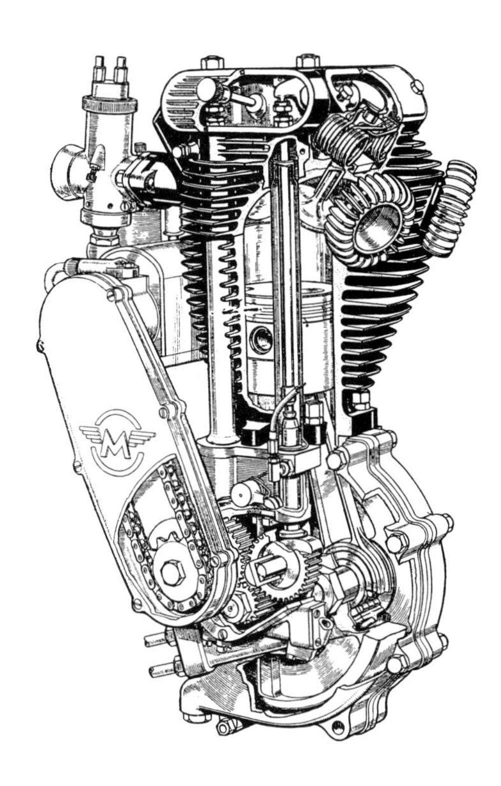

By the 1938 model year the new 'Clubman Super' Matchless engine had enclosed valve gear. Note the twin-port cylinder head.

tunnels formed in the casting. The pushrod tubes, which enclosed the pushrods between the crankcase and the head, mated at the bottom of the tunnels, and special rubber washers were employed to provide an oil-tight seal when the cylinder head was tightened down.

The lubrication system closely followed existing Matchless practice, but of course the other ohv singles still had exposed valve springs.

The lower half of the new engine was based on the existing Clubman format, but several alterations had been made to the crankcase, and these improvements were incorporated in all overhead-valve Matchless models for 1938. The oil leads to the pump had been redesigned, and the feed and return pipes now made a wide sweep from the tank to the crankcase.

In the three-fifty the engine was produced as a single-port model, with the exhaust pipe on the offside (right) of the motorcycle, but in the five-hundred the head was of the twin-port variety. Equipment of both followed that of the other Clubman models, in other words, with cradle frames, four-speed foot-change Burman gearboxes and separate magnetos and dynamos. The 347cc 38/G4 Super Clubman cost £62 10s; the 498cc 38/G90 Super Clubman £65 10s.

The remaining Clubman models in the 1938 range had the new crankcases, but otherwise the engines were unaltered. All models except the 246cc ohv de luxe had vertical Amal carburettors, and every model in the Matchless range now came with 14mm spark plugs.

Modified Cycle Parts

Several changes had been made to the cycle parts: mudguards were flared with centre ribs fitted, whilst the rear chain-guard had been extended down on the outside, so that the final drive-chain was almost totally enclosed. The tyre pump on all Clubman models was now carried on this chain-guard instead of the front fork.

A low-lift spring-up rear stand was another new feature of these machines, whilst the side stand was retained in only the Competition models of the single-cylinder range. All the ohv models – with the exception of the single-port two-fifty standard Clubman (38/G2) – had a new single-piece 3gal (14ltr) fuel tank; this was rubber-mounted on four frame lugs. And perhaps much more significantly to future Matchless history, there was a large, winging 'M' motif in chromium on either side, which of course was to be adopted as the marque's logo for the remainder of the company's life.

The colour scheme of all the models was black and chromium, but the two Super models had red panels on the sides and top of the chromium-plated fuel tanks, and red and gold-centred wheel rims.

Tyre sizes of the Super models were 3.00 × 19 ribbed front and 3.50 × 19 'Universal' rear; these were of Dunlop manufacture, whilst those fitted to the other singles were Firestone's.

In the issue dated 29 September 1938 *The Motor Cycle* began its review of the 1939 Matchless range thus: 'Continuing their policy of producing reliable, high-class machines which are notable for their mechanical silence, the makers of Matchless motorcycles have adopted total enclosure of the valve gear throughout their range for 1939.' As before there were three separate series: the Clubman, the Clubman Special and the Tourist. And for 1939 the new cylinder-head design on the Super Clubman models was adopted on all new 350 and 500 ohv machines.

A change to crankcases of larger diameter and bigger flywheels on the 500cc ohv singles had been made, to improve the slow running and increase the smoothness of these engines.

The pair of 250cc now had vertical Amal carburettors in common with the other models in the range. These engines also featured a redesigned cylinder head with a modified inlet port, which, it was claimed, improved slow running and acceleration.

More Bodywork Changes

Apart from the engine changes outlined above, a number of modifications had been carried out to the remainder of the motorcycle. All the 1939 models had welded exhaust-system fittings instead of clips, resulting in both greater strength, and also improved appearance. High- or low-level exhaust systems were optional on all ohv models. The rear fork-ends of the frame had been modified so that pillion footrests could be fitted, and folding footrests with stock Matchless rubbers could be supplied as a cost option. This last modification did not apply to the side-valve 250, only to the coil-ignition model.

The trio of 250cc machines – side valve; ohv (coil) and ohv (magneto) – all had a heavier front-fork spring designed to eliminate what *The Motor Cycle* called 'clashing' on bad road surfaces and to reduce vibration of the spring itself as far as possible. On the magneto model a steering damper was fitted, and all three machines had an adjustable fork damper.

Alterations had been made to the brakes of all models over 250cc. Special steel pads were fitted to the brake shoes on the cam-operating faces, so that the expander cam put pressure on these plates instead of directly on the aluminium shoe. This was claimed to mean less frequent brake adjustment.

A new side stand of the spring-up type had also been made available. It featured a single arm and was mounted on the nearside (left) footrest hanger, and was available at extra cost on all 1939 Matchless models.

War Ends Play

As history records, the invasion by Germany of Poland on 1 September 1939, and the subsequent decision of France and Great Britain to declare war on the Nazi regime two days later on 3 September, meant that everyone was forced on to a wartime footing. And so Matchless made the transition from civilian to military production. However, unlike the previous conflict, it was devoted entirely to the manufacture of motorcycles for the armed forces. And as revealed in Chapter 5, Matchless with its W/G3L was to build one of the greatest of all military motorcycles – and to pioneer the use of the telescopic front fork in Great Britain.

3 V-Twins

World War I – or as it was more commonly referred to at the time, the Great War – ended with the Armistice on 11 November 1918. And within the remarkably short time of just ten days, almost fifty British motorcycle manufacturers had announced that they would be resuming civilian motorcycle production. This was, of course, good news for everyone. At last this fearsome conflict, which had taken such a vast toll of human life and suffering, was at an end. The returning former servicemen, many of whom had known only trench warfare for months or years, were looking to find a peacetime job and thus some form of transport. In those days only the very well off could consider a car, and for the majority, personal transport meant two wheels: so the motorcycle industry was looking forward to what it hoped, and fully expected to be, a period of major growth and record sales.

However, things were not quite as straightforward as it might have seemed. Yes, there was a big demand, but there was also a severe shortage

Matchless produced a long line of V-twin-engined machines; this example dates from 1912. Features included chain and belt drives, forward-mounted magneto and single carburettor between the 'V' of the cylinders.

The 1919 Model H sidecar outfit with swinging-arm frame and electric lighting; it cost a formidable £140.

of materials, which meant that supply simply couldn't keep up with demand; and the situation was not helped by the restriction imposed by the British government. But in 1919 the Ministry of Munitions finally released its control over what were termed 'strategic materials', thus allowing civilian production to resume – which included, of course, motorcycles and associated products.

Post-War Production

The first post-war model produced by H. Collier & Sons was known as the Victory – because it was essentially the machine which the Plumstead company had produced for the British allied forces during wartime. Powered by a 976cc (85.5 × 85mm) JAP side-valve V-twin, this bike was given the model code 8B/2. There was also the Model H, a de luxe sidecar outfit featuring a swinging-arm frame, three-speed hand-change gearbox, all chain drive, and patented quickly detachable wheels. The specification included a folding luggage rack in the sidecar, together with electric lighting. However, as Peter Hartley pointed out in his 1981 book *Matchless, Once the Largest British Motorcycle Manufacturer*: 'The price was a formidable £140, a 40 per cent rise over the cost of the equivalent rigid-framed outfit with electric lighting in 1914.'

A team of Matchless V-twin sidecar combinations successfully participated in the ACU Six Days Trial towards the end of 1919. In typical pioneering fashion, Charlie Collier won a silver medal, whilst team-mate Rex Mundry went even better with a gold, and G.D. Hardee secured a bronze. Mundry was also awarded a special trophy by the National Benzole Association for the top performance by a bike running on benzole (the idea behind this being to encourage its use instead of petrol, since the latter was in short supply following the war).

Also late in 1919 the Colliers took a stand at the London Olympia Motorcycle Show. Their main exhibit was the Model H, based heavily on the firm's 1914 sidecar outfit Model 8B; it went on to prove a remarkable sales success, continuing until 1928. Equipped with a Lucas magdyno, Lucas electric lighting and horn, sidecar hood and pillion pad, it cost £200, although the basic model could be supplied for £30 less.

The Colliers also continued their pre-war interest and participation in racing and record breaking, and the engine configuration generally used in the first few years of peace was the V-twin. At first the problems of peacetime production meant that racing took something of a back seat, but by mid-1920 things had improved, allowing Charlie Collier to get back in the saddle himself. The machinery was usually 496cc Matchless MAGs or 994cc Matchless JAPs. Besides Charlie Collier, other notable Matchless competitors of the day included Captain O. M. Baldwin, Captain

Jack ('Mad Jack') Woodhouse, and Tommy Eve (the latter riding a 330cc Matchless MAG V-twin).

The Model J

In October 1920 H. Collier & Son were able to introduce their first big new solo motorcycle following the end of the war. Called the Model J, it offered potential customers the choice of either a JAP or MAG V-twin. Then a year later, in November 1921, the Olympia Show was the setting for the launch of the 1922 Matchless range, comprising five different variations of the two basic types of Matchless V-twin, the Models H and J. All these could be supplied in either solo or sidecar guise, and with either JAP or MAG engines.

For the remainder of the decade, Olympia was often the setting for the launch of new Matchless models. The 1923 exhibition marked the arrival of a new 976cc JAP V-twin-powered sports solo, the Model J/S. Its features included B & B carburettor; total loss (drip-feed) lubrication; three-speed Sturmey Archer gearbox with hand-change; all chain drive; and rigid frame. Its 'very basic sporting specification', as one commentator described it, meant that the price could be limited to £110, with a tuned engine available for an additional £5!

Unsuccessful Car Production

It was around this time that Matchless dabbled in four wheels, when in April 1923 a light-tourer, the Model K, was placed in limited production. The engine was a horizontally opposed, air-cooled flat twin that featured overhead valves, unlike the power unit of the prototype Model H motorcycle of 1915. With bore and stroke dimensions of 89 × 102mm respectively, the model K displaced 1,249cc, the largest Matchless engine up to that time.

Other interesting features of this car included unit construction, which enabled shaft drive to the rear wheels via a differential. The engine was given detachable cylinder heads and barrels, with each alloy piston being equipped with three rings. One of the Model K's most unusual features, however, was its body construction, which used no chassis as such, instead relying on its strength by a series of integral panels and side members. At the front, a plate formed the rear engine support and bodywork, whilst panels and the like were a mixture of pressed steel and wood.

But with fierce competition, sales of the Model K were never great, and it therefore came as no surprise that production ceased before the end of 1924. Matchless thereafter concentrated upon its core business, motorcycles; or to be exact, motorcycles and sidecars. In those days, as elsewhere in the British motorcycle industry, sidecars were big business, and many firms, just like Matchless, made their own sidecar models during the 1920s.

A New V-Twin

For the 1925 season there was a brand new 982cc (85.5 × 85.5mm) side-valve 50-degree V-twin engine, designed and built by Matchless themselves. But as Peter Hartley recalled in 1981, 'This engine bore a strong resemblance to the JAP engine it replaced'. This Matchless-built power unit was in line with Collier policy of the time – that of becoming self-sufficient as regards engine supply, rather than reliant on outside suppliers as in the past. The M/3S was the model code of the motorcycle powered by the new engine, and this bike replaced the 1924 Model M/2 (powered by the 976cc JAP motor). In reality Matchless were by now switching much of their production into a new range of single-cylinder machines, which ultimately would be produced in side-valve, overhead valve and overhead camshaft forms (*see* Chapter 2). But the V-twin was still to play an important role in Matchless fortunes for many years yet.

The 1929 Model Range

By the time the 1929 Matchless range was announced in the autumn of 1928, only models with the company's own V-twin were listed, namely the X9.9HP and X/R9.9HP Sports. Both employed the 982cc (85.5 × 85.5mm) side-valve, 50-degree V-twin, the X/R variant having a higher compression ratio (up from 4.4:1 to 4.8:1), special valve springs and nickel-plated cylinders. Power was up from 20bhp @ 4,000rpm on the standard model, to 26bhp @ 4,200rpm.

The factory's catalogue for 1929, showing the V-twin X and X/R models. The illustration has the version with Lucas magdyno electric lighting.

The 1929 X/R Sports

Engine:	Air-cooled sv 50-degree V-twin, enclosed valves, three-cam timing gear
Bore:	85.5mm
Stroke:	85.5mm
Displacement:	982cc
Compression ratio:	4.8:1
Lubrication:	Pilgrim mechanical oil pump, with incorporated sight-feed glass
Ignition:	Lucas magneto
Carburettor:	Amal, two-lever, semi-automatic
Primary drive:	Chain
Final drive:	Chain
Gearbox:	Three-speed, hand-change, Sturmey Archer; four alternate sets of gear ratios available
Frame:	All-steel tubular construction
Front suspension:	Matchless girder forks
Rear suspension:	Rigid
Front brake:	8in, drum
Rear brake:	8in, drum
Tyres:	Palmer Flexicord 3.50 × 26 front and rear

General Specifications

Wheelbase:	56in (1,422mm)
Ground clearance:	5in (127mm)
Seat height:	26½in (673mm)
Fuel tank capacity:	2gal (9ltr)
Dry weight:	340lb (154kg)
Maximum power:	26bhp @ 4,200rpm
Top speed:	78mph (126km/h)

1929 Matchless V-twin engine and Sturmey-Archer gearbox.

The Matchless slogan at that time read: 'The Machine that sets the fashion to the world', and the company described the X/J V-twin thus: 'The most handsome motorcycle on the road is the Model X/J with its twin silencers (stacked bunk-bed fashion, and sporting fishtail ends) and graceful black and white tank.'

Morgan

The Morgan Motor Company of Malvern Link, Worcestershire, was founded in 1910 and became famous for its three-wheel cars, usually fitted with large capacity V-twin motorcycle engines. The power unit was mounted at the front, and drove the single rear wheel via a propshaft running through a large tube, which was the main chassis element. Initially JAP engines were used, and by the outbreak of World War I, production of Morgan cars was approaching 1,000 a year. Sales were helped by numerous successes in racing and trials, the most important being victory in the French Cyclecar Grand Prix at Amiens, and a gold medal in the Six Days Trial, both in 1913.

Post-war, the three-wheelers continued to sell well and to win every kind of competition, and whilst basically changing very little, they gained more power from their V-twin engines, neater bodywork, front-wheel brakes, electric starting, geared-down steering and other worthwhile features. Engine options at that time included Anzani, Blackburne and Precision V-twins, as well as the popular JAP.

Three-wheelers were banned from racing after an accident in 1924, but in 1927 the Morgan Club was reorganized as the Cyclecar Club, and by running competitions open to all cyclecars, it managed to re-establish the three-wheeler in racing – bringing, as one commentator described it, 'endless success' for the marque. In 1929 Gwenda Hawkes set a kilometre class record of over 115mph (185km/h) with her Morgan. By this time the Morgan three-wheeler range covered everything from pukka racing models to four-seater tourers.

During 1933 Morgan began to use Matchless V-twin engines, these being specially developed for the purpose by the Plumstead factory. The first such engine was a watercooled side-valve unit, this being followed by an overhead valve air-cooled model. This latter engine was given a thorough testing by G.H. Goodall in the International Six Days Trial.

The air-cooled ohv engine had deep vertical ribs on the cylinder head, and the rocker gear was fully enclosed and mechanically lubricated; further, there was an adjustable oil feed to each inlet-valve guide. As with the water-cooled engine, the starting handle engaged directly on to the crankshaft, through the timing case. Coil ignition was employed, the distributor being mounted on the timing case.

From November 1933 a model with a four-cylinder Ford engine appeared, alongside the JAP and the recently introduced Matchless twins. In 1935 Morgan 'reluctantly' dropped the popular but scarce JAP engine, and thereafter the Matchless was the standard twin.

In December 1935 Morgan launched its first four-wheeler, and not a moment too soon, as sales of three-wheelers had begun a dramatic decline, partly because of cheaper four-wheel competition, and partly because of the improving general state of the economy. The newcomer, named the 4/4, used a 1,122cc Coventry Climax engine, and although not as fast as the three-wheelers, it soon began to sell well, helped by a licence agreement by the French Morgan agent.

Largely due to its rural location, the factory survived World War II undamaged. A few cars were built from spares in 1945, but production did not start properly until late 1946, and then almost entirely for export, especially the United States. But there was little export potential for the three-wheelers, however, as other countries did not offer the same tax concessions/driving laws as Great Britain, and in February 1952 the Morgan three-wheeler era came to an end.

If the truth be known, the lion's share of Morgan three-wheelers had JAP engines rather than Matchless power, as unfortunately the Matchless involvement came just as the demand for such vehicles went into terminal decline. And because the company had to use the speciality version of the V-twin engine, rather than standard motorcycle units, the whole exercise cost Matchless, and later AMC, a tidy penny.

V-Twins for the 1930s

For the 1930 season the V-twins had their model prefixes changed to X/2 for the basic version, whilst the other, more sporting bike was referred to as the X/R2, the latter featuring chrome-plated wheel rims, nickel-plated cylinders and additional performance. For 1931 the Vs became the X/3 and the X/R3: new features were new-type cylinders with heavier finning round the exhaust ports; a four-speed gearbox; and a new fuel tank.

These were extremely worrying times for the Colliers, as the Wall Street stock-market crash in October 1929 was causing an increasingly difficult economic climate: by late 1930 the economic gloom had transferred across the Atlantic to Continental Europe, and also to Great Britain. As Matchless had just launched their new V-four 600cc Silver Hawk, development on other models had taken something of a back seat.

Alterations to the V-twins for 1932 included new handlebars and a new oil filter, the latter of

1931 Matchless range of sidecars offered by the Plumstead factory, for a range of clientele.

1931 X/3 V-twin 990cc, 26bhp at 4,500rpm; £60 standard (shown) or £69 in De Luxe with air filter, electric lighting, speedometer and so on.

The 990 Tourist Model 36/X4 of 1936. On the Standard model the switch and ammeter were carried in the headlamp shell, but on the De Luxe version there was an instrument panel mounted above the handlebars.

which had been adopted across the range. Because of the continuing bleak economic climate little change occurred until the end of 1934, when the 1935 model line-up was announced. Even then, changes to the side-valve V-twins were limited to larger big-end bearings, whilst the diameter of the main shaft had been increased to 1½in (38mm). A wider chain line had been provided to give greater clearance for oversize tyres, while minor details, such as saddle springing and battery mounting, had been improved. Buyers now had a choice between

The 1936 Tourist Model 36/X4

Engine:	Air-cooled sv 50-degree V-twin, enclosed valves, forked connecting rods; iron heads and barrels
Bore:	85.5mm
Stroke:	85.5mm
Displacement:	982cc
Compression ratio:	5.5:1
Lubrication:	Dry sump, duplex horizontal reciprocating rotary plunger pump
Ignition:	Magneto
Carburettor:	Single Amal instrument
Primary drive:	Chain
Final drive:	Chain
Gearbox:	Four-speed, hand-change
Frame:	All-steel tubular construction
Front suspension:	Girder forks
Rear suspension:	Rigid
Front brake:	8in drum, cable-operated
Rear brake:	8in drum, rod-operated
Tyres:	3.25 × 26 front and rear

General Specifications

Wheelbase:	N/A
Ground clearance:	N/A
Seat height:	N/A
Fuel tank capacity:	3½gal (16ltr)
Dry weight:	N/A
Maximum power:	28bhp @ 4,200rpm
Top speed:	80mph (130km/h)

1928 Matchless 990cc (85.5 × 85.5mm) engine was introduced in 1925 as M/35, continued in production until late 1928.

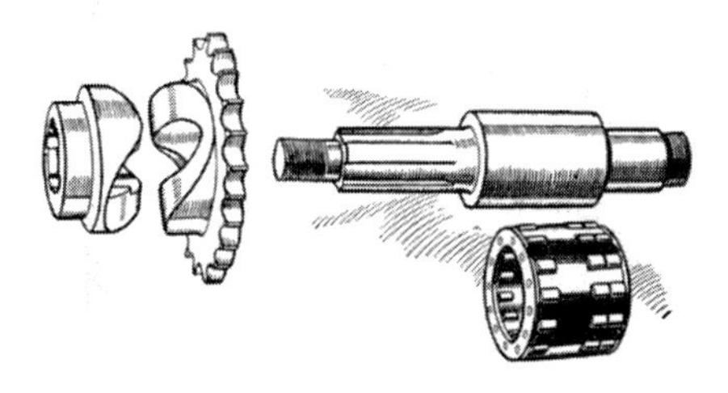

ABOVE: *Drawing showing mainshaft and the three-row bearing on which it was carried. The transmission shock absorber was carried on the splines formed on the end of the shaft. The shock-absorber spring and nut are not shown here.*

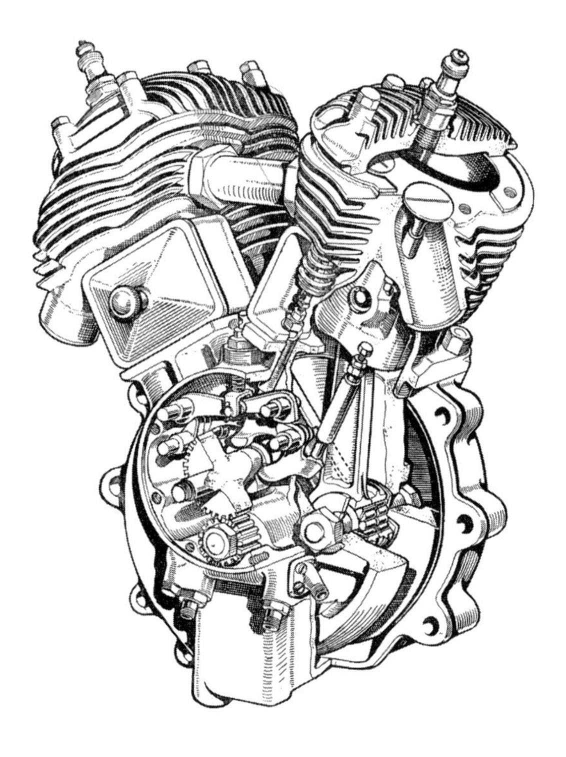

RIGHT: *Engine from Matchless X/4. Features included detachable cylinder heads and forked connecting rods with four rows of rollers for big-end bearing. The valves were totally enclosed.*

hand- or foot-change for the four-speed Burman gearbox.

Due to the falling of various currencies and the rising of others during the financial turmoil of the early 1930s, the price structure for motorcycles in Great Britain bore no relationship to those of only a few years earlier. On the 27 September 1935 (when the 1935 model range was announced), the V-twins were as follows: the 35/X4 £68 15s, and the 35/X4 de luxe £72 10s.

There was little change between the 1936 and 1935 side-valve V-twins; most significantly, the rear frame members were now heavier. The standard model now cost £69 15s, and the de luxe model £73 10s; the latter had a handlebar-mounted instrument panel, chromium-edged mudguards and a speedometer as standard.

Major Changes for the 37/X

When the 1937 Matchless range was announced on 8 October 1936, enthusiasts for the marque's now long-running 982cc side-valve V-twin got a surprise: just when everyone thought it had been taken as far as it could be, the company brought out a model that demonstrated a major rethink.

First, for 1937 it was only offered in a single guise, the 37/X, and Matchless said it was now only being produced 'purely for solo and single-seater sidecar work'. This was because the frame had been redesigned and was now only fractionally longer than that of the 500cc single-cylinder range. The short wheelbase frame required a number of alterations to the engine.

A separate magneto was mounted in front of the unit, whilst the dynamo, driven by a chain enclosed in the primary chaincase, was mounted in the engine plates above the gearbox. The exhaust port design had been considerably modified, and on both cylinders the exhaust pipes emerged almost at right angles, the cooling of the lower halves of the cylinders and valve chests being much improved.

Sports-type front forks were fitted, with tapered, round-section, tubular girders and duplex shock absorbers. Hubs and brakes had been uprated, whilst the quickly detachable rear wheel, as fitted to all the latest Matchless models except the two-fifties, was employed. The wheel featured a long spindle running right through the hub, and the detachable portion of the wheel was held to the brake drum by three dowels and three studs, the latter provided with easily removable nuts.

The short frame, neatly flared mudguards with centred ribs, and a new 4gal (18ltr) fuel tank, gave the 1937 V-twin a much more compact and sporting appearance than its forebears. At £72 10s, the price was actually less than the outgoing 1936 de luxe. However, the speedometer was now an additional £2 10s.

The dwarf tappet chests, which were fitted to the singles (*see* Chapter 2), and in which the valve springs were insulated from engine heat, were to be found on the 1938 V-twin when it arrived in September 1937, each valve guide being equipped with a grease nipple. In the crankcase the driving side main-shaft bearings had been redesigned, the assembly now consisting of deep-groove ball-and-roller bearings. The clutch diameter had been increased to enable it to cope better with the immense torque produced by the big engine.

The brakes featured one-piece cover plates and anchor plates, whilst an extended rear brake pedal provided smoother action. The price had increased to £77 10s.

The End of the Line

In what were to be the last few months of peace, the 1939 model Matchless range was announced to the public at the end of September 1938. Except for a number of what *The Motor Cycle* described as 'practical improvements', the 39/X side-valve V-twin was retained in its 1938 guise, with only one change exclusive to the model. This was the provision of dampers on both sides of the forks, each one with its own hand adjuster; the price remained unchanged.

Although the Model X big V-twin was still listed in the 1940 Matchless catalogue, very few examples were actually built. As this model was not re-introduced after the end of the war in 1945, the 1930s effectively saw the end of the X family. No more V-twin Matchlesses were ever built, so this truly was the end of the line.

4 Silver Arrow and Silver Hawk

The Silver Arrow, designed by the Collier brothers, Charlie and Harry, arrived mid-way through November 1929; its 397cc (54 × 86mm) engine was a narrow-angle V-twin, with the crankshaft in its conventional position (across-the-frame). Note this example is essentially stock, except there is no fishtail on the silencer.

The Motor Cycle called it 'The Master Design of Master Designers', and they were talking about the brand new Silver Arrow four-hundred narrow-angle V-twin. This exciting machine made its bow to a large and critical assembly of journalists on Tuesday 12 November 1929, in the drawing room of the Hyde Park Hotel, London. In addition to the models in the hotel, there were others being demonstrated in Hyde Park. Even the national daily newspapers had been invited to ride the new machine. Harry Collier and his brother Charlie had designed it, although they were quick to recognize the valuable assistance they had received from the heads of various departments in their company. Said Harry: 'We have aimed at retaining the orthodox, whilst incorporating the refinements we thought desirable. For instance, we should not have deployed a spring frame had it not been that for the overseas market we think it desirable.'

A comprehensive two-page advertisement was used for the launch, and the following assertions were made in it for the Silver Arrow:

> The Motorcycle … is as silent, as smooth running, and as comfortable as a high-grade car. The Matchless 'Silver Arrow' has a vibrationless, monobloc twin-cylinder engine, a remarkably effective spring frame that is adjustable whilst riding, dry sump lubrication, chromium plating, enclosed valves, detachable cylinder head, inter-connected brakes, prop stand, detachable rear mudguard, direct drive magneto, and a host of other advanced features. The engine can be started by a child.

LEFT: Matchless sales brochure illustration for the Silver Arrow side-valve narrow-angle V-twin.

BELOW: A drawing of the Silver Arrow engine showing the car practice of the bottom end and side-valve layout.

The Silver Arrow

Engine Design

The Silver Arrow (and the later four-cylinder Silver Hawk) was, like Edward Turner's Ariel Square Four, in many ways a brilliant design which was unfortunate enough to be conceived at just the wrong moment in history. *The Motor Cycle* described its engine as having 'Delightfully clean lines, reminiscent of modern car practice.' At first glance, the new powerplant gave the impression of being a straight four, but actually it was a twin – and a V at that – with the crankshaft in its conventional position (across the frame). The cylinders' angle, however, was exceptionally narrow, a mere 18 degrees.

With a bore and stroke of 54 × 86mm (giving a displacement of 397cc), it is evident that, even for the time, the stroke was exceptionally long. This, Charlie Collier said, was to provide 'flexibility and smooth running'. Also, even though it was an exotic design, the new Matchless was not intended as a sports bike, rather a 'good-mannered' de luxe tourer. It also featured side valves instead of overhead ones, with a firing angle of 26 degrees.

Mounted on the compact crankcase assembly was the cylinder barrel assembly; earlier reference to 'monobloc' meant that the cylinders were cast in a single block. A single cast-iron casting was attached to the cylinder block by twelve studs, and formed the two semi-tubular combustion heads. A definite advantage was the fully enclosed

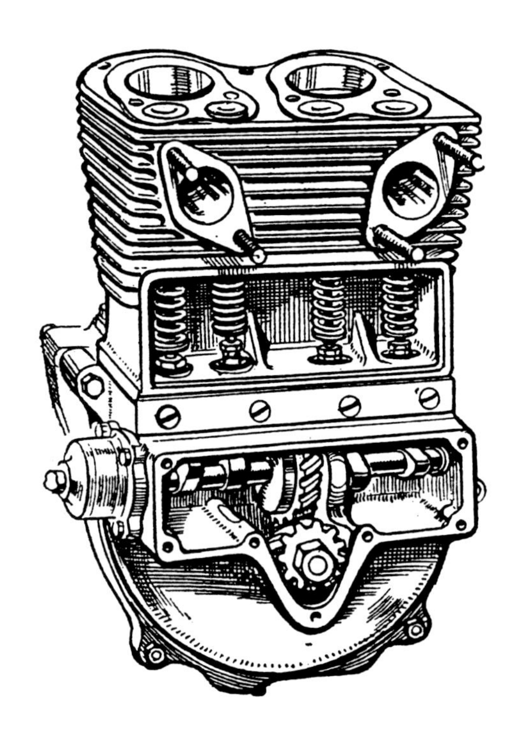

valve gear, still something of a rarity at that time. There was a chromium-plated cover that was easily removed by courtesy of a single knurled knob, for valve adjustment purposes.

As with the existing side-valve models in the Matchless range, the spark plugs were set centrally in the cylinder heads, whilst a copper-asbestos sealing gasket was used for the head joint. The valves were placed on the offside (right) of the engine, as was the cast-iron exhaust manifold, which was retained in place by a quartet of studs; the single Amal carburettor was bolted centrally on the near (left) side. Obviously, the ingoing gas therefore had to pass from one side of the engine to the other. This was achieved by way of a cored passage between the two cylinders, so cooling them and at the same time becoming pre-heated.

The two pistons had a compression ratio of 5.6:1, and were of aluminium alloy (when iron was still in widespread use for those components). Each piston had two rings, their crowns cut at an angle, thus allowing a conventional combustion-chamber shape. The single camshaft (supported by three bearings) was set at right angles to the crankshaft, from which it was driven by skew gearing. At the rear end of the camshaft there was a rubber-block connection through which the magneto (or optional magdyno) could be driven.

Lubrication, as with the remainder of the 1930 model year Matchless range, was of the dry-sump type — though the Silver Arrow had no external oil pipes. At the front of the crankcase, and immediately behind the front wheel, there was a bolted-on oil tank (with its connecting pipework to and from the tank drilled in the crankcase itself).

The big-end eyes were slightly offset, and operated side by side on the single crank pin, with a set of rollers for each connecting rod. A roller bearing was also fitted on the drive side of the crankshaft, whereas the timing side bearing, which was force-fed with oil, was a plain bush.

As mentioned earlier, a feature of the Matchless four-hundred narrow-angle V-twin was the ease of starting. Because of this, no valve lifter (a common feature on motorcycles of the time) was considered necessary; as *The Motor Cycle* said, 'No exhaust valve lifter is fitted, it being found that, with cylinders so small as 200cc, no effort was required to rotate the engine against compression.' To stop the engine – which, owing to the carburettor being equipped with a throttle stop, ticked over with the throttle lever closed – there was a magneto cut-out button mounted on the handlebars; when the 'full electrical equipment' option was taken up, it was placed on the console behind the headlamp.

Frame Design

The sprung frame design was, as a journalist of the day reported, 'ingenious in its simplicity'. The centre portion was of the diamond variety with three straight, large-diameter tubes. The top tube (which Matchless described as 'the tank rail') carried close to its rear end a pair of compression springs, one on each side. These were attached to a triangular rear section, which pivoted immediately behind the saddle tube. 'Silentblocs' (a special form of rubberized bearing) were used as the pivot bearings, so that in theory there was nothing to wear, and no side play until the bearings themselves failed.

At the rear end of the 'tank rail' was a huge T-lug. This carried a pair of rubber buffers, whose purpose was to prevent any possibility of the springs closing up solid in the event of the motorcycle hitting a really deep pothole – and a pair of slotted steel plates acted as saddle spring mountings, and formed the necessary friction surfaces for two hand-adjusted shock dampers, one on each side of the bike. A simple means of compensating for wear of the fibre discs in the dampers was provided.

A hand-operated, three-speed Sturmey-Archer gearbox was located immediately to the rear of the crankcase and in front of the saddle tube, so that the pivot of the rear section of the frame was not concentric with the final-drive sprocket. In practice, however, the alteration in chain tension had a negligible effect. To allow for the spring frame's action, the rear brake featured a special slotted link mounted on the pivot bolt of the rear frame. The gearbox shell was prone to cracking between the nearside layshaft and the mainshaft bearings.

Another interesting feature of the Silver Arrow design was its interconnected brakes, 8in in diameter and of Matchless design and manufacture. Webb-type girder front forks were employed, but again, these were of Matchless manufacture, with shock absorbers that were adjustable whilst riding (just as the factory claimed).

The basic, unequipped version cost £55, but for an additional £8 2s 6d (making £63 2s 6d in total) a 'fully equipped' Silver Arrow could be ordered. For this additional cost the buyer received a Lucas magdyno lighting set, an electric horn, a gearbox-drive Smith's Chronometric speedometer, and an illuminated instrument panel. A further 15s bought a detachable luggage carrier. Standard equipment included centre and front wheel stands; deeply valanced front mudguard; a large Lycett 'Aero' saddle with roll back; all-chain transmission (primary and final drives); and extensive chromium plating, including petrol tank, exhaust system, valve inspection cover and control levers.

Matchless claimed a top speed of 65mph (105km/h), and *The Motor Cycle* found that the Silver Arrow 'had a useful top-gear range of 8 to 63mph' (13 to 101km/h).

When the 1931 Matchless model range was announced a year later in early October 1930, the factory's publicity material said of the Silver Arrow: 'This machine has proved so satisfactory during the 1930 season that it is being continued with detail alterations only except for the provision of a new design petrol tank and the fitting of a four-speed gearbox'. The price of the standard A/2 remained the same, but the fully equipped model was now referred to as the Silver Arrow De Luxe and cost £64.

The Silver Hawk

But the really exciting news for the 1931 model year was the new six-hundred four called the Silver Hawk. Designed by the youngest of the three Collier brothers, Bert, the newcomer was a masterpiece, certainly as regards its engine unit. In their 9 October 1930 issue *The Motor Cycle* described its arrival thus: 'To prophesy that the Matchless will be the talk of the Show is equivalent to betting on a certainty. Last year at Olympia the "Silver Arrow" created a furore; this year it will be the "Silver Hawk", a four cylinder overhead-camshaft of 597cc.'

The Silver Hawk four was in fact the only newcomer to the factory's range, and in creating it, Bert Collier had aimed at providing 'a machine which combines docility, silence, smooth running and comfort with a really high road performance'.

Introduced at the end of 1930, just as the full force of the Great Depression, caused by the October 1929 New York stock exchange crash, reached Europe, the 597cc Silver Hawk four was launched into a market bereft of customers.

This latter segment saw the makers claim 'a top gear range from 6mph [10km/h] to over 80mph' (130km/h). Whilst the four-hundred Silver Arrow twin was never claimed to be anything but a mild-mannered touring bike, the Silver Hawk was built primarily as a sports model, and was thus a very different motorcycle. Sadly its launch came at the very height of the Great Depression, when millions of people in Britain (and elsewhere in Europe and America) were out of work.

However good the product, the priorities of just surviving meant that the majority of customers for whom the Silver Hawk had been designed were simply unable to make a purchase of such a luxury item in those times of economic gloom.

Engine Design

In essence the Silver Hawk engine was a pair of Silver Arrows, but in place of the side-valve twin there was a narrow-angle V-four with a single overhead camshaft. The cylinders were cast in a single unit, heavily finned and which featured air passages around the head, thus providing cooling to the rear cylinder (always a problem on Edward Turner's Ariel Square Four design).

The cylinder block was mounted on the particularly compact crankcase, in which was a simple, built-up two-throw crankshaft supported by three main bearings. Phosphor-bronze bushes, positively lubricated, were to be found on both the timing and drive sides of the crankshaft, whereas the central bearing was of the roller type, mounted in an aluminium plate; this plate formed a partition between the two halves of the crankcase, by which it was clamped and held rigidly in place. Interestingly there were no conventional flywheels, but instead, what could be described most simply as crank cheeks and bob-weights.

Silver Arrow connecting rods and big-end assemblies were employed – in other words the rods had their big-end eyes very slightly offset, and were mounted in pairs on the two crankpins with a set of rollers for each rod/big end. There is no doubt that in designing the six-hundred four, Bert Collier had utilized various features from the smaller, older twin. This also made good commercial sense, as it not only kept down development costs, but also made use of existing test programmes.

The drive to the overhead camshaft was achieved by means of the offside (right) of the engine, a drive from the crankshaft by bevel gears, and a vertical shaft to operate the camshaft in the cylinder head. The shaft incorporated Oldham's couplings to overcome any possibility of misalignment under working conditions, and the system featured the required 2-to-1 gear reduction by means of bevel gears at the top. A single camshaft, parallel to the crankshaft, was used, this operating the eight valves via straight rocking levers.

Like the cylinders, the heads were formed in a single one-piece casting, which had copper asbestos gaskets and a twelve-bolt fixing. The valve-head diameter was $1\frac{1}{16}$in (28mm), and involved the use of combustion chambers which, in plan view, were ovals, the cylinder barrels at the top being suitably cut away to conform to the same pattern. The valves, which featured $\frac{5}{16}$in (8mm) stems, were set vertically in relation to the cylinder bores and were completely enclosed, yet readily accessible for adjustment purposes after the removal of two cover plates, each held in place by a knurled hand-nut.

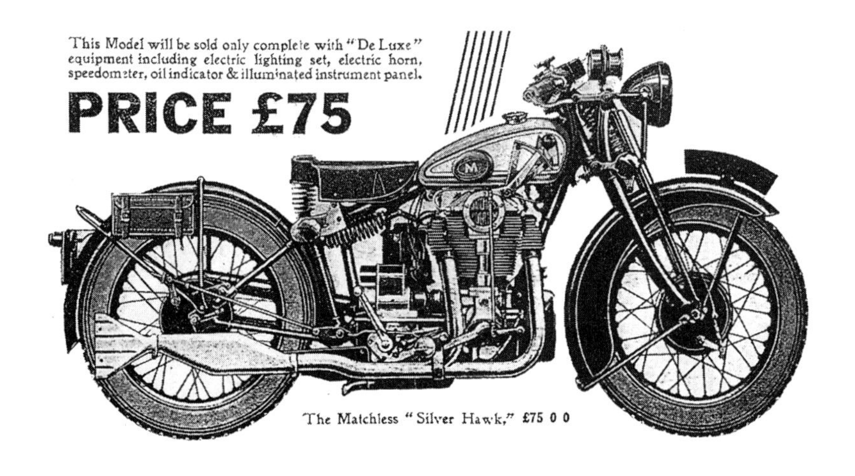

Capable of speeds of over 80mph (129km/h) in top gear, the Silver Hawk V-four's overhead camshaft engine was a compact and powerful unit. It was finally taken out of production in mid-1935.

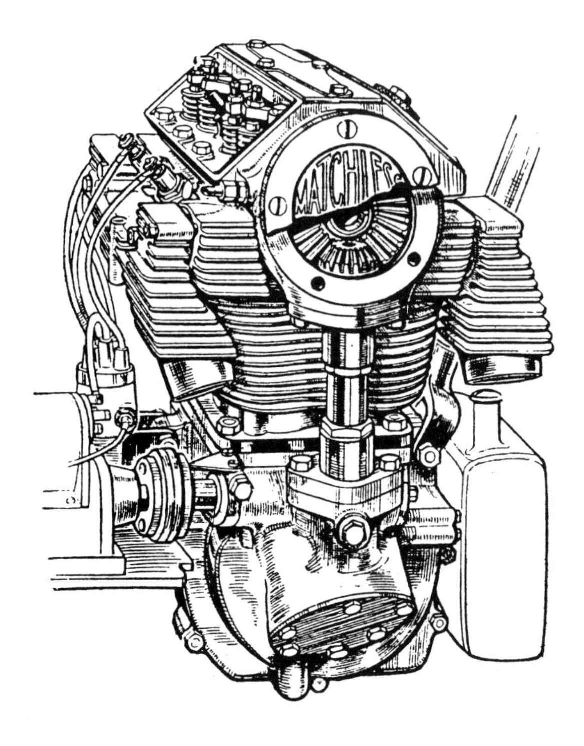

The four-cylinder engine, showing bevel gears, valve gear, dynamo, shaft drive and oil tank (the latter at the front of the crankcase).

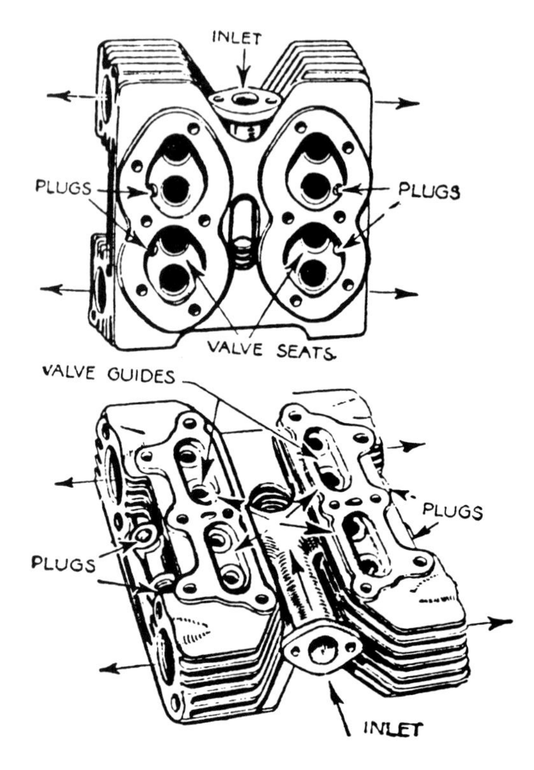

One-piece cylinder-head casting of the V-four engine.

At 50.8 × 73mm, the bore and stroke dimensions were still long-stroke, whilst a 'very clever' induction system (*The Motor Cycle*) had been adopted to ensure perfect mixture distribution to each of the four cylinders. From the single flanged carburettor on the nearside (left) there was a cored passage to the centre of the cylinder head; from this position there were passages, each of the same length, to the four cylinders.

A pair of exhaust ports exited towards the front of the machine, with two to the rear. Instead of four exhaust header pipes, Bert Collier had provided his design with two finned manifolds, thus cutting the number down to two, which were led into a single rearward-facing silencer on the offside (right).

As with the Silver Arrow four-hundred, the four-cylinder model had alloy pistons, with two rings – the lower being the oil scraper – and $1\frac{1}{16}$in (17mm) gudgeon pins. The large size of these latter components showed a degree of over-engineering which could be seen throughout much of the engine. This was intended to provide the unit with a long service life. With a compression ratio of 6.1:1, the engine produced 26bhp.

The dry sump lubrication, much akin to the Silver Arrow, had been retained, with the oil tank being bolted to the front section of the crankcase, as per Silver Arrow practice. A reciprocating and rotating plunger pump driven from the crankshaft drew lubricant from the tank, and provided, under pressure, a quantity of oil to the big-end and main bearings, whilst the remainder went via a sight feed (in the handlebar instrument panel) to supply the top bevel gears and camshaft drive. The latter supply kept the bevel chamber full, thereafter it overflowed into the cambox, lubricating the valve gear, including the rockers, and flowed downwards to the oil tank. A needle-controlled bypass allowed a small quantity of the return flow to be diverted to the duplex primary chain (the Silver Arrow having a simplex chain).

This duplex primary chain was housed in an oil bath and kept automatically tensioned by a form of spring loading produced under Weller patents. This system employed a pair of spring steel strips that bore constantly on the upper and lower runs of the chain. As with the Silver Arrow, the Sturmey-Archer gearbox was operated by hand via a tank-mounted control lever.

Much of the remainder of the machine followed the lines of the Silver Arrow, including the sprung frame and girder front forks – although, unlike other Matchless models of the era, ignition was by coil, rather than magneto.

Compared with the four-hundred Silver Arrow at £64, and the 990cc side-valve V-twin X/3 De Luxe also at £64, the new six-hundred Silver Hawk retailed at £75.

Testing the Silver Hawk Four

In their 2 April 1931 issue *The Motor Cycle* carried a three-page feature entitled 'Westward by the Silver Hawk Express'. The essence of this was a 630-mile (1,000km) weekend test, taking in the London to Land's End route. As 'Torrens' related:

> Six hundred and thirty miles covered in the period from noon, Saturday, to latish Sunday evening sounds more like work than pleasure, yet it was pleasure – sheer, unadulterated fun, and one of the most glorious weekends I have ever had. ...One is always suspicious of something new, the pressmen particularly so – once bitten, twice shy – and I make no excuse for setting off on my trip to Cornwall in a distinctly cynical frame of mind. That the design was absolutely sound I was certain, but there was a lurking fear of impending disappointment – of the performance being only so-so. ... But I returned convinced that no finer machine had ever left the Matchless works, and that on all-round performance it had very, very few equals.

So why had Torrens come to this conclusion? Well, even from the start of his journey one could see that he was impressed:

> Threading my way through West London with the streets congested with people flocking to the Boat Race gave ample opportunity for finding out that the Silver Hawk is really flexible. Ten miles an hour on the top gear of 5.7:1 is well within its compass, and by easing the clutch (as the makers suggest in their instruction booklet, for the clutch runs in oil), one can slip effortlessly away from a walking pace. And if a gap in the traffic presents itself, a flick of the wrist sends the bus surging forwards. Its acceleration is magnificent, and so is the cruising speed. ... At 50mph [80km/h] the engine of the machine tested was unnoticeable – there was just the roar of the wind in my ears, and barely a sound from the engine or exhaust could be heard; 76mph [122km/h] under slightly adverse conditions was the best speed recorded, so it is reasonable to suppose that with a rider unencumbered with pack and haversack, and lying down to it, the honest-to-goodness maximum would be 80mph [130km/h].

But what Torrens really admired about the Silver Hawk was 'the way one can use its speed', and in the very way it behaved on the road: 'The spring frame was excellent, and the only guide to its presence in the specification was the exceptional comfort of the machine.' On corners the handling was 'just about perfect; there was no tail wag, chopping or pitching, even when roughish bends were taken nearly flat out by way of experiment, my whole impression was of handling a first-class three-fifty and not a 413lb [187kg] six-hundred at all.' (In fact this final comment was inaccurate, as officially, Matchless sources quoted 370lb (168kg) for the solo Hawk.)

Updates for the 1932 Season

During mid-September 1931, details of the Matchless range for the 1932 season were published. The four-hundred Silver Arrow had few changes. There was a new oil filter (adopted throughout the entire Matchless range) and cleaner handlebars. But chief modifications were the use of deeper piston rings and an improved set of ratios for the four-speed gearbox (also made on other Matchless models using the Sturmey-Archer four-speed box)

The Silver Hawk six-hundred four was substantially unchanged except for improvements made throughout the range. Second gear in the four-speed box was now 9.2:1 instead of 12.4:1, the top three ratios being, for solo work, 5.7, 6.9 and 9.2:1 – and bottom gear 17:1. A higher bottom gear was available to order. Another important alteration concerned the lubrication system, which had been modified to provide low oil consumption figures (Torrens had noted, '500 miles per gallon!')

Prices of both the four-hundred V-twin and six-hundred four remained unchanged.

The continuing economic gloom meant that the Matchless range, including the Hawk and Arrow models, remained substantially the same for the 1933 season when the range details were announced at the end of September 1932. Probably the most noticeable feature (which was applicable to all models) was the alteration in the design and finish of the fuel tanks. Gone was the chromium tank with its white panel, to be replaced on the Arrow and Hawk models with a black tank panel, with an embossed 'M' in chromium. Otherwise for 1933 the two models were unchanged in specification and price.

The Silver Arrow is Axed

During 1933 the four-hundred Silver Arrow was axed, after suffering a combination of high production costs and low sales; the Silver Hawk four, however, was retained for the 1934 season. The latest edition was very similar to the previous one, although it incorporated the new range features for that year; this included deeper mudguards, whilst the chromium 'M' on the tank was now retained by screws, as on other models. The 1934 price was £73 10s. In 1934, the Hawk finally received the new-style silencers that had been used on some models since 1932, and the deeper, chrome-edged mudguards that had been introduced on other models the previous year.

In September 1934, when the 1935 Matchless range details were released, it was seen that the Silver Hawk was now coded 35/B (the year and series number). A noticeable alteration (to all the range) was the adoption of chromium-plated wheel rims and the substitution of an enamelled gold line in place of the chromium edging for the mudguards – though these were still retained on the Silver Hawk. And the Silver Hawk was the only machine in the Matchless 1935 model year line-up to retain the fish-tailed silencer in preference to the latest tubular pattern. The price had now risen to £78 10s.

The End of the Road

Finally, in mid-1935, the Silver Hawk four-cylinder machine, which had remained largely unchanged for the previous five years, was removed from the Matchless range. Like the smaller Silver Arrow narrow-angle V-twin, the ohc four-cylinder Hawk had been saddled with the double disadvantage of high production costs and a high purchase price, in a market dominated during its life by economic depression.

Also, even though everyone who rode the machine was hugely impressed, there is no doubt that the early version's high oil consumption, combined with a tendency for overheating problems in the engine top end when given full throttle treatment for long periods, caused customer dissatisfaction. Finally, it was reported that setting up the bevel gears correctly was almost impossible once the bike had left the factory's area of mechanical assembly. Others seemed to set up the bevel gears so they were either too tight or too loose, resulting in whining or rattling, respectively.

Even with the above comments, the fact remains that the Silver Hawk ohc four – and to a lesser extent the Silver Arrow V-twin – was a notable design worthy of a better fate than history records. Had it been put on to the market at any other time, it would have achieved a different outcome. As it was, just as the world was pulling itself out of recession, the Silver Hawk left the scene, and one can only imagine what 'could have been'.

5 Wartime

Late 1939, and this civil defence volunteer had offered up his Matchless Model X V-twin for the war effort. Many such civilian bikes were employed for such duties during the early war years.

Behind the Norton 16H and the BSA M20, the Matchless G3/L was the most numerous of the various motorcycles used by the British military services during World War II. However, a bombing raid on the city of Coventry one night in November 1940 was the real reason why so many G3/L models were to be built. Why? Well, the original plan by the War Office had been to mass-produce Edward Turner's Triumph 3TW 349cc ohv parallel twin (contract number C8331). And in fact the first batch of these machines was awaiting delivery when the raid took place. However, virtually all the bikes were destroyed, together with the drawings, tooling and spares, and the Triumph factory itself.

AMC and Matchless had been trying to win a major military contract to supply motorcycles for many years; these attempts can first be traced back to 1929 when the War Office selected a T/4 three-fifty side-valve single for evaluation purposes. However, in the event the military chose a Douglas design (the L29 flat twin).

Next, in 1930 and 1931, came more extensive testing of the Silver Arrow four-hundred narrow-angle V-twin (*see* Chapter 4). This resulted in the purchase of thirty-seven machines, but no further examples were ordered (this was seen as a combination of the type's unsuitability for military service, and the prevailing world economic situation).

The 36/G3 Clubman

During 1935 Matchless were requested by the War Office to supply an example of their 348cc (69 × 93mm) model 36/G3 Clubman overhead-valve single for evaluation. Subsequently the machine was delivered and thereafter put through an extensive MEE 10,000-mile (16,000km) reliability test that year. The main problems encountered by what was still essentially a series-production civilian model were soft hairpin valve springs, collapsed rear-wheel bearings, sprockets, and – probably most seriously – a gearbox that wore to such an extent that it had to be replaced at 8,800 miles (14,160km). Matchless attended to the valve-spring problem by substituting the superior coil springs from the AJS version. Fortunately the G3 had enough positive features for the War Department to order small numbers of the model under contract between 1936 and 1939.

These pre-war bikes continued to feature the duplex cradle frame and a similar specification to the original 1935 machine. However, annual improvements were made, including a change to 14mm spark plugs, the enclosure of the valve springs, a new crankcase and cosmetic changes (which included the fuel tank). In addition some machines were equipped with air filters.

The G3/L

During 1940 – and before the air raid that destroyed the Triumph works – the War Office had already instigated a programme to encourage manufacturers, including Matchless, to reduce the weight of their motorcycles. The Woolwich factory thus embarked on a weight-pruning

The wartime G3/L with Teledraulic front forks proved one of the most successful of all military motorcycles of World War II; over 55,000 were delivered to the War Department.

exercise, which was to result in the G3/L ('L' being for 'light') prototype: this was 56lb (25kg) lighter than the stock civilian model, and included a single front downtube frame.

Most interesting of all was the fitment of the then – at least as regards British bikes – patented teledraulic front forks, a design that relied heavily on a pre-war German BMW design (*see* panel). There is no doubt that the new forks were not only technically superior to the existing girder type as found on other British machinery of the period, but they also improved the bike's aesthetic appearance, giving the newcomer an extremely modern look.

At least two prototypes of the special lightweight G3 were constructed. But despite it being highly thought of, the War Office had decided to order the Triumph 3TW lightweight ohv twin –

The AMC Teledraulic Front Fork

A 1945 advertisement proclaiming the virtues of AMC's Teledraulic front forks. These were the first telescopic forks fitted to a British-made production motorcycle.

The story behind the development of the AMC teledraulic front forks is not one simply of design and manufacture, but of competitors, contracts and ultimately tragedy. Back in the 1930s the Isleworth, Middlesex, company of AFN Ltd held the British import rights for the German range of BMW cars and motorcycles. And in 1935 BMW had introduced the world's first production oil-damped telescopic front forks to the motorcycle world. First seen on the R7 prototype, these forks entered series production with the R12 and R17 models. In addition the German marque also used developments of these forks on its racing and record-breaking machines.

Also in 1935, Jock West, who was later to join AMC, had begun work at AFN. As a result of his riding ability (he had successfully raced Ariel, Triumph and AJS machines) Jock was subsequently invited to become a member of the official BMW works racing team, and he went on to win the Ulster Grand Prix on more than one occasion on one of the German flat-twin models – and of course more famously finished runner-up behind BMW team-mate Georg Meier in the 1939 Senior TT.

However, before this, in 1937 Jock West had been instrumental in organizing for AMC to purchase a set of BMW motorcycle telescopic front forks, via AFN. This all came about because he was on such good terms with the Collier brothers who then owned AMC. Having taken delivery of the forks, AMC set about making their own version of the telescopic forks, under the Teledraulic trade name. Like the BMW components, the Matchless Teledraulics operated on the action of compression of an extended coil spring in each fork leg by means of an aluminium slider. The alloy moving slider members of the Teledraulic fork assembly supported the front wheel, mudguard and brake anchorage, and most important of all, housed the hydraulic damping mechanism. The operation of this mechanism depended upon the movement of small, disc-like damper valves, having a limited range of movement. These disc-type valves were designed to obstruct progressively the transfer of oil, employed as the damping medium, between damper compartments whilst the slider was moving. This served to slow down movement at the moments of both impact and rebound, whilst coil springs took up the inertia of the moving parts of the forks as it attempted to bottom out.

The majority of the development work in transferring the technology to actual production was carried out by the youngest of the Collier brothers, Bert, who was then manager of the AMC works at Plumstead until his untimely death on the 31 October 1941, whilst carrying out further tests on the public highway near Sevenoaks, Kent. He was taken to hospital with a fractured skull, from which he died; he was only thirty-four years of age.

This came only weeks after the Teledraulic front forks had made their debut on the new 348cc W41/G3L military model. It should also be noted that these forks were the first British-made examples of the telescopic front fork to feature a hydraulic damping on a production bike.

As is charted elsewhere, although the principle of the Teledraulics remained, the actual fork design underwent continual development over many years of service during the 1940s and 1950s, to improve both its operation and serviceability.

G3/L engine with rear-mounted, magdyno, four-speed, foot-change Burman gearbox and overhead valves.

that was, of course, until the Luftwaffe intervened! And so with Triumph effectively sidelined, Matchless were able to offer a viable alternative in the shape of a production version of the Model G3/L.

Despite the prototype having been evaluated and tested during 1940, the first production G3/Ls were not available until the latter half of 1941 – and it wasn't until mid-1942 that the type was in widespread use. Because quantity was demanded as the highest priority, the production Model G3/L was not quite as light as the prototypes; also, to begin with the machines featured 'luxuries' such as ribbed mudguards, metal Matchless tank badges, rubber handlebar grips and rubber knee pads. Control levers were initially either Amal (single) or Bowden (combination pattern), and the machine's crankcase usually marked with an A or B to signify the type fitted. However, this practice was relatively short-lived, and subsequently universal components were fitted, to make the stocking of spare parts easier in service. Pannier frames were fitted to virtually all the G3/Ls built from late 1942, so that the standard military canvas bags could be carried.

Another feature that was soon replaced in production was the single fuel tap. The disadvantage of this was that the fuel tank had to be drained prior to its removal, so twin taps were soon specified. Another early problem was the lack of a front stand, making wheel removal very difficult; again this was soon attended to, and a suitable stand added. As new contracts for large batches arrived, so Matchless sought to make improvements; but the constraints of wartime economy soon meant that the metal tank emblems were replaced by transfers, rubber knee grips were dropped and handlebar rubbers replaced by canvas components, and mudguards were plain.

The engine's valve timing was improved, to give easier starting, and the teledraulic front forks were modified (the yokes and lugs strengthened). A comprehensive Vokes air-filter system was also fitted to most later machines. Although the G3/L was highly regarded by those who rode her, the same could not be said for the men who serviced the Matchless single. A major problem, as compared to the more bulky (and much heavier) Norton and BSA side-valve singles, was the sheer compactness of the Matchless, which meant that access to certain components was difficult and often time-consuming. For example, for virtually all engine maintenance the fuel tank had to be removed – and even to replace the oil filter the rider's saddle had to be taken off! But the most serious problem was that associated with the removal of the dynamo: this was situated under the magneto and embedded in the engine plates, and the entire primary chaincase and clutch had to be taken out first! In addition, the primary chaincase was prone to leaking, whilst the innovative teledraulic front forks caused difficulties for workshop staff only familiar with the traditional girder variety.

The toolbox (on the offside of the machine) had to be packed in numerical order as follows:

Rider's handbook
Toolbag
Chain rivet extractor

Tyre-repair kit
Rear chain spares
Insulating tape
Tyre levers (2)
Tyre pressure gauge
Webbing straps (2)
Coil of wire.

Official figures show that 55,030 G3/Ls were actually delivered; this includes an order placed in March 1944 for a total of 10,000 bikes, but subsequently reduced to 6,089.

The 1942 G3/L

Engine:	Air-cooled ohv single with vertical cylinder; iron head and barrel; vertically split aluminium crankcases, fully enclosed valve gear; coil valve springs; built-up crankshaft; roller-bearing big end; gear-driven cams
Bore:	69mm
Stroke:	93mm
Displacement:	348cc
Compression ratio:	5.9:1
Lubrication:	Dry sump
Ignition:	Magdyno, Lucas
Carburettor:	Amal 275 ⅞in bore
Primary drive:	Chain
Final drive:	Chain
Gearbox:	Four-speed, foot-change, Burman
Frame:	Diamond type with single front down-tube
Front suspension:	AMC teledraulic forks
Rear suspension:	Rigid
Front brake:	5.5in, SLS drum, single-sided
Rear brake:	5.5in, SLS drum, single-sided
Tyres:	3.25 × 19 front and rear

General Specifications

Wheelbase:	54in (1,372mm)
Ground clearance:	5.5in (140mm)
Seat height:	30in (762mm)
Fuel tank capacity:	3gal (14ltr)
Dry weight:	344lb (156kg)
Maximum power:	16bhp (7.3kg)
Top speed:	71mph (114km/h)

As with other wartime models, the G3/L was also subject to alteration either because of material shortages, or shortages of certain manufacturers' components. And so (for a short time only) the aluminium timing cover for the engine was substituted for a cast-iron assembly; whilst during 1942 a shortage of Lucas electrical parts led to a batch of some 5,000 G3/Ls being equipped with Miller components – although the magneto remained a Lucas assembly throughout. The final examples of the military G3/L featured Vokes air filters factory-fitted to the top of the fuel tank, a feature which caused Matchless to have to reintroduce the knee-grip fastening holes to allow the mounting of the filter. In addition, one G3/L was constructed using a swinging-arm frame, the rear shock absorbers being based on components from the company's teledraulic front forks.

The G3WO

The next most numerous Matchless model to see service during World War II was the G3WO three-fifty ohv single, supplied between 1940 and 1942. A total of some 18,500 were produced – these being in excess of the various small batches of the G3 model supplied between 1935 and 1939 inclusive. The G3WO can be viewed as an interim model between the largely civilian pre-war G3 and the lighter, teledraulic-forked G3/L.

Matchless had announced several changes during the autumn of 1939 for its 1940 model-year bikes, and these changes affected the marque's WD specification G3. These can be listed as follows:

- revised frame with a single front downtube;
- AJS-type cylinder head with coil valve springs;
- redesigned cylinder barrel (incorporating the cutaway of some finning);
- fitment of a second toolbox above the existing one.

Production of the G3WO and G3/L overlapped during late 1941 and early 1942, and this led to the last machines supplied using G3/L components

A 1940 advertisement for the G3WO ohv single-port three-fifty; basically a militarized version of the pre-war civilian model.

such as crankpins and brake shoes; in fact, the final fifty bikes were specials – featuring more G3/L items – including the new teledraulic front forks.

Because of its extra weight the G3WO was not as popular as the G3/L, particularly off-road.

The 990cc ohv V-Twin Project

In addition to its contract work for both the G3WO and G3/L three-fifty singles, Matchless (via the AMC parent company) were involved in the 990cc ohv V-twin project, which although badged as a Sunbeam, was nevertheless Matchless-powered. AMC had acquired the Sunbeam company during 1938, and although they subsequently sold it to BSA during the war, when the machine was built in 1942 Sunbeam was still under AMC control.

The machine was intended as a sidecar tug, the 990cc engine driving a four-speed gearbox, with a reverse ratio. There was also optional sidecar wheel-drive, which could be employed on the road. There were two exhaust header pipes connecting to a large, single hi-level silencer on the offside (right). Ignition was by a forward-mounted magneto, with the dynamo sited above the gearbox; lubrication was by dry sump.

The engine was mounted in a substantial double cradle frame with an abundance of ground clearance, and was equipped with specially constructed, heavy-duty teledraulic front forks. Final drive (from the gearbox to the rear wheel) was by way of chain and could be connected, or not, to operate the sidecar wheel. Unlike the Norton of the same era, this sidecar outfit could be driven on the road with the drive engaged. Other details of this impressive machine's specification included bulbous knobbly tyres, comprehensive mudguarding, and a 4gal (18ltr) fuel tank.

Although AMC did win a contract for the design, this came at the height of the G3/L's production and so the Woolwich factory simply couldn't cope; production was to be undertaken by the Standard car firm. However, in reality this did not occur, as by then suppliers of the four-wheel American Jeep were coming on stream, and the whole order was cancelled.

But although only the single prototype example was constructed, it remained the most serious British attempt to build an all-terrain sidecar machine comparable to the German BMW R75 and Zündapp K750 outfits.

Matchless the Innovator

In conclusion it can be said that in the G3/L Matchless built one of the very best motorcycles employed by the British armed forces during the 1939–45 period, and one which lasted from the early 1930s to the late 1960s. And in military guise the G3/L was particularly notable for introducing the telescopic front fork into mass production for the British motorcycle industry. It was very much a case of where Matchless led, others were destined to follow.

6 Heavyweight Singles

Fresh from its wartime production spearheaded by the famous G3/L three-fifty single, AMC announced its civilian production plan in early July 1945. At that time the service contract for the military G3/L was still ongoing – the Allied forces were still at war with Japan – and so the two 'civilian' Matchless models that the company said 'would be available in a few weeks' were therefore necessarily based on the army machine – which, as *The Motor Cycle* pointed out, was 'one of the Army's favourite motorcycles'. Both bikes featured the frame, forks (the by now famous Teledraulics) and the general features of the G3/L, the lighter military model developed from the pre-war G3; they were designated the 348cc 350 Clubman Model G3/L, and the 498cc 500 Clubman Model G80.

Two Bikes for the Post-War Civilian Market

Thanks to chromium plating, the lustrous black enamel – the fuel tanks were lined with black and silver – and such components as rubber knee-grips and footrest rubbers, it was, as one journalist put it, 'difficult to imagine that the new "Clubman" models have any connection with the WD [War Department] machine we all know so well. They look what they are: a pair of sleek, modern overhead valve singles.'

A Burman four-speed, foot-operated CP gearbox provided closer bottom and second gears than were provided by the box fitted to the WD G3/L. Top gear in the case of the three-fifty remained 5.8:1 and third gear 7.5:1, but second and bottom were 10.3 and 15.4:1 instead of 12.2 and 18.5:1. The compression ratio of the 348cc Clubman G3/L was also different: there was no compression plate, as on the WD version, which meant that the compression ratio was 6.3:1 in place of 6:1. Another feature was the larger-bore Amal carburettor, namely 1in as against ⅞in.

The lively five-hundred fitted to the G80 model was similar to the engine listed for 1940. It featured heavier flywheels than the early 1939 engine, and a different inlet-valve timing. The compression ratio was 5.9:1. Gear ratios in this larger-engined model were 5.25, 6.8, 9.3 and 13.9:1. Another feature of this larger model was a cylinder-head steady, which ran from the rocker box to the top tube of the frame.

Many pre-war singles had been of the twin-exhaust-port type, but both these new machines released in the summer of 1945 had a single port, with the exhaust header pipe arranged to pass above the offside (right) footrest on the three-fifty,

Burman CP gearbox fitted to the G3/L and G80 from 1945 until 1951.

During the immediate post-war era a popular choice with many enthusiasts was the rigid frame G3/L three-fifty single, a motorcycle that had built a good reputation during the war years and was destined to do the same in peacetime. This photograph dates from 1948.

and below it in the five-hundred (the latter featuring a pipe diameter of 1¾in (44mm)). Both engines had totally enclosed valve gear, with coil instead of the hairpin valve springs found on the pre-war Matchless singles (*see* Chapter 2). In fact the wheels and the final drive chain were the only exposed moving parts, the rear chain being guarded at its top run, and with a deep flange running downward to protect the chain from mud from the tyre.

The 1946 G3/L

Engine:	Air-cooled ohv single with vertical cylinder; iron head and barrel; vertically split aluminium crankcases; fully enclosed valve gear, valve springs; built-up crankshaft; gear-driven cams
Bore:	69mm
Stroke:	93mm
Displacement:	348cc
Compression ratio:	6.3:1
Lubrication:	Dry sump
Ignition:	Magdyno
Carburettor:	Amal type 76 1in
Primary drive:	Chain
Final drive:	Chain
Gearbox:	Four-speed, foot-change, Burman
Frame:	Diamond type with single front down-tube
Front suspension:	AMC Teledraulic forks
Rear suspension:	Rigid
Front brake:	5.5in SLS drum single-sided
Rear brake:	5.5in SLS drum single-sided
Tyres:	3.25 × 19 front and rear

General Specifications

Wheelbase:	54in (1,372mm)
Ground clearance:	5.5in (140mm)
Seat height:	30in (762mm)
Fuel tank capacity:	3gal (14ltr)
Dry weight:	344lb (156kg)
Maximum power:	16bhp @ 5,600rpm
Top speed:	71mph (114km/h)

The 1946 G80

Engine:	Air-cooled ohv single with vertical cylinder; iron head and barrel; vertically split aluminium crankcases; fully enclosed valve gear; coil valve springs, built-up crankshaft; roller bearing big-end; gear-driven cams
Bore:	82.5mm
Stroke:	93mm
Displacement:	497cc
Compression ratio:	5.9:1
Lubrication:	Dry sump
Ignition:	Magdyno, Lucas
Carburettor:	Amal Type 89 1 3/32in
Primary drive:	Chain
Final drive:	Chain
Gearbox:	Four-speed, foot-change, Burman
Frame:	Diamond-type with single front down-tube
Front suspension:	AMC Teledraulic forks
Rear suspension:	Rigid
Front brake:	5.5in SLS drum
Rear brake:	5.5in SLS drum
Tyres:	3.25 × 19 front and rear

General Specification

Wheelbase:	54in (1,372mm)
Ground clearance:	5.5in (140mm)
Seat height:	30in (762mm)
Fuel tank capacity:	3gal (14ltr)
Dry weight:	353lb (160kg)
Maximum power:	23bhp @ 5,400rpm
Top speed:	81mph (130km/h)

Other features of the two singles included separate Lucas dynamo and magneto; fabric oil filter; internally illuminated Smiths speedometer head mounted on the top cross-member of the AMC Teledraulic front forks; 7in (178mm) headlamp; side and centre stands; fabric-type handlebar grips; 3gal (14ltr) fuel tank, with twin taps; ½gal (2ltr) oil tank; and 3.25 × 19 block-section Dunlop tyres.

In December 1945 two patents (specifications 572,520 and 572,581) were issued under the name of Associated Motor Cycles. The first concerned improvements in cam action adjusters for rear wheels, to ensure correct wheel alignment being maintained; the change would eliminate the possibility of human error associated with the draw-bolt method of wheel adjustment, and would obviate the dependency of the usual cam method upon accurate positioning of the cam stops on frame fork-ends – a difficult operation in a brazed-frame. The other patent concerned the arrangement of the AMC long-life oil-tight bearing for pivoted fork-type rear springing, employing porous oil-impregnated bronze bushes fed by lubricant within the bearing tube.

These, and other innovations, were being considered for production as Matchless (and AJS) prepared for the competitive environment of the post-war civilian motorcycle marketplace.

Improvements for 1947

When details of the 1947 Matchless (and AJS) motorcycles were published at the beginning of November 1946, there were numerous improvements to be seen. Several of these had come from a 'suggestions book' maintained by Jock West, AMC sales manager: this was something unique in the British motorcycle industry at the time. One example of those points he had jotted down concerned the oil-bath primary chaincase: this now had a longer screw in the band which held the two halves together, because it had been found that the rubber sealing washer was liable to expand after use, and as a result, an owner might experience problems refitting the band. Simple as this particular alteration might have appeared, it was nonetheless a good illustration of the attention to detail that was being made by AMC at that time.

Changes had also been made to the well-known AMC-made Teledraulic front forks. These now featured new springs that had been wound in such a way as to provide three different rates: the coils were set at different distances apart, and the springs, claimed AMC, afforded 'a soft, easy movement at initial deflection of the forks, and increasing resistance with increased fork travel.' Buffer springs had been added to reduce the fall of the wheel, and this had meant that the front brake cable could be shortened 3¼in (83mm), therefore providing a neater arrangement of the cable, which now had a guide on the nearside fork blade.

Another important change was that the gudgeon-pin bosses were now set ½in (13mm) lower in the Lo-Ex (Low Expansion) split-skirt piston assembly, and the connecting rod had been reduced in length by an equal amount. The intention had been to reduce pistol slap, which had become a feature of the latest Matchless (and AJS) motorcycles, with rather larger piston clearances; the latter were intended to greatly reduce the likelihood of piston seizure during the running-in period. At the same time, the oil circulation had been doubled. The oil-pump speed had been increased by the introduction of a two-start worm on the timing-side engine shaft, and a larger feed pipe, measuring 7⁄16in (11mm), from the oil tank, and larger ducts in the engine to suit.

In the case of the 350cc engine, the lubricating oil operated at an appreciably lower temperature owing to a change in the exhaust pipe design. Previously the pipe had been fitted in as close as possible to the crankcase and timing chest, above the rider's footrest. Now it was arranged *beneath* the footrest, which, in addition to improving the appearance of the machine, resulted in a greater range of adjustment for the footrest – and as already stated, cooler running. The pipe was still well tucked away, thus providing sufficient ground clearance.

Another, more detail change was a new front number plate and its fixings, described by *The Motor Cycle* as 'altogether neater'. The development team had placed rubber between the mudguard and the channelled member which now formed the mounting of the front plate.

Chromium-plated wheel rims and handlebars had now been standardized: the rims featured black centres lined in silver (gold on AJS models), and all wheel spokes were cadmium plated. The Matchless chromium-plated winged 'M' now adorned the fuel-tank sides. A pillion seat and carrier were now available, the cost for the two being an additional £2 11s 11d. A lifting handle on all models was now integral with the rear mudguard stays, making for a much neater arrangement.

AMC made much of its factory finish, saying:

> The durability of enamel is proportional to the stoving temperature, and no stove enamel allows the employment of so high a baking temperature as does black. What is especially pleasing about the latest productions is the exceptionally high quality of the finish. All enamelled parts have three coats of Pinchin Johnson's best black enamel on a rustproof Bonderized base.

The British prices as at 24 October 1946 (including UK purchase tax) were as follows: the 350 Clubman Model G3/L, £134 12s 5d; and the 500 Clubman Model G80, £147 6s 5d.

Matchless and AMC Models for 1948

The 1948 AMC programmes for Matchless and AJS machines were announced to the public in mid-October 1947, and as *The Motor Cycle* reported, there were 'a number of interesting and important changes'. Whilst the range of machines was unaltered, the improvements were many and significant. Thus essentially there were the four Matchless (and four AJS) models, a three-fifty and five hundred in each marque, and each of these in roadster and competition guises (the latter is fully covered in Chapter 10).

All engines were of the single port, ohv single-cylinder type, mounted in cradle frames. The main differences between the Matchless and the AJS machines were that the latter had engines with the magneto mounted between the cylinder base and the front down-tube, and a black-and-gold paint job, whilst the former had the magneto to the rear and a silver-and-black finish.

No changes had been made to the engines except for the oil pump and its housing. The pump spindle, its cam screw and pin had been strengthened, with the object of increasing the factor of safety; this coming after changes to considerably increase the flow rate the previous year. AMC recommended a period of 5,000 miles (8,000km) between oil changes.

There were major changes to both the steering and the braking; sales chief Jock West made the following comment: 'Associated Motor Cycles maintain that perfect high-speed steering is not enough; the rider should also have absolute confidence at low speeds – be complete master of his machine – and this is so, right from the slowest of traffic crawls'.

To this end the company had carried out an extensive test programme in the matter of steering layout.

For the 1948 model year there was a new steering-head angle, and a new rake and trail of the front forks. The aim had been to provide a motorcycle that could be ridden feet-up almost to a standstill, was really light to handle at low speeds, yet would maintain perfect stability at high speeds. As *The Motor Cycle* was able to report: 'A short run on one of the new models showed that the steering is exceptionally good, and under traffic conditions close to remarkable'.

One also has to remember that both Matchless and AJS roadster models benefited greatly from AMC's support and participation in trials and scrambling at the highest level; furthermore, in Hugh Viney it also had probably the finest rider of the era at its disposal, to provide feedback which could usefully be used in the series-production models.

Important modifications had also been made to the now-famous AMC Teledraulic front forks. For 1948 the hydraulic damping had been considerably simplified, yet was as effective as before. Immediately above the piston, which was fitted at the lower end of each 1⅛in (28mm) chrome-moly fork stanchion, there was a light alloy shuttle of slightly smaller external diameter than the piston, with an internal diameter fractionally larger than the stanchion. When the front wheel encountered poor road surface (a pothole, for example), the slider moved upwards, compressing air in the upper part of the fork tube; this forced oil through four ¼in (6mm) holes in the tube, raising the shuttle off its seat on the piston and automatically centring the shuttle relative to the main tube and the slider, thus cushioning the fork action. Should the shock be particularly violent, one of the patented taper plugs would come into action, providing an increasingly rapid cut-off and, at extremes, almost complete cut-off, thus acting as a hydraulic buffer.

On rebound the shuttle was forced downward, sealing itself on the piston, and thus sealing the lateral passage through which the oil passed, causing the oil to return to the fork tube via the predetermined passages between the bore of the shuttle and the fork tube. The arrangement was continued whereby the main fork springs, one per leg, were wound so as to provide a progressive action, but thanks to the elimination of the previously fitted distance piece, the springs were now 1½in (38mm) larger than before. With this new set-up the amount of oil per leg was 'critical' (AMC), the factory's official recommendation being 6oz of Mobiloil 'Artic' per leg, against 6½oz previously.

Another important feature of the 1948 range was that new, larger brakes were specified for all models: 7in diameter, with ⅞in-wide linings. The drums were cast in Chromidium, and quite apart from the excellent construction of the hubs themselves, they were fitted with (*Motor Cycling*) 'some of the most rigid, deep section aluminium-alloy brake shoes that have ever been fitted to production models'. When tested by *The Motor Cycle* the opinion was that here was 'a pair of brakes which are free from lost motion and from sponginess, and, while extremely light in operation and thoroughly progressive, are outstandingly effective'.

There were also a series of more minor changes. These included a larger (3.50 section) rear tyre on the G80; improved saddle-spring mountings, giving improved comfort on both the three-fifty and five-hundred; revised fuel piping (providing easier access to the carburettor for maintenance); revised exhaust-pipe bend (on the 500 only); a neater, chromium-plated battery strap; one-piece 'M' badges on the fuel tank; chromium-plated rings part-way down the front fork cover tubes; and neater toolbox fixings.

Cover from the 1949 Matchless Clubman brochure, published in October 1948.

Matchless Single-Cylinders for 1949

When the Matchless 1949 range was announced at the start of October 1948 they were all single-cylinders: the new parallel twin was not unveiled until a few weeks later, on the eve of the London Show. There were over a dozen modifications, some of major importance – such as the redesigned frame and cylinder heads – others far less so.

As in the past the frame remained of the cradle type, but the seat tube was now further back; this gave additional clearance at the carburettor, enabling a flat, cylindrical Vokes air filter to be fitted (as a cost option). In addition, the new frame allowed a larger oil tank, capacity ½gal (2ltr), to be fitted. Another feature was that a sidecar connection point was provided at each rear fork and lug.

Other changes as a result of the redesigned frame were that the chain line had been widened by 3/16in (4mm) so that a 4in- (100mm-) section rear tyre could be fitted if required; whilst the engine was now 7/16in (11mm) lower, which improved accessibility and also lowered the centre of gravity. AMC also claimed 'improved roadholding'. But the frame was still rigid, with no form of rear suspension.

Both the cylinder head and rocker box had been redesigned, mainly because a switch had been made from coil to hairpin valve springs. The AMC development engineers considered that these springs gave better service at very high engine revolutions. In addition, the valve-stem caps had been dispensed with; instead, the valve-stem ends were now hardened.

A new aluminium-alloy rocker box, which also enclosed the valve springs, was retained by a total

The G3/L's bigger brother, the 497cc (82.5 × 93mm) G80, c. 1949.

of nine bolts. A boss in the rocker box housed the exhaust-valve lifter; this took the form of a simple cam which, when brought into operation, pressed down on the exhaust rocker arm. This cam, its shaft and the external lever were a one-piece stamping; a torsion spring round the shaft returned the cam out of contact with the rocker when the handlebar lever was released. With the exhaust-valve lifter mechanism now being in the rocker box in place of the timing gear, the crankcase exterior had been cleaned up considerably. A deeper cover plate was fitted to the new rocker box, this providing improved access for rocker adjustment.

The cylinder-head finning had been revised to prevent 'fin ringing', whilst the top of the cylinder bore now featured a spigot for locating into the cylinder head; but the joint between the cylinder and head was still made by means of a gasket at the faces.

The dynamo armature speed had been increased. The sprocket on the engine mainshaft was now larger, resulting in the armature being driven at 1½ times engine speed; thus the charging rate when travelling slowly was improved. Another electrical change was a right-angle extension of the battery platform to provide a new mounting for the lighting voltage-regulator.

Other changes were new handlebars, new headlamp shell and rectangular rear lamp (with modified number plate), whilst the saddle was now adjustable for height at the nose as well as at the springs. New saddle springs reduced lateral sway. There were also synthetic rubber seals for the wheel bearings, and a square-section footrest bar that was integral with the nearside (left) hanger; this latter assembly being secured by a single nut against the boss of the hanger on the other side.

When the new Matchless G9 (and AJS Spring Twin) five-hundred vertical twins were announced in mid-November 1948, AMC also stated that the new spring frame was to be made available for the single-cylinder models for an additional £20 6s 4d. Many customers opted to pay the extra charge for the improvements this conversion to the swinging-arm frame offered, in comfort, handling and a more modern appearance. The rear-suspension units were of AMC's own manufacture and were referred to as being of the 'candlestick' type – much narrower both top and bottom from the famous 'Jampot' type which came next.

Further Refinements for 1950

Various improvements and modifications were planned for the 1950 season, as recorded by *The Motor Cycle* in its 13 October 1949 issue:

Prototype Frame

In July 1946, AMC and their designer Philip Walker applied for a patent regarding a new part-pressed, part-tubular frame, this eventually being accepted in November 1949 under Patent No. 631,946. However, following the death of former Ariel and Triumph tester/tuner Freddie Clarke whilst riding a machine with this new frame, the project was abandoned; nevertheless it is important to record its details, if for no other reason than to give an insight into how AMC (and thus Matchless) were thinking when spring frames were in their infancy. As *The Motor Cycle* said in 1950: 'From any review of frame design over the last few decades, it might reasonably be concluded that British manufacturers have been far less inclined to break away from the orthodox tubular frame, usually with brazed joints, than manufacturers in other parts of the world.'

So who would have imagined that such a conservative firm as AMC might have designed a fabricated, part-pressed, part-tubular frame incorporating features such as Patent No. 631,946? In fact, except for Freddie Clarke's untimely accident, it could have seen production in the company's roadsters, instead of the race-derived AMC spring frame!

The prototype was extensively tested by the Woolwich works. The design featured a box-section sheet metal beam, at its front end attached to the steering head, extending back to take the place of the top tube in a conventional frame. The tail of this beam fitted between the side members of a sheet-metal 'saddle' which replaced the orthodox seat tube. Various methods of securing the components of the beam and 'saddle' were provided for by the patent, and Philip Walker even envisaged that it could be formed integrally. Either sheet steel or duralumin could be used, but Walker considered the latter preferable.

The beam was straddled by the fuel tank, which rested on soft insulating material, and was held in position by a single long bolt that passed through the beam and screwed into a captive nut in the crown of the tank tunnel; an alternative method of attachment provided for a bolt through a bridge-piece section across the base of the tunnel, abutting to the underside of the beam and keeping a tank projection in line with a seating in the upper face of the beam.

Across the two rails formed at the top of the 'saddle' was a duplex seat of the type then fitted as standard on Matchless G9 Super Clubman twins. Rear ends of the rails formed an attachment for the twin rear shock absorbers.

The swinging-arm fork pivoted on lugs that were attached to the side-members of the 'saddle' and which could either be cast or built up. To these lugs were attached the cradle tubes of the frame. Transversely mounted across the side-members was the oil tank, this latter component forming an additional bracing member.

A passage through the oil tank registered with the carburettor air intake; this passage joined with a semicircular duct leading up to a filter element situated between the rails of the 'saddle'. The official patent stated:

> The object of the passage and duct is to provide an easy path of flow for air into the engine and a confined space immediately in alignment with the carburettor venturi passage, so that liquid fuel which is normally ejected at certain engine speeds by blowback resulting from valve-opening overlap may be trapped and contained in an air column that is subsequently drawn into the engine. A certain degree of fuel economy is thus assured.

Essentially, the experimental frame set out to provide an integrated assembly and thus to save weight. This theme was continued by incorporating built-in side panels within the frame structure, with doors giving access to storage compartments within. The patent specification envisaged one container to house the battery and small electrical components, the other for tools.

Of course, a frame made up of tubes and sheet metal was by no means new in concept, Italian designers having already exploited this idea for several years previously. But what made the AMC patent exciting was the favoured use of aluminium sheet, as this offered great strength combined with weight-saving, and also gave a cleaner external appearance to the motorcycle. But Freddie Clarke's death caused the whole project to be abandoned.

Further refinements of standard models and competition machines are announced by Associated Motor Cycles for the 1950 AJS and Matchless ranges. As widely known, these two marques have much in common; the most obvious difference, other than the finish, is that on single-cylinder engines the AJS has the magneto mounted at the front of the cylinder, and on the Matchless the magneto is behind the cylinder.

A minor change, already introduced in production but which could well be described as a modification for 1950, was that the steering-crown

1950 Matchless G80, the last year of the iron cylinder head.

lug was a steel stamping, with the fork leg clamps pinned and brazed in position. This steel stamping incorporated the steering stops, and was both stronger and lighter than the previously used malleable casting.

Brakes were unchanged except that, for the 1950 model year, the rear pedal was of a slightly different shape – more 'directional', as one journalist described it at the time. All models, including the singles, now featured a long shoe-plate torque arm for the front brake. This, it was claimed, provided smoother braking under hard application than the previous set-up, where the shoe-plate was retained by two bolts passing through a lug on the fork slider.

Both front and rear mudguards had been redesigned: they were now of deep section, with a circumferential rib to provide greater stiffness. The front mudguard stay was of tubular one-piece construction, flattened and curved where it ran under the mudguard blade (previously, the stay had been of the pressed-steel variety). The rear mudguard, also supported by tubular stays, was given a detachable tail section to help wheel removal.

A centre stand was given to models fitted with the swinging-arm frame, whereas the old rigid frame retained the almost vintage rear-wheel type; there was also a toolbox between the chain stays of the rigid models.

The silencers of the single-cylinder models had been redesigned, and were now described as being 'offset'; this was done to avoid grounding. Footrests had also been modified considerably, so that each combined footrest and hanger was fitted inside the frame tubes, and the hanger boss had twelve internal splines to fit on a square-section clamping rod. Rear hubs were now wider. As a

Scottish enthusiast Alastair McWilliams with his 1951 Matchless G80S ohv single, East Fortune, June 2004.

The 1950 G80S

Engine:	Air-cooled ohv single with vertical cylinder; iron head and barrel, vertically split aluminium crankcases; fully enclosed valve gear; hairpin valve springs; built-up crankshaft; roller-bearing big end; gear-driven cams
Bore:	82.5mm
Stroke:	93mm
Displacement:	497cc
Compression ratio:	5.9:1
Lubrication:	Dry sump
Ignition:	Lucas magneto
Carburettor:	Amal type 891 3/32in
Primary drive:	Chain
Final drive:	Chain
Gearbox:	Four-speed, foot-change, Burman
Frame:	Two-part with single front down-tube
Front suspension:	AMC Teledraulic forks
Rear suspension:	Swinging arm with twin AMC 'candlestick' shock absorbers
Front brake:	7in, SLS drum, single-sided
Rear brake:	7in, SLS drum, single-sided
Tyres:	Front 3.25 × 19; rear 3.50 × 19

General Specifications

Wheelbase:	55.2in (1,402mm)
Ground clearance:	5.5in (140mm)
Seat height:	31in (787mm)
Fuel tank capacity:	3gal (14ltr)
Dry weight;	390lb (177kg)
Maximum power:	23bhp @ 5,400rpm
Top speed:	80mph (129km/h)

result, the taper roller bearings were placed slightly further out from the centre, and provided more support. These bearings were now separate races, which could be detached complete from the hollow spindle. The diameter of the solid spindle had been increased to ½in (13mm), whilst the Amal carburettor now came with a longer body, making the previous intake distance piece unnecessary. A small 'M' badge was placed on the nearside of the crankcase. The prop-stand was modified, allowing the pivot bolt to pass through the frame tube and thus provide greater support. There were also new-type tank bolts with hexagon heads, and distance pieces that allowed the bolts to be fully tightened, yet ensured the rubber buffers were correctly compressed.

All the above changes, other than the rear mudguard, applied to the spring frame.

Significant Changes for the 1951 Singles

The big news for the 1951 singles – announced in mid-September 1950 – was the introduction of die-cast DTD 424 light-alloy cylinder heads and alloy pushrods. The advantages, the factory claimed, were 'cooler running, the possibility of

A 1951 G3/LS three-fifty, showing the introduction of the alloy head on roadster singles, also alloy pushrods, all-ball-race dynamo and flexible horn mounting.

Easter Saturday, Brough Airfield, East Yorkshire, April 1951: AMC works rider Mick Featherstone with his special 'works' Matchless G80 racer with AJS 7R hubs, Teledraulic forks, swinging-arm frame, 'Candlestick' rear shocks and plenty of tuning.

employing slightly higher compression ratios, increased economy and, of course, lighter weight.' The new heads featured cast-in austinetic valve inserts, and they also provided a slightly different angle for the exhaust port and for the header exhaust pipe. The compression ratio for the G3/L was 6.35:1, and for the G80 6:1; and by removing a compression plate on the 500cc engine, 7.24:1 was available – suitable for better quality fuels available in countries such as the USA.

There was also a new clutch (shared by the twins and the competition models), based on racing experience gleaned with the AJS 7R. This clutch had a steel-drum housing for the plates, and the guides for the driven plates were formed inside the drum by means of slats spot-welded in position.

The primary chaincase sealing had also received attention, and the long-established V-section rubber band ditched in favour of what AMC called a 'mushroom'-section sealing band. This formed a gasket between each half of the chaincase, also fitting into the light-alloy retaining strap.

Developed as a result of their participation in scramble and moto-cross events, AMC introduced their now-famous 'Jampot' rear shocks for all touring types as well as their competition/racing models for the 1951 season. These had a much fatter appearance than the 'candlestick' units they replaced. It was claimed that the new shock absorbers would provide slightly less fork-arm movement than had been the case before, but would 'definitely avoid all tendency towards "bottoming" when used either over really rough country (in competition) or poor surfaces out on the street.'

The front suspension was entirely redesigned for 1951 (again with help from the works competition department) and would, it was claimed, provide 'complete freedom from oil leaks', the loading on the hydraulic seals of the forks having been considerably reduced. The fork drain plugs had also been redesigned.

An early 1950s swinging-arm G80 converted for racing; photographed by the author at a CRMC meeting at Donington Park in 1985.

All 1951 models benefited from an improved type of Lucas 6-volt dynamo: this instrument provided a sturdy ball-type bearing at the commuter end, and afforded good access to the brushes for maintenance purposes.

All models also featured a new, flexible horn mounting, since the older, rigid type of horn bracket had tended to break.

Notable Changes for the 1952 Model Year

An instantly noticeable change to the 1952 series engines in the Matchless single-cylinder range was to the magneto and timing case. Essentially, the magneto was taken from behind the cylinder, to a position in front of it – as had been the case for AJS engines for several years; also a new timing case was provided. One of the reasons for this change was to make it easier to inspect and remove the dynamo. The magneto shield for all the singles had been redesigned and cleaned up, the clips and bolts done away with, and the shield retained from underneath the platform.

Another notable change for the 1952 model year was that the single-cylinder models were now equipped with a new type of timing-side main bearing: this incorporated a large flange, permitting an extremely fine clearance to be employed without the risk of seizure. The compression plate for the 500cc roadster engine was no longer fitted; instead, alteration to the compression ratio could be achieved by fitting a higher compression piston, now listed by the factory.

A modification to the cylinder head was that the cast-iron pedestal which formerly retained the open ends of the duplex hairpin valve springs had been abandoned in favour of a steel channel in which the springs lay and automatically aligned themselves. Another advantage of the change was that the assembly was much easier to install; it was possible to do it by hand, though a small factory workshop tool had been made available.

A new, improved Burman gearbox, type B52, superseded the CP component fitted previously. In all its main details this new gearbox was similar to that developed for the AJS 7R racing model. It was lighter and shorter, the shafts were more rigid, and sturdier engagement dogs were employed; it was also claimed that gear-change quality was improved. The sequence of foot-lever movements remained unchanged. The clutch-cable adjusting screw on the new gearbox was located on the top of the cover and faced forward and upward, and this improved adjustment considerably.

Another transmission improvement concerned the primary chaincase: an inspection plate was installed that gave access to the clutch thrust-rod adjustment and also to the clutch-spring adjusters, without having to remove the case itself.

The Burman B52 Gearbox

The Burman B52 (Burman 1952) gearbox was introduced in August 1951. It was intended to replace the existing BA (heavy) and CP (light) models. AMC had been closely involved in its development, it being based on the Burman box employed on the AJS 7R racing model.

Like the 7R unit, the B52 had as its general feature a very short and sturdy gear train, plus an improved and greatly simplified foot-change mechanism, superior oil sealing and an improved clutch. As was traditional amongst British motorcycle producers, the new Burman gearbox was four speed, and the layout entirely conventional for the era, with the sleeve gear concentric with the mainshaft and running in ball-race bearings. Interestingly on the 7R, the bearings were rollers.

The layshaft was underneath and rotated in bushes. Gear selection was by moving one gear on each shaft, and the selectors were controlled by a drum cam operated directly by a change mechanism housed under the gearbox over cover. Under this also went the kickstarter quadrant and a new form of clutch lift mechanism – although the old type was also offered to those companies (not AMC) who preferred it. The new design employed three ball bearings held between two steel pressings with ramp recesses to take them; one pressing held in the end housing, whilst the other turned by the clutch cable so the balls ran up the ramps and operated the pushrod.

The clutch itself had four or five friction plates, depending upon use, and an adjuster screwed into the outer (pressure) plate. Access to this was via a small cover added to the primary chaincase for the 1952 machines. A cable adjuster screwed into the gearbox outer end cover, and access for hooking the cable to the lift mechanism was by removal of a screwed cap.

Burman & Sons Ltd had their works in Wychall Lane, Birmingham.

To comply with government restrictions on the use of plating (caused through shortages of materials), changes had to be made in the appearance of Matchless (and AJS) machines for 1952. Even so, chromium plating was retained for the exhaust system, handlebars, handlebar controls, gear levers and filler caps. Wheel rims were no longer chromium plated, but instead employed a matt anuminized finish developed by AMC and known as 'Argenizing'. Wheel rims were first Bonderized and then sprayed with the Argenizing solution. After baking for 1½ hours, a finish resembling smooth matt aluminium was produced. This finish was very thin, but also very hard – essential for withstanding tyre changing and the like.

Lined, black enamel fuel tanks were retained, but the large winged 'M' of the Matchless had to be replaced by a much smaller winged 'M' mounted on a circular red background. This new badge was a light alloy die-casting; before that a chromed steel pressing was used. Tank lining was as before, with Matchless models using silver, but with a red line superimposed on the silver, together with the addition of a fine inner line.

Another change to the finish was that the light alloy fork slider bottom cover was now left unenamelled; instead it was buffed and polished. The steel front brake plate had been superseded by a light alloy component, which was also polished. Pushrod cover tubes, steering-crown dome nuts, fork nuts and the like were bright cadmium-plated.

A newly designed handlebar headlug clamp (top yoke) permitted a much neater speedometer mounting. The handlebar clamp was now retained by three recessed Allen screws, for which a key was provided in the toolkit. This kit itself had been revised, and now included a box spanner for use when adjusting the clutch via the primary chaincase clutch inspection cover plate mentioned previously.

The wiring had also been tidied up, coloured cables being employed throughout, making for easier identification. The new wiring also included the positive-earth system. And to make life easier for the automatic voltage control regulator, this unit was now flexibly mounted on the rearward side of the battery carrier. There was a new Lucas headlamp, too, this featuring a square-pattern lens designed to provide a more powerful main beam, and an even spread of light when the dip filament was used. Finally, the external appearance was altered by an underslung 'gondola'-type pilot lamp.

Roadster prices for the 1952 Matchless single-cylinder models as at 13 September 1951 were as follows:

- G3/L 348cc rigid £172 10s;
- G3/LS 348cc spring-frame £192 4s 6d;
- G80 498cc rigid £190 7s 10d;
- G80S 498cc spring-frame £212 2s 3d.

A Host of Alterations for the 1953 Range

There were, once again, a host of alterations when the 1953 Matchless range was announced in mid-September 1952, many involving the single roadster models. The most notable of these changes was the fitting of dual seats as standard equipment (pioneered on the twin-cylinder models), and a new front brake of increased power.

Although a dual seat had been standard equipment on the G9 Super Clubman twin from its introduction in late 1948, the singles had had to make do with the traditional AMC sprung single saddle and a separate pillion pad. But now a new dual seat was standardized on both the twins and the singles for the 1953 model year. This new seat was the same length, but it was narrower, and was equipped with red piping (blue on the AJS). It was undoubtedly practical, but it also gave the single-cylinder family a much more modern appearance. Certainly it was an improvement as regards comfort – at least as far as the pillion passenger was concerned!

The front brake had been redesigned – although there was in fact very little that was different in the appearance of the new brake as compared to the former assembly. The changes and improvements came in the detail: to start with, the brake shoe plate had been moved anticlockwise through a number of degrees, whilst the cam lever had been turned relative to the camshaft, so that the lever projected forwards instead of backwards; the cable stop was moved to match, and was now at the front of the fork leg. AMC claimed that the new position of the cam lever 'provides maximum mechanical efficiency on the leading shoe instead of the trailing shoe, and hence better stopping power.'

There was also a chromium-plated top piston ring, AMC's contention being that extensive testing (of various five-hundred G80 engines) had shown that using the chromium-plated ring reduced bore wear by no less than a third.

Other changes were a new primary chaincase sealing band; a new-type Lucas rear light; revised petrol piping; and modified front-fork top covers (these could now be moved for packing purposes when the headlamp assembly was removed).

On the Matchless (and AJS) singles, the magneto weathershield had been shortened, and was now mounted to the magneto base-plate bolts; there was also an improved sweep for the high-tension lead from the magneto pick-up, a 90-degree type of pick-up having been achieved. The rear mudguard was a bolted up two-piece affair, rather than being hinged as one assembly. This made the job of painting at the factory easier.

1953 advertisement showing the latest G3/L model, now with forward-mounted magneto.

There were improvements to both the centre stand and rear lifting handle on the spring-frame models. The finish for all machines was in black stoved enamel. Wheel rims were Argenized on bikes for the home market, but for 1953 the rims on export machines were once more to be chromium-plated, and plated fuel tanks were now available at extra charge.

Earls Court Show, 1952

The Matchless stand at the London Earls Court Show in November 1952 was number 17, and since Great Britain was returning to a buyers' market, most manufacturers, including Matchless, had gone to a considerable amount of trouble to provide impressive and interesting displays. An unusual feature of the company's stand was a display of machine components in both rough and finished states. These items were laid out on a special counter that extended for the entire width of the stand; they were screwed down – an indication that even in those days, certain members of the public might simply walk off with a set of pistons or a crankshaft! In fact there was just about every component from the Matchless parts list.

Another display was a framed collection of colourful envelopes received from Matchless enthusiasts from all parts of the world; these were displayed under the caption: 'British Made – World Famous'. *The Motor Cycle* in their Show Report issue dated 20 November 1952 had this to say:

> The display is as sparkling as any at Earls Court. The machines are finished in gleaming black. Light-alloy sliders of the Teledraulic forks are highly polished. The small, winged M tank motif, which is die-cast in light-alloy, is mounted on a circular red background. Tanks are lined in silver and red. The standard of delivery time of Matchless models is held by many to be second to none at the present time. The show models appear to bear this out, since the controls for throttle, clutch, brake, air and ignition operate with the silky smoothness of those on a machine groomed for strenuous and exacting competition work.

The 1954 Range

When the 1954 Matchless range was launched in September 1953, the most noticeable change was the full-width, light-alloy front hub. A new design of fuel tank had been standardized on all the 500cc bikes (both singles and twins), whilst the singles of that displacement now had automatic ignition advance and rotating magnet magnetos. In addition, internal modifications had been carried out to all the single-cylinder engines to improve power output, durability and mechanical quietness.

Shortly before the 1954 range was officially announced, Phillip Walker, AMC's chief designer, was interviewed about the engine updates. He was asked why the flywheel weight of the 1954 single-cylinder engines had been reduced by 3–4lb (about 1.5kg) a pair, since many people – including the interviewer Alan Baker, the technical editor of *The Motor Cycle* – considered this a 'retrograde step'? Walker's answer was as follows:

> It is true that some loss in low-speed torque is an inevitable result of lightening the flywheels. But the modern single is extremely docile. My feeling is that, bearing in mind the rapid changes in speed of modern traffic, the need is for increased responsiveness. Engines have to be lively if they are to give the utmost rider-satisfaction. And this, I feel, is more important than low-speed slogging. It is no secret, of course, that really heavy flywheels are desirable for trials engines where low-compression ratios, retarded ignition and ultra-low speeds are de rigueur.

A notable engine modification on the singles was a stiffened-up crankshaft assembly to cope with the increase in power output. The timing-side mainshaft diameter had been increased from ⅞in (22mm) to 1⅛in (28mm). In addition, the shaft was now a keyed parallel fit in the flywheel instead of a taper fit. This new layout provided a more rigid set-up, and also an easier one to manufacture.

As mentioned previously, the crank flywheels had been reduced in weight and thereby engine

A 1955 G80S. The ignition system on the five-hundred singles had been changed to a Lucas SR1 rotating magneto with auto advance for the 1954 season. To accommodate the mechanism, a bulge appeared at the top of the engine timing cover, as shown.

liveliness had been enhanced – without any serious impairment of low-speed smoothness.

New cams and a larger inlet port and carb size were responsible for the considerably improved power output of both the 350 and 500cc engines:

1954 carburettor sizes (1953 figures in brackets):
1$\frac{1}{16}$in (1in) G3/L and G3/LS;
1$\frac{5}{32}$in (1$\frac{3}{32}$in) G80 and G80S.

The cams provided a slightly higher lift than the 1953 type, and the timing was also altered a little; it was notable that the different characteristics of the two sizes of engine had required an appreciably different exhaust-valve timing, though identical exhaust cam profiles were employed for both.

The increase in carburettor and inlet port sizes had not, as one might have expected, resulted in a loss of low-speed torque in favour of an increase of top-end power. If anything, both low- and high-speed figures had improved.

The five-hundred single-cylinder engine had proved rather sensitive to ignition advance. Therefore, in view of the reluctance or laziness of many owners to use a manual control to the best advantage, centrifugal automatic control had been adopted for the G80 series. Its incorporation had necessitated a bulge on the magneto-drive cover, so there was now an easy means of identifying the engine size. And in the light of racing experience, Phillip Walker and his development team had equipped the five-hundred single with a rotating-magnet magneto, a Lucas SRI assembly.

The search for mechanical quietness had been the driving force behind the provision of a positive oil feed to the valve-stem ends on both capacities of the AMC single. A longitudinal groove was machined in the rocker arm, and the oil, after lubricating the rocker spindle, emerged and ran along the groove, under centrifugal force, to the pad which bore on the valve stem.

On all models the bottom front engine-mounting bolt, which also connected the cradle to the front down-tube, had been increased in size from $\frac{5}{16}$in (8mm) to $\frac{3}{8}$in (9mm) to improve rigidity.

The new AMC full-width alloy front hub certainly afforded the 1954 Matchless (and AJS) singles and twins with a 'neat, handsome and modern appearance' as one journalist of the day described the new component, as compared to the outgoing, single-sided brake.

The new hub shell was a strong, ribbed, light-alloy die-casting that was easy on the eye and easy to clean. Straight spokes were a distinctive feature, and had the advantage of being stronger than the usual curved type; because of this a slight reduction in gauge size had been found possible.

A flanged, 7in (178mm), cast-iron brake drum was shrunk into the hub shell and bolted through the flange. AMC also claimed that this brake was waterproof, the conical face on the inside of the spoke flange acting as a water-flinger device.

Also new was the cast-alloy shoe plate, of slightly domed exterior and equipped with a grease nipple for the cam spindle. The shoe's operating mechanism and anchorage were virtually identical to the 1953 components. A light-alloy circular plate closed the offside (right) of the hub shell.

With the relaxation of nickel restrictions, chromium plating made a return for components such as wheel-rims, the latter having enamelled wells with silver lining for the Matchless models (gold for AJS).

There were several more minor changes for 1954, and these were as follows:

- domed clutch cover with eight screws replaced previous small inspection cover;
- twin pilot lights;
- flared mudguards;
- new side-stand spring;
- flexible fuel lines;
- cable lubricators;
- voltage regulator repositioned under-seat;
- larger fuel tank for the G80 series; the same as the G9 twin.

Prices as at 10 September 1953:
348cc G3/L, £166 16s;
348cc G3/LS, £191 8s;
498cc G80, £184 4s;
498cc G80/S, £208 16s.

Evolutionary Development for the 1955 Range

According to *The Motor Cycle*, modifications to the 1955 range of Matchless (and AJS) machines could be called 'evolutionary development'. It went on to report:

> Numerous refinements are incorporated in the range of AJS and Matchless machines for 1955. As is widely known, the two makes have much in common and are famous for the mechanical quietness of their engines and excellence of machine finish. There are no new models, and the changes to existing models are with a view to increased component life, improved accessibility, enhanced appearance, and better protection for the machine and rider from water flung up by the front wheel.

Clevis-end AMC 'Jampot' rear shocks; the full-width alloy rear hub and large toolbox dates this machine from 1955 onwards.

This is an early swinging-arm G80 photographed in 1974 whilst touring Czechoslovakia. It is basically a 1955 bike but much modified, with alloy mudguards, fork gaiters, chromed tank (with earlier Matchless 'M' badges), panniers, aftermarket seat and tank bag.

Automatic advance and retard, fitted a year earlier to the 500cc singles, was standardized on the 350cc range.

On all single-cylinder engines, longer life and more silent running of the crankshaft main bearings were claimed from two notable bottom-end changes. The flange of the timing-side bronze bush had been beefed up, whilst the diameter of the inboard drive-side ball-race bearing had been increased.

One or two cases of noisy operation of the automatic advance mechanism at low engine speeds had been reported. This problem had been attacked by fitting plastic sleeves over the retard limit stops to cushion the return of the operating fingers.

There were several modifications that were common to all engines. Previously, air filters (an optional extra) had been of differing types on the singles and twins – one type had not been standardized throughout the range. The lubrication system had been tidied up on all models by repositioning the main feed and return pipes below the oil tank. Previously, when viewed from the offside (right) of the motorcycle, the pipes lay side by side; in the revised layout, one pipe was behind the other.

The full-width, light alloy front hub with straight spokes had been one of the outstanding innovations of the British motorcycle industry in 1954, and for the 1955 season the hub had been improved, giving it a more rounded appearance. This had been achieved by making the centre cooling fins deeper than the outer. And now there was the same type of hub on both wheels; the wheel being quickly detachable on rear-sprung machines (the rigid-framed G3/L and G80 were still being offered).

Yet another important innovation for 1955 was the introduction of the brand new Amal Monobloc carburettor. Developed over a two-year period, the new instrument had three main priorities: improved performance; economic manufacture; easier to tune and maintain. In

Matchless G80S of 1955 vintage, with the last of the small toolboxes, alloy full-width rear hub and 'Jampot' rear shocks.

Toolbox as fitted to the early swinging-arm singles, from 1949 through to 1955.

general, it has to be said, in retrospect it achieved all three goals.

The most striking external difference between the Monobloc and the old-type Amal carburettor it replaced was that the float chamber was no longer a separate unit; a single, very neat die-casting in Mazak zinc-base alloy provided both mixing and float chambers. The throttle slide featured a full skirt, and a separate, detachable pilot jet was utilized. The float needle, operated by a hinged float, was a nylon moulding.

The Monobloc carb also embodied two-way compensation to provide a richer mixture for accelerating and a weaker cruising setting. This compensation was achieved by the simple means of a bleed hole near the base of the needle jet. There were three basic Monobloc types: 375, 376 and 389.

A year earlier a 3¾gal (19ltr) fuel tank was standardized on 500cc roadsters; in the 1955 range this tank was also fitted on the 350cc models. A combined mounting for the oil tank and battery carrier had been designed that was both tidier and stronger than the 1954 type. The frame set tube had also been modified and provided with a malleable casting, so a hole could be provided to take the air filter hose.

Other changes for 1955 singles included the following:

- larger diameter front forks;
- modified 'Jampot' rear shock absorbers;
- pressed steel lugs for pillion footrests;
- deeper headlamp shell carrying the speedometer;
- deeper chainguard;
- rear reflector;
- new front mudguard without front stay;
- rigid-frame models with barrel saddle springs.

A New Frame for 1956

There was a new frame for all roadster models, singles and twins, for the 1956 model year. In this design the seat tube, instead of running diagonally from under the seat to the engine and gearbox plates, now ran vertically at the rear of the gearbox. Lateral rigidity had been improved compared to the earlier spring frames by housing the swinging-arm pivot in a substantial, malleable-iron lug clamped between the cradle tubes and brazed to the lower end of the seat tube.

Conventional brazed and bolt-up construction was employed, and considerable attention had been applied to make the frame more suitable for sidecar duties.

At the same time the end of the line had been reached for the old rigid frame, single-cylinder models. *The Motor Cycle* in their 8 September 1955 issue commented:

> That no solid-frame machines are to be produced by the Plumstead concern in the coming year is hardly surprising in view of current trends. Rear springing is gaining popularity in trials just as quickly as it did for sidecar work. And, of course, production and servicing efficiency can be improved as the number of different models in a given range was decreased.

For 1956, the roadster singles were given higher compression ratios. That of the G3/LS three-fifty went up from 6.5 to 7.5:1, whilst the G80/S was increased from 6.3 to 7.3:1. To prevent the possibility of the exhaust valve guide on the singles moving when hot, circlip location had been increased earlier in 1955. Another change was the inclusion of a magnetic sump oil filter, shared with the twins.

A 1956 G80S with the Burman B52 gearbox, Amal Monobloc carburettor and the new-for-year long, thin oil tank and new frame with vertical seat tube.

A 1956 Matchless brochure illustration of the G80S. Described as 'Fast but tractable, robust yet light, this 85mph [137km/h] big single is utterly dependable and maintains its performance indefinitely.'

The introduction of the new frame for both the single and twin roadster models brought with it the integration of the oil-tank and toolbox assemblies. These now filled much of the area to the rear of the carburettor to the front of the rear shock absorbers, on both sides of the motorcycle. At the same time the capacity of the oil tanks had risen from 4 to 5½ pints (1 to 2½ltr). The two assemblies were bridged at the front by a detachable steel pressing. If the optional air filter was fitted, it was concealed behind this cover. The 'toolbox' housed the 6-volt battery at its forward end. The battery was secured by a quick-release rubber strap, instead of the conventional British-style metal strap. At the upper right of the toolbox was the automatic voltage control unit, mounted in sponge rubber.

Other changes for 1956 are listed below:

- cover over gearbox with primary chain adjuster underneath;
- front brake cam lever above wheel spindle;
- rear brake adjuster at front end of brake rod;
- aluminium rear brake backplate;
- horn under seat;
- revised, longer dual seat;
- modified front fork legs;
- cables group and routed to fork crown;
- combined horn and dipswitch.

Details of the 1956 Matchless prices for the roadster singles, published on 15 September 1955 were as follows:

- 348cc G3/LS, £204 12s;
- 498cc G80/S, £216 12.

Prices included UK purchase tax.

Improvements for 1957

The two notable changes for 1957 – announced in late September 1956 – were the introduction of the newly released AMC-made gearbox (described in Chapter 8), and the replacement of the company's own 'Jampot' rear shock absorbers by ones of Girling manufacture. It was the first time since rear springing had been introduced in the 1949 programme that proprietary shocks were employed in place of AMC-manufactured units. The AMC gearbox also saw the adoption of

MATCHLESS Clubman Range and Prices 1957

ISSUED OCTOBER 1956

		PRICE £	s	d	PURCHASE TAX £	s	d	TOTAL £	s	d
Model G3/LS	350 cc. o.h.v. Single	170	10	0	40	18	5	211	8	5
Model G80S	500 cc. o.h.v. Single	180	10	0	43	6	5	223	16	5
Model G9	500 cc. o.h.v. Vertical Twin	205	0	0	49	4	0	254	4	0
Model G11	600 cc. o.h.v. Vertical Twin	210	0	0	50	8	0	260	8	0
Model G3/LC	350 cc. o.h.v. Trials	177	0	0	42	9	7	219	9	7
Model G3/LCS	350 cc. o.h.v. Scrambles	182	0	0	43	13	7	225	13	7
Model G80/CS	500 cc. o.h.v. Scrambles	196	0	0	47	0	9	243	0	9
Model G45	500 cc. o.h.v. Road Racing	325	0	0	78	0	0	403	0	0
Electric Lighting on Trials and Scrambles Models		8	5	0	1	19	7	10	4	7

Prices are subject to alteration without notice.

MATCHLESS MOTOR CYCLES
LONDON, S.E.18.

The Matchless price list for 1957, issued in October 1956.

ABOVE: *A 1957 348cc G3/LS – the last year of the front-mounted magneto. Note the differences with the 1956 G80S, namely the AMC gearbox, Girling rear shock absorbers and rear chainguard.*

LEFT: *The appearance of the Matchless (and AJS) heavyweight singles, the G3/LS and G80S models, was radically changed by the adoption of the AC generator and coil ignition in place of the long-running magneto.*

a Norton-type clutch with shock absorber, so there was no engine shock absorber. Another change was a smaller dome in the primary chaincase.

A new inlet cam was given to the singles, in a quest for more speed and acceleration; otherwise the engines of both the three-fifty and five-hundred single remained unchanged. The only other components to be altered were the oil tank and toolbox lid, which both received a series of three small ribs either side of the Matchless logo in the centre of each, plus push-on oilpipe lines. Besides these there were minor cosmetic alterations, mainly aimed at tidying things up, and improvement to the five-pin drive of the quickly detachable rear wheel on all roadster models.

Finally, a mid-season alteration to the Teledraulic front fork damping was continued for 1957. On both shock and recoil movements the hydraulic action was more progressive in action, resulting in a decrease of front-end pitching.

Prices had again risen, and on 27 September 1956 were as follows (including the UK purchase tax): the G3/LS, £211 8s 5d; and the G80S, £223 16s 5d.

A Change in Appearance for 1958

The external appearance of the Matchless (and AJS) heavyweight single-cylinder engines was radically changed for the 1958 model year by the adoption of AC generator and coil ignition in place of the long-running dynamo and magneto set-up. Not only this, but the familiar pressed-steel (and leak-prone!) primary chaincase was dropped in favour of a brand new, cast-aluminium case; this was also used to provide a rigid mounting for the stator of the crankshaft-driven alternator. Because there was no longer a magneto and dynamo, both sides of the engine had a considerably different look to them.

Located on an extension of the offside (left) end of the crankshaft, the alternator used on the roadster singles was the Lucas RM15; this was similar to the already well-known RM13 model in featuring a rotor of 2¾in (70mm) diameter, but it was approximately ¼in (6mm) wider. Three ¼in BSF studs and nuts held the stator in place in the dome of the chaincase outer half. Since the running clearance between rotor and stator was only 0.015in (½mm), clearance was needed to ensure co-axiality of the two components. Firstly, a spigot formed on the rear of the chaincase inner section registered in a hole bored in the crankcase nearside (left) co-axial with the main bearing housing. Secondly, two dowels in the chaincase inner section ensured accurate location of the outer half. Both halves of the chaincase were clamped to the crankcase by a stud screwed into a boss just behind the main bearing housing. Of ⅜in (9mm) diameter, one of these dowels was hollow and fitted over the stud; the other dowel was of 5/16in (8mm) diameter, and was pressed into the near-most portion of the joint face.

The new aluminium primary chaincase was highly polished, the two halves held together by fourteen screws. Two flush-fitting aluminium plugs in the outer half of the case incorporated milled slots to help removal and replacement. One of the plugs was for checking primary chain tension, and filling the case with oil to the correct level; the other provided access to the clutch adjustment screw in the centre of the pressure plate.

In place of the outgoing timing cover (which embodied the inner portion of the magneto chaincase) there was a deep, circular, light-alloy casting that contained the automatic advance and retard, plus the contact breaker assembly. This housing was secured to the crankcase by five screws, and the unit driven by an extension of the inlet camshaft, the latter being tapered and threaded to suit. Access to the contact breaker for adjustment involved removal of only two screws and an aluminium cover. The single circular ignition coil was mounted under the top frame tube, just aft of the steering head.

The cylinder finning of the three-fifty cylinder barrel had been increased, and in addition, on both engine sizes, the space previously occupied between the front engine plates by the magneto had been superseded by a channel-section member. In the absence of a dynamo the rear engine plates were now solid, and were bridged by a modified clip-on cover which concealed the gearbox draw-bolt.

The electrical cables from the stator passed through a synthetic rubber grommet situated in the inner half of the chaincase, and were led over the gearbox (where they were hidden by the engine-plate cover) and up behind the bulkhead that bridged the front of the oil tank (on the offside) and the toolbox (on the nearside). A four-way snap fastener at that point meant that the cables could be disconnected as required.

The rectifier was placed beneath the seat nose, just aft of the battery and inboard of the tool compartment, to which it was attached by a single bolt; so if it had to be replaced, this was a simple task. The procedure was, first, to take off the dual seat by removing its two rear securing bolts and loosening the nuts holding the forked ears at the front. Then the leads were disconnected from the rectifier, a nut was undone inside the toolbox, and the rectifier lifted away. There was also more room in the toolbox itself, as the voltage control unit was no longer needed.

As with all Lucas AC sets at that time, an emergency-start facility was provided, whereby the

A 1958 G80 CS in export guise with lighting equipment – really a road-legal scrambler – an early trail bike, in fact.

majority of the generator output was directed to the ignition coil, so the engine could be kick-started even if the battery had gone flat. The generator output balanced the full lamp load at an engine speed of 1,400rpm: this was equivalent to 22mph (35km/h) in top gear on the five-hundred, or 18mph (29km/h) on the three-fifty. A lighting modification common to all the roadsters (both singles and twins) was a change from two separate pilot lights to the more conventional arrangement of one small bulb in the reflector.

Various other changes were made to the Matchless models that year: for instance, the three-fifty single's frame design was brought into line with that of the five-hundred by unification of the attachment lugs for the subframe and the rear of the fuel tank. Also the gearchange in the AMC gearbox, introduced the previous year, was lightened by way of a lower-rate selector spring; this modification also applied to the roadster twins and competition bikes. The Girling rear shock absorbers were shortened on both the single and the twins, a modification that made the seat height lower; another change was that chromium plating was now used in the middle of the wheel rims in addition to the sides.

Once again prices rose. The new price list was published on 12 September 1957, with the G3/LS at £233 18s 2d, and the G80S at £247 12s 7d (both including UK purchase tax).

The Heavyweight Singles Take a Back Seat

The G3/LS and G80S roadster singles saw little change, except for deeper section mudguards, for some two years between the end of 1957 and the end of 1959. A major reason were developments in both the twin-cylinder family and the new 'lightweight' family of two-fifty and three-fifty models – to say nothing of the time spent on the new G50 road racer and the off-road competition bikes.

In fact, during this period it would be true to say that the bikes, now known as the 'heavyweight singles', took very much a back seat. Even the Earls Court Show in November 1958 concentrated heavily on other models, and the only bike to be given even a mention was a G3/LS with an optional white and chromium finish! And that from no fewer than twenty-three bikes on the Matchless stand at the annual London showcase for the British industry.

Alterations for the 1960 Model Year

The major change for heavyweight singles and twin-cylinder Matchless and AJS models for 1960 was a brand new frame. Of full cradle layout, it featured duplex front downtubes that ran back to pass beneath the engine and gearbox. A single 1½in (38mm) diameter, twelve-gauge top tube and a vertical seat tube completed the main frame, which was built up on the time-honoured Matchless principle of malleable-iron lugs brazed in position; *The Motor Cycle* described as 'massive indeed' the cast lugs that formed the steering-head and swinging-arm pivot housing. The rear subframe was bolted to lugs just below the rear of the gearbox and the very front of the dual seat. AMC sources said that the new frames increased rigidity, and an increase in front fork trail provided improved steering and handling abilities. Another change was that the three-point fuel-tank mounting, previously a feature of the two-fifty G2 model, was now employed on the new frame, with two mountings at the front and one at the rear.

Another alteration for the 1960 model year was that the gearbox internal ratios had been revised to give more even spacing, reducing the gap between third and top. Therefore bottom was now slightly higher at 2.56:1 (previously 2.67), second remained unchanged at 1.77, and third was increased from 1.33:1 to 1.22:1.

The cylinder head of the five-hundred single had been redesigned. The combustion chamber shape was now hemispherical, with a new flat-top piston featuring small recesses for the valves; but the compression ratio at 7.3:1 remained unchanged. The inlet tract, now best described as an arc between the inlet valve and the carburettor, had been designed to promote the swirl of gases – another bonus being that the valve stem and protruding portion of the valve guide were now at one side of the tract, where AMC claimed 'they offer less restriction to gas flow'.

In parallel with the new combustion chamber shape and inlet port was a valve included angle reduced to 39 degrees. The felt oil filter fitted previously had been superseded for 1960 by one featuring wire gauze of two different mesh sizes. Other changes included a new Lucas 12-amp hour battery of more compact design; a smaller headlamp shell, still housing the speedometer; and a two-level dual seat.

More Conservative Change for 1961

With such major changes the previous year – duplex frames and new cylinder heads – the 1961 changes were considerably less sweeping, with more emphasis on detail improvements across the range. All single-cylinder models were given a modification intended to strengthen the drive to the rotary reciprocating oil pump. Both the crankshaft worm and the oil-pump pinion had a redesigned tooth form, thus improving their engagement.

With the introduction of the Lightweight G5 350, AMC management had expected that sales of the old Heavyweight G3 would fall, and that it could therefore be 'pensioned off'. But they were to be proved wrong, because in fact it was the newcomer that proved hard to sell! And far from sales falling off, demand for the G3/LS actually increased during 1960, which meant that production had to be increased for 1961.

Detail changes included an external circlip at the upper end of the inlet valve guide for the 498cc G80 engine, to ensure positive guide location when the engine was really warm and working hard. Cosmetically, there were changes to the mudguards, tank badges and colours. The deeply valanced front and rear guards had been shortened; tyre clearance at the leading edge of the front component had also increased. There was now a smart two-tone paint finish of Cardinal red and Arctic white – though it was still possible to order an all-black finish.

As for prices, at 25 August 1960 (when the 1961 range was announced) the G3 was listed at £236 8s 6d, and the G80 at £249 13s 10d; both including UK taxes. Chromium-plated fuel-tank panels cost an additional £2 8s 10d.

The following news snippet in the 16 February 1961 issue of *The Motor Cycle* is an apposite reminder of just how popular Matchless single-cylinder models had remained with foreign police and military contracts: 'Just completed – ahead of time – is the delivery of 300 Matchless 347cc (G3) models for use in the Dutch Army. The machines were built to an army specification; the total value of the order was £45,000.'

By the beginning of 1961 there were over 400 dealers selling Matchless motorcycles throughout Great Britain, with just about every well known dealership selling the marque. Of course, this was just before the influx of Japanese marques, an invasion that was soon to see the likes of Honda, Suzuki and Yamaha recruit many of these very same dealers over the next few years; and it was the same for the export market. And as outlined in Chapter 7, within the next five years AMC was to fall from its position as a market leader, and descend into financial meltdown. Of course it was much the same for the rest of the British motorcycle industry: a sad picture indeed.

Just two weeks before the announcement of the 1962 model range, sales director Jock West resigned (*see* Chapters 7 and 8) at the end of August 1961. The AJS and Matchless range were launched in mid-September.

Big News for 1962

The big news regarding AMC heavyweight singles for the 1962 season was a short-stroke three-fifty engine. As *The Motor Cycle* said:

> You want a big, lively roadster with the relatively low insurance rates of a three-fifty? Then for you AMC have extensively redesigned the single-cylinder

A 1962 G3S Mercury Sports, with chrome-plated mudguards and massive tank badges. Coil ignition had arrived for 1958, the duplex frame in 1960.

> engine of the Matchless G3 and AJS 16. As a result, maximum power is boosted from some 19 to 23bhp at 6,200rpm without sacrifice of tractability, and the engine is said to give a pleasant top-gear surge when the twistgrip is tweaked at around 55 to 60mph [88 to 96km/h]. And since the engine is now a shade shorter, with the pushrod tunnels cast in the cylinder barrel and head, it has a cobby appearance, giving the models a more up-to-the-minute air.

Both the bore and stroke had been revised and were now 74 × 81mm instead of the former 69 × 93mm, and advantage had been taken of the increased bore size to provide bigger valve sizes. Choke diameter of the Amal Monobloc carburettor had also been stepped up, from 1 1/16in (26mm) to 1 1/8in (28mm); whilst the exhaust pipe diameter had been increased by 1/8in (3mm) to 1 5/8in (40mm).

The light alloy head had had its included valve angle slightly reduced; compression ratio had been increased from 7.5 to 8.5:1.

From now on, with the exception of the road racers (AJS 7R and Matchless G50), every model in the two ranges was given a name as well as a catalogue code number. The Matchless G3 and AJS Model 16 became, respectively, the Mercury and Sceptre. In addition, there was now a 'hot' version of each, the Mercury Sports (G3S) and Sceptre Sports (Model 16S), the latter having dropped handlebars and bright chromium finish to the mudguards and chainguard. But it should be noted that the Sports models didn't have any increase in performance … and as history now shows, the names never became popular, and were rarely referred to by owners.

The Five-hundred Single

The 498cc single – in which the bore and stroke of 82.5 × 93mm remained unchanged – became the Matchless G80 Major and AJS Model 18 Statesman; unlike the smaller-engined versions, there were no sporting variants of the larger models. There was, however, a whole list of what are best described as minor modifications:

- new soft-rubber tank mountings, including a sponge rubber pad at the rear;
- revised oil tank – breather tower incorporated;
- ignition key in place of knob switch;
- roll-on centre stand;
- stronger kickstarter spring;
- new horn – smaller, lighter and louder;
- larger fuel tank;
- new, larger tank badges of zinc-alloy and chrome plated;
- battery reverted to former larger dimensions, with enclosure box enlarged to suit.

Testing the G3 Mercury

A comprehensive road test of the G3 Mercury appeared in the issue of *The Motor Cycle* dated 18 May 1962. The tester began by saying:

> Any descendant of the ubiquitous G3 Matchless has to uphold a tough, almost historical reputation. Did not the wartime G3, in the hands of countless Don Rs [slang for 'despatch riders'], help to make history? Sceptical old sweats may rest assured, the latest version, the Mercury, is an extremely worthy scion of the DR model. Soft, woolly power and oodles of bottom-end slogging characterized the original G3; and although the engine revved willingly, the power tailed off in the upper ranges. Revamping the unit has resulted in appreciably more punch higher up the rpm scale, and that without any loss of tractability.
>
> [The revised engine for the 1962 model year] was noticeably lively, producing a harder punch and developing considerably more urge in the middle rpm range. The model was happy to cruise all day on two-thirds throttle, at close on 70mph (110km/h). A further twist of the grip produced even more urge, and it was possible to hold a steady 70mph for long stretches. Most main-road gradients were surmounted effortlessly in top gear.

And with a timed maximum speed of 78mph (125km/h) and excellent fuel economy – 67 mpg at a constant 60 mph – the 1962 G3 Mercury was in many ways the 'best of breed'. The main criticism concerned, once again, excessive exhaust noise, also insufficient ground clearance, only 'adequate' lighting, a shade 'top heavy' handling at low speeds, poor 'plastic' handlebar grips and a weak horn. Against this, high speed stability, brakes, comfort, ease of starting, routine maintenance, gearbox action and mechanical quietness all received praises. The price, including UK purchase tax in May 1962, was £248 4s 5d.

The 1963 Matchless Range

Yet more development work had been carried out in the spring and summer of 1962, so that when the 1963 Matchless range made its debut that autumn, there were yet more changes. In addition, the poor-selling 'sports' three-fifty was axed, although its chrome-plated mudguard remained an option.

One of the changes for 1963 was a new front hub with fewer (five) fins and wider brake shoes. Another was a new subframe and rear swinging arm; there were now standard Girling shock absorbers without clevis ends, a restyled and more rounded oil tank and matching toolbox. 18in wheels replaced the former 19in ones, there was a narrower dual seat, D-section mudguards,

Blackpool Motorcycle Show, May 1963. Centre stage is the 350 G3 Mercury single, for £249 12s.

A Matchless G80, a 1963 model with new front hub with five fins and wider brake shoes, new subframe and swinging arm, revised (rounded) oil tank and toolbox, revised mudguards, new silencer and 18in wheels.

direct-action stop-light switch, a new cigar-shaped silencer without the traditional AMC tail-pipe, and a revised fuel tank with knee grips in the recesses. Yet another modification was a switch from taper rollers to ball races for the wheel bearings. The seat height was also reduced, thanks in major part to the reduction in wheel size.

At the very end of 1962, AMC had closed the Norton works at Bracebridge Street, Birmingham, and moved everything south to Plumstead; so now Matchless, AJS and Norton were to be built under one roof, so to speak. And by the autumn of the following year the first sign of what was to be called the 'Norton influence' began to make itself felt in the Matchless and AJS model ranges, with all the roadsters being equipped with Norton Roadholder forks and full-width alloy hubs, 8in (203mm) at the front, and the AMC duplex frame modified to suit.

Scrambler-Based Engines for 1964

Another major change for the 1964 model year was that the remaining roadster singles (plus the trials three-fifty) had their engines replaced by ones based around the scrambles power unit. So in both the three-fifty and the five-hundred assemblies the stroke was set at 85.5mm, bore sizes being 72 and 86mm respectively. On the smaller engine the compression ratio was 9:1; on the five-hundred 7.3:1. Pushrod tunnels were integral with the cylinder, and all engines featured head sleeve nuts screwed to extended crankcase studs.

Internally there was a substantial steel-connecting rod, single row, aluminium-caged roller big-end (similar in design to the G50 road racer), steel flywheels, and a timing-side roller plus plain bronze bush to replace the old flanged main bearing.

Another Norton component, the gear-oil pump, replaced the long-running AMC reciprocating plunger type; this was driven in typical Norton fashion by a worm nut which also held the timing pinion in place. The Matchless lubrication system was modified with a direct feed into the end of the crankshaft to the sides of the big-end rollers, whilst the rocker lubrication was now taken from the scavenge line and so was less intrusive.

LEFT: For 1964 the G3 (Mercury) and G80 (Major) gained Norton Roadholder front forks and Norton brakes: an 8in front and 7in rear. They then remained largely unchanged until production ceased in late 1966.

BELOW: The GB500 Clubman's racer was built in the mid-1960s; the original prototype is seen here with the Jack Emmott-prepared G85CS Scrambler engine. A combination of AMCs financial collapse and a relatively high price put a damper on sales.

The 1964 G3

Engine:	Air-cooled ohv single with vertical cylinder; alloy head; iron barrel; vertically split aluminium crankcases; fully enclosed valve gear; hairpin valve springs; built-up crankshaft, roller-bearing big-end; gear-driven cams; integral pushrod tunnels in barrel
Bore:	72mm
Stroke:	85.5mm
Displacement:	348cc
Compression ratio:	9:1
Lubrication:	Dry sump; Norton gear-oil pump
Ignition:	Battery/coil 6-volt
Carburettor:	Amal monobloc 389 1⅛in
Primary drive:	Chain
Final drive:	Chain
Gearbox:	Four-speed, AMC
Frame:	Duplex full-cradle
Front suspension:	Norton Roadholder forks
Rear suspension:	Swinging arm with twin Girling shock absorbers
Front brake:	8in, SLS, Norton full-width hub
Rear brake:	7in, SLS, Norton full-width hub
Tyres:	3.25 × 18 front and rear

General specifications

Wheelbase:	55in (1,397mm)
Ground clearance:	6in (152mm)
Seat height:	30in (762mm)
Fuel tank capacity:	4gal (18ltr)
Dry weight:	382lb (173kg)
Maximum power:	18bhp @ 5,750rpm
Top speed:	78mph (125km/h)

The 1964 G80

Engine:	Air-cooled ohv single with vertical cylinder; alloy head; iron barrel; vertically split aluminium crankcases; fully enclosed valve gear; hairpin valve springs; built-up crankshaft; roller-bearing big-end; gear-driven cams; integral pushrod tunnels in barrel
Bore:	86mm
Stroke:	85.5mm
Displacement:	497cc
Compression ratio:	7.3:1
Lubrication:	Dry sump; Norton gear-oil pump
Ignition:	Battery/coil 6-volt; alternator
Carburettor:	Amal monobloc 389 1⅛in
Primary drive:	Chain
Final drive:	Chain
Gearbox:	Four-speed
Frame:	Duplex full cradle
Front suspension:	Norton Roadholder forks
Rear suspension:	Swinging arm with twin Girling shock absorbers
Front brake:	8in, SLS, Norton full-width hub
Rear brake:	7in, SLS
Tyres:	Front 3.25 × 18; rear 3.50 × 18

General Specifications

Wheelbase:	55in (1,397mm)
Ground clearance:	6in (152mm)
Seat height:	30in (762mm)
Fuel tank capacity:	4gal (18ltr)
Dry weight:	394lb (179kg)
Maximum power:	28bhp @ 5,600rpm
Top speed:	84mph (135km/h)

The End of an Era

And really from then on, development of the AMC Heavyweight single-cylinder line came to an end, even though production was to continue for another three years or so. Why? Well, by now the factory's management were firmly locked into a downward spiral of what in today's commercial world would be described as 'downsizing'; but unfortunately this only created more problems than it solved, since less production meant fewer sales and of course less money. And in contrast to this situation, from what had been a highly profitable organization at the end of the 1950s, by the end of 1963 Associated Motor Cycles was running at a loss.

From then on, things simply got worse as each year unfolded. This caused the management to seek ever more ways of cost-cutting, and also some truly feeble and unpopular ways of attempting to

ABOVE: The prototype GB500 in action during a recent classic race meeting. It was originally constructed by Green Brothers of South Norwood, and was raced by development rider Terry Sparrow, c. 1967.

LEFT: Much modified heavyweight Matchless single, one of seven such machines constructed during the 1980s by Ernie Dorsett, using diesel power.

Tony Kay with his own brand of sporting Matchless, a hybrid G80CS/G85CS engine in a special frame. The café racer spec includes disc front brake, alloy rims, clip-ons, rear sets, alloy tank, steering damper, hi-level exhaust and rev counter. It was built in the 1970s long after production had ceased at Plumstead.

sell their motorcycles. Typical was the move to offer the Matchless G3 and G80 singles with *Norton* badges screwed to the tank sides. This had the effect of upsetting all three sets of enthusiasts for Matchless, AJS and Norton – and is vivid proof of just how out of touch and desperate the decision makers at Plumstead had become.

This standardization had robbed the big singles of their identity – and Matchless owners, although they had for years accepted the badge-engineering of their brand and AJS, had still viewed a Matchless as just that. But with the Norton forks, hubs plus coil ignition, the 'cigar'-shaped silencer and the unloved tank badge designs, the bikes had lost their appeal to the very customers who had continued to buy versions of the three-fifty and five-hundred singles down through the years.

During 1966, AMC's financial position worsened (fully covered in Chapter 7), and production of the roadster singles came to an end. The official receiver was called in, and eventually, in September 1966, Manganese Bronze took over the remains of AMC, registering the new company as Norton-Matchless. The new range of bikes comprised the twin-cylinder models and only one single, the G85CS scrambler (*see* Chapter 10). So as far as the traditional heavyweight Matchless singles were concerned, this was the end of an era.

But for many, the G3 and G80 were classical examples of the British singles at their very best, offering a robustness and reliability that few others could match, combined with economy, safe handling and braking, plus a high level of finish.

7 The AMC Empire

The company registered as Associated Motor Cycles, popularly known as AMC, came about as a result of various takeovers: in 1931, at the height of the Great Depression, Matchless had acquired AJS from the Steven's Brothers; then following the takeover of Sunbeam by ICI (Imperial Chemical Industries), in August 1937 Matchless subsequently acquired the Sunbeam marque from ICI. This meant that the Colliers now owned three quite different marques – Sunbeam, Matchless and AJS; all famous brand names in their own right. The directors of the Matchless company decided that a more suitable name was needed, to encompass all three. And so on 12 October 1937 the company was re-registered as Associated Motor Cycles Ltd.

As the 1930s came to a close, AMC had a level of financial stability that was the envy of the remainder of the industry, achieved 'through basically good management' (quoted Peter Hartley). At the same time, Matchless engines were being supplied to several other companies: Brough Superior, Calthorpe, Coventry Eagle, Morgan (cars) and OEC. AMC were therefore one of a select band of manufacturers that included J. A. Prestwich and the Burney & Blackburne concern, plus of course the Villiers factory in Wolverhampton.

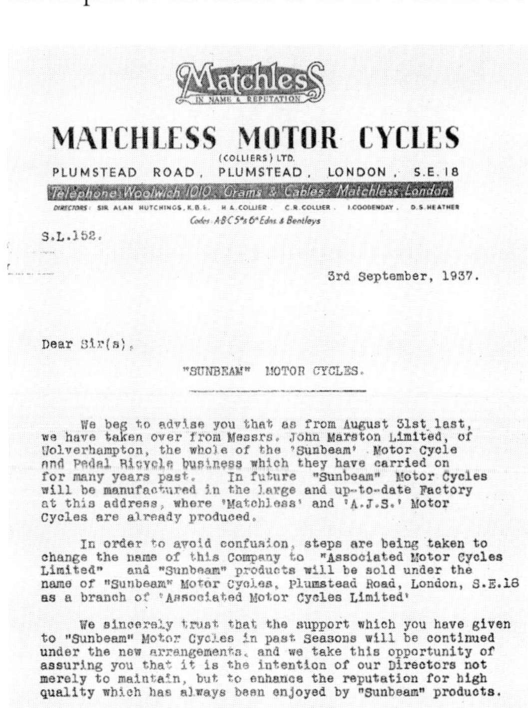

Matchless
IN NAME & REPUTATION

MATCHLESS MOTOR CYCLES
(COLLIERS) LTD.
PLUMSTEAD ROAD, PLUMSTEAD, LONDON, S.E.18
Telephone Woolwich 1010. Grams & Cables: Matchless London
DIRECTORS: SIR ALAN HUTCHINGS, K.B.E. H.A. COLLIER. C.R. COLLIER. I. COODENDAY. D.S. HEATHER
Codes ABC 5th & 6th Edns & Bentleys

S.L.152.

3rd September, 1937.

Dear Sir(s),

"SUNBEAM" MOTOR CYCLES.

We beg to advise you that as from August 31st last, we have taken over from Messrs. John Marston Limited, of Wolverhampton, the whole of the 'Sunbeam' Motor Cycle and Pedal Bicycle business which they have carried on for many years past. In future "Sunbeam" Motor Cycles will be manufactured in the large and up-to-date Factory at this address, where 'Matchless' and 'A.J.S.' Motor Cycles are already produced.

In order to avoid confusion, steps are being taken to change the name of this Company to "Associated Motor Cycles Limited" and "Sunbeam" products will be sold under the name of "Sunbeam" Motor Cycles, Plumstead Road, London, S.E.18 as a branch of 'Associated Motor Cycles Limited'

We sincerely trust that the support which you have given to "Sunbeam" Motor Cycles in past Seasons will be continued under the new arrangements, and we take this opportunity of assuring you that it is the intention of our Directors not merely to maintain, but to enhance the reputation for high quality which has always been enjoyed by "Sunbeam" products.

continued ....

ABOVE: Front cover of the 1938 Sunbeam range brochure.

LEFT: Letter dated 3 September 1937 advising dealers that Matchless had purchased the Sunbeam business, and that the parent company's name would be changing to Associated Motor Cycles Limited (AMC).

Post-War Recovery

In 1940 AMC sold the rights to the Sunbeam brand name to the BSA Group in Birmingham. As related in Chapter 5, only Matchless motorcycles were built by the Group during the war years, largely the Teledraulic-equipped G3L three-fifty ohv single. Events that crucially affected AMC during the war years were the deaths of Bert Collier, in 1941, and Harry A. Collier in 1944; so when the war ended in Europe on 8 May 1945, only Charlie Collier remained. This was a much more serious blow than anybody outside the family could have envisaged, since young Bert Collier was just beginning to show he had all the hallmarks of being a brilliant designer, whilst the oldest brother, Harry A. Collier, was, at the time of his death, AMC chairman.

Jock West

Born in Belvedere, Kent, John Milns (Jock) West has a pivotal role in any history concerning the products and politics of AMC and therefore the Matchless marque.

After entering an apprenticeship in heavy engineering, Jock began racing in 1928 on a Zenith 350cc, after an earlier introduction to the sport of motorcycling via a Levis 211cc two-stroke in 1924. Jock was to race a vast range of bikes over the next quarter of a century, in a wide variety of competitions including grass track, Brooklands, the Isle of Man TT and international Grand Prix events. As for the machinery, they were Hartley Ariels, works Triumph, AJS, NSU, Vincent and, in the period immediately preceding World War II, supercharged BMW twins. The latter came about when in 1935 Jock West joined the AFN concern, at that time the British concessionaires for BMW cars and motorcycles. This led to an invitation from the German company to meet them at the Eilenreide races, near Hanover, early in 1937. This meeting resulted in an important milestone in the Englishman's career as he left Germany with the promise of a bike for that year's Senior TT.

The sleek black supercharged twin duly arrived, and with it Jock battled for the lead with Norton's Freddie Frith until the BMW's fuel tank sprang a leak – resulting in Jock having to push in to finish sixth. Later the same year he won the Ulster Grand Prix on the same machine. Then the following year, 1938, he was fifth in the Senior TT and again won the Ulster GP, plus third in the Belgian Grand Prix.

As recorded in Chapter 5, Jock West had been instrumental in arranging for a set of BMW's revolutionary telescopic front forks to be sold to AMC; the technology gain resulting in the G3/L Matchless becoming the first British production motorcycle to sport telescopic forks (in 1941). Then just before the outbreak of World War II in September 1939, Jock finished runner-up to team-mate Georg Meier in the Isle of Man, but was forced to retire after disputing the lead with Dorino Serafini (Gilera) during the German GP.

Jock West served throughout the war in the Royal Air Force Volunteer Reserve, rising eventually to the rank of Wing Commander. Even before the war was over he had been offered the post of sales manager with AMC in Plumstead, a position he took up within hours of being demobbed. Then shortly after beginning his job at AMC he learnt that he had been awarded the OBE in the 1946 New Year's Honours List. This news was made public at the AMC victory party held at the beginning of 1946 to celebrate the end of six hard years of conflict.

Besides his responsibility of generating sales in the immediate post-war period, Jock also managed to pursue a racing career on various AJS machines. He finally hung up his leathers at the end of 1950. Even so, as sales boss, Jock West still managed to ride many thousands of miles a year on the latest AMC products, which from 1953 also included the Norton marque. In fact it was the Norton marque that really finally decided Jock to go. During the mid-1950s he had spent a lot of time and energy getting the James Company (also part of AMC) back on its feet; this meant that he was in Birmingham a lot. But when AMC wanted him to do the same at Norton, he refused. Also he had had a furious row with fellow director Donald Heather who had authorized the James scooter project, when Jock had said it wouldn't sell.

So at the end of August 1961 came the shock announcement that J.M. West, OBE, had resigned his post as sales director of Associated Motor Cycles Ltd. Coming only five years from the group going into receivership, there is no doubt that he got out just at the right time – and even if others couldn't see it then, the writing was already on the wall. Furthermore the James scooter proved to be a financial and sales disaster, so Jock had been right. Jock West then joined dealers Glanfield Lawrence, and later BMW Concessionaires in Portslade, Brighton to successfully relaunch his career.

Another event of note for the company was that Jock West joined AMC as sales manager as soon as he was demobbed from the Royal Air Force; he was to have a pivotal role in the products and politics of AMC.

In the first two years of peace almost every motorcycle built – both Matchless and AJS – went for export, with the USA featuring prominently. At this time the importer into the USA was the Indian Sales Corporation of Springfields, Massachusetts. The company was doing well, as their annual general meeting report made abundantly clear; published at the beginning of 1947, it made interesting reading, giving an insight into how the group was performing – and how it viewed its workforce. The chairman was full of praise:

> Once again I feel sure you would not like me to conclude without paying a tribute to the company's staff, which from top to bottom have worked loyally, honestly and faithfully, achieving a higher output per man-hour than was previously attained. The details are as follows: on the basis of 'target hours' introduced pre-war and the criterion today, one man-hour in 1939 produced one and a half 'target hours'; in 1946 one man-hour produced two and one third – or, in other words, 1946 output per man was 55 per cent higher than in 1939. Yet another point is that, since the introduction of the five-day week last month, the output per man-hour has still further increased. Everyone at the Plumstead factory can be proud of these figures achieved, not only by a concentrated production programme, but also by honest toil in the factory. Other motorcycle manufacturers can show good output per man-hour figures and, in general, the industry can claim to have made a brilliant recovery from the dislocation of war.

The Francis-Barnett Takeover

In June 1947 AMC took over the Coventry-based Francis-Barnett concern. Gordon Francis and Arthur Barnett had been related by marriage before joining their names to form the marque in 1919. During the 1920s and 1930s they had enjoyed considerable sales, and had established an excellent reputation with their slogan 'Built like a bridge'. Post-war they had built Villiers-powered autocycles and lightweight motorcycles.

At the time of the FB takeover Charlie Collier and D.S. (Donald Spencer) Heather were joint managing directors of AMC, with Samual Rollason Hogg as chairman. The other members of the board were Gordon Francis, Sir Alan Hutchings, Jack Kelleher and Arthur Sugar, the latter being the company secretary.

The James Takeover

After the Francis-Barnett acquisition, the next marque to be swallowed up by AMC was the James concern based in Greet, Birmingham, in November 1950. James's had been founded in 1880 by Harry James to manufacture bicycles, and when he retired from the business in 1897 it went public, leaving his manager, Charles Hyde, as managing director. In turn, Hyde quit and Fred Kimberley became works manager in 1902 when the first James motorcycles were constructed – and he was still there at the time of the AMC takeover almost fifty years later! In 1952 Fred Kimberley was made president of the Motorcycle Manufacturers Union.

During the 1920s James built a vast array of models, from cheap commuter, lightweight two-strokes, through to a series of top quality but expensive four-stroke V-twins and singles; the company even offered its own range of sidecars. During the early 1930s, however, James, like others, was greatly affected by the depression and thereafter concentrated on Villiers-powered two-strokes. In 1940 the factory was destroyed; it was rebuilt, however, and managed to build some 6,000 machines for the war effort.

Following the AMC takeover James was ever more closely connected with Francis-Barnett, until 1962 when the Francis-Barnett production line was transferred to the James factory at Greet. After this the combined companies became accused of blatant badge engineering, which didn't do either marque, or AMC, any good at all.

It is also important to point out that AMC sales boss Jock West spent a lot of time and effort on the James side during the 1950s, rebuilding its sales successfully.

AMC Fortunes in the 1950s

The Norton Takeover

On the 25 February 1953, at AMC's annual general meeting, it was revealed that a plan existed for the group to acquire the issued share capital of the famous Norton marque. It was also revealed that Norton would continue as a separate organization under the existing managing director, Gilbert Smith (who had been with the Bracebridge Street works since 1916), and that in the words of AMC chairman, S.R. Hogg, 'the Norton factory team will continue to compete in the major events.' But in reality Norton was a bad move, because although its racing successes were legendary, its range, except for the Dominator twin, was obsolete, with much investment required. In addition the share capital and financial control of Norton had in fact been acquired by the Pearl Assurance Company, and for the first time in its history AMC had to allow outside investors to have a say.

1954 – a Bad Year

Nineteen fifty-four was a bad year for the group. First, on Monday 23 August 1954 the joint managing director of AMC, Charlie Collier, died suddenly in his office at the Plumstead works. It was typical of 'Mr Charlie', as he was affectionately known, that he should be busy at the factory until the very end. Sixty-nine years old, he worked a full day, taking a special interest in the service and spares side of the business. He also brought a deep knowledge of the motorcycle industry to AMC, something that with his passing would suffer in future years.

Then, only a few short weeks later, H.J. (Ike) Hatch, who was AMC's development engineer, died at the beginning of October 1954, aged sixty-eight.

1953 AJS promotion material centring upon the marque's sporting successes in scrambles, trials and road racing.

1954 AJS 498cc Model 20 Spring Twin – basically a badge-engineered Matchless G9.

At the end of 1954 AMC announced that it was to quit racing, at least with full GP bikes, although it would continue to support selected riders on production models (the AJS 7R, the Matchless G45 and Manx Norton). The author is sure that had Charlie Collier not died, this decision would not have been taken – at least not so quickly. This view is corroborated by long-time AMC man, Wally Wyatt, who when interviewed in 1984 said: 'If anything went wrong we would soon know about it. Old Charlie Collier was a great man – he was always in the factory walking around. In fact AMC went downhill from the day he died.'

Jock West had been firmly against the purchase of Norton, fearing that he would be faced with having to lend a hand, as he had with James. As one commentator said,

> He made it clear that the AMC board of directors should not expect him to do at Norton's what he had done at the James factory, for the hours involved had taken their toll of him, and he did not relish the prospect of repeating such an exercise if a similar situation arose again.

But of course it did, and in 1954, a few months after the arrival of Norton to AMC's portfolio, Jock West was offered the vacant seat on the AMC board, if he would sort out the Norton sales problem. Despite his earlier misgivings, he accepted the post and thus the task, and the result was an improvement in Norton's future. This was helped by the introduction of the 88 (and later 99) sports versions of the twin-cylinder models. The upsurge in Norton sales then led to Jock being offered, in 1958, the managing directorship of Norton Motors, with the upcoming retirement of the long-serving Gilbert Smith. This time, however, Jock said no, and thus Bert Hopwood was appointed. Even so, regular visits to both James and Norton continued as part of the sales director's role.

Jack Williams was brought in to fill the void left by Ike Hatch's death, as chief development engineer at AMC. Today he is best remembered for improvements made to the AJS 7R, and for his

Early 1950s advertisement for AJS and Matchless from north London dealers Slocombes of Neasden.

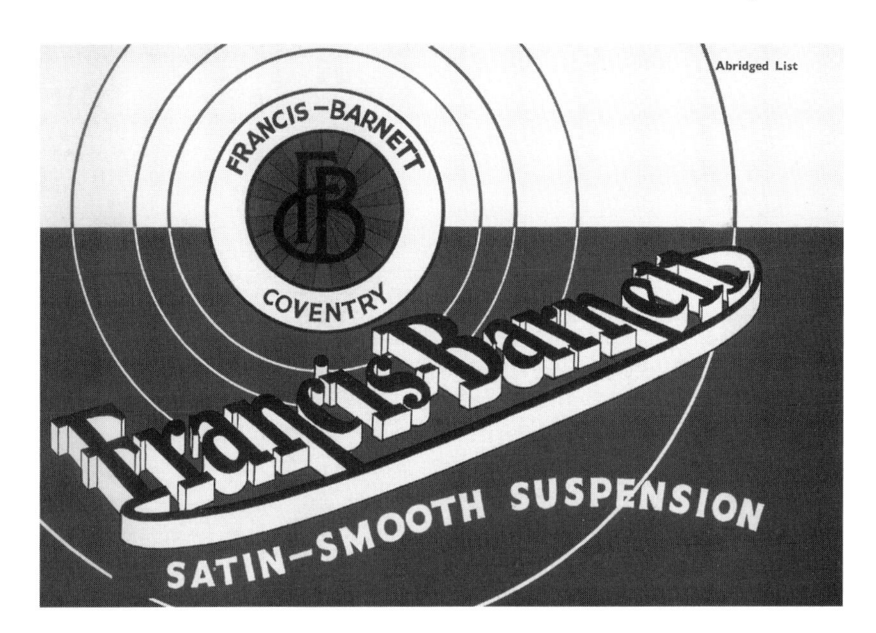

Coventry-based Francis-Barnett had joined the AMC family in June 1947, followed by rivals James (in November 1950). This Francis-Barnett brochure is dated from September 1953 (for 1954 models).

work in bringing to production the new Matchless G50 five-hundred single. However, he was also involved in the continuing development of both the single and twin-cylinder roadster during his time at the Plumstead factory.

A Return to Road Tests

Since the late 1930s AMC had effectively imposed a ban on allowing the motorcycling press, including *The Motor Cycle* and *Motor Cycling*, to test their latest products. But in April 1958 the AMC board of directors partly relented by authorizing a one-off high-speed effort by *The Motor Cycle*'s Vic Willoughby. This test, involving one of the then new Matchless 592cc G11CS Sports Twins, took place at the Motor Industry Research Association's proving ground near Nuneaton in the Midlands. Using MIRA's 2.82 mile (4.2km), triangular, banked outer circuit, Willoughby achieved 102.926 miles (165.608km) in one hour, with a fastest leg of 103.9mph (167.2km/h).

In attendance was AMC's chief development engineer, Jack Williams and race mechanic Jack Emmott. Shortly after the completion of this highly successfully run, Alan Baker, *The Motor Cycle*'s technical editor, went down to the AMC factory in Plumstead to witness the engine of the Matchless twin being taken apart, and to report on its mechanical state of health.

Lifting the cylinders showed that the piston rings were in excellent condition, except for a slight picking up on the thrust face of the offside (right) piston. And the camshafts, followers, rockers and both the big and small ends, together with the crank and gudgeon pins, were also unworn. This, and the fact that there was, as Laurence Hartley recalled, 'the complete absence of oil leaking from the power unit', brought a successful conclusion to what had proved an excellent piece of publicity. Incidentally, the much travelled photographer and author Michael Marriott had joined the advertising and publicity department at AMC in February 1958, and this project had been his first for his new employers.

In late March 1958, S.R. Hogg had resigned from the boards of Associated Motor Cycles and its subsidiaries, and Donald S. Heather became the new chairman. Heather also retained his position as managing director of the parent company. Donald Heather had joined the old Matchless company in 1924, became secretary, then joint managing director and, finally, managing director after the death of Charlie Collier in 1954.

AMC Acquires Brockhouse Engineering

In 1959 AMC acquired the Brockhouse Engineering Group, who themselves had purchased the ailing Indian Motor Cycle Co of Springfield, Massachusetts, USA in 1951. Indian motorcycle production had continued until 1953; thereafter production of a 250cc side-valve single had continued at Southport, Lancashire for the next six years. Meanwhile Indian (i.e. Brockhouse) had acted as importers for a whole host of British marques into the USA during the 1950s, including Norton, Vincent, Royal Enfield, AJS and Matchless. But after AMC acquired Brockhouse, the Indian import activities ceased the following year, in 1960. Instead the New Jersey-based Berliner Corporation were to take over the imports of AMC products, including Matchless, AJS, Norton and James. Berliner were also, at various times, the Stateside importers for the German Zündapp and Italian Ducati factories.

More badge-engineering, the AJS16MS, aka Matchless G3/LS of 1957.

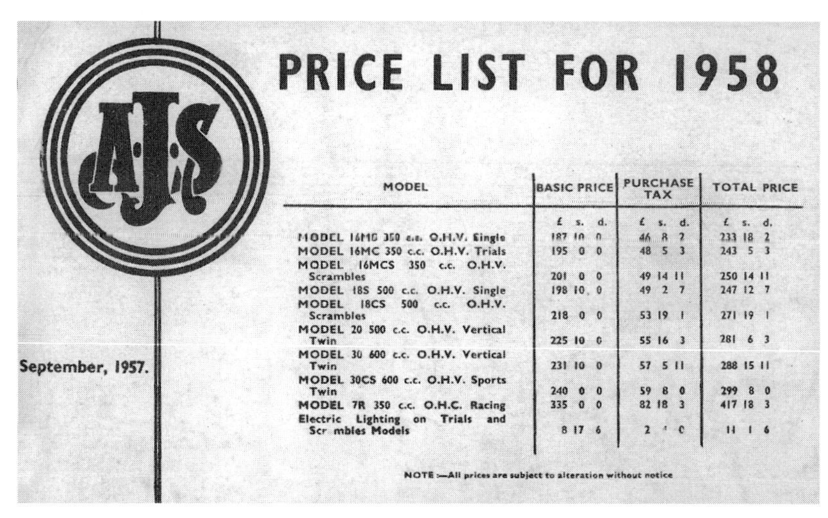

PRICE LIST FOR 1958

AJS

September, 1957.

MODEL	BASIC PRICE			PURCHASE TAX			TOTAL PRICE		
	£	s.	d.	£	s.	d.	£	s.	d.
MODEL 16MS 350 c.c. O.H.V. Single	187	10	0	46	8	2	233	18	2
MODEL 16MC 350 c.c. O.H.V. Trials	195	0	0	48	5	3	243	5	3
MODEL 16MCS 350 c.c. O.H.V. Scrambles	201	0	0	49	14	11	250	14	11
MODEL 18S 500 c.c. O.H.V. Single	198	10	0	49	2	7	247	12	7
MODEL 18CS 500 c.c. O.H.V. Scrambles	218	0	0	53	19	1	271	19	1
MODEL 20 500 c.c. O.H.V. Vertical Twin	225	10	0	55	16	3	281	6	3
MODEL 30 600 c.c. O.H.V. Vertical Twin	231	10	0	57	5	11	288	15	11
MODEL 30CS 600 c.c. O.H.V. Sports Twin	240	0	0	59	8	0	299	8	0
MODEL 7R 350 c.c. O.H.C. Racing	335	0	0	82	18	3	417	18	3
Electric Lighting on Trials and Scr mbles Models	8	17	6	2	[illegible]	0	11	1	6

NOTE :—All prices are subject to alteration without notice

AJS 1958 price list; all except the 7R 350cc road racer had direct Matchless clones.

The Beginning of the End

On the 31 August 1960, Donald Heather retired from the post of managing director of AMC, although he retained his position as chairman of the board of the group; from the same date, Arthur Sugar and Jack Kelleher were appointed joint managing directors. Other board members at that time were Tom Cowell and Jock West, whilst R.S. Mays-Smith continued as group secretary.

But things were far from being well at AMC. At the beginning of 1960 a shareholder's committee had been formed and an extraordinary general meeting called, at which the committee had requested that all the directors resigned – with the exception of Jock West. However, somehow the board sweet-talked the protesters to such a degree that when the meeting ended, the mass resignation that had been called for did not happen.

But what this *did* cause was the ultimate resignation, in 1961, of the one man who had the shareholders' confidence: Jock West. Jock went first to retailers Glanfield Lawrence (as a director), and later to BMW Concessionaires in Portslade, Brighton. The reasons behind his resignation are discussed elsewhere, but suffice it to say that he was tired of cleaning up the mess caused by others.

On 1 October 1961, W.J. (Bill) Smith, who up to that date had been general sales manager of Norton, took over the duties of home and export sales manager from Jock West. Then at the end of 1961 the group had to announce that it had turned the previous year's profit of £219,000 into a £350,000 loss (this was about £3.5 million in today's money). The fallout from this was that in February 1962, Donald Heather had been replaced by Tom Cowell as chairman of the AMC Group board; the latter now consisted of Arthur Sugar and Jack Kelleher, with R. S. Mays-Smith the remaining director, and W. A. Hildreth the company secretary.

Associated Motor Cycles then introduced what it called the 'Standardization Programme'. But this could not be instigated until Matchless, AJS and Norton were on a single site, with the same applying to James and Francis-Barnett. The result was that the Norton factory in Bracebridge Street, Birmingham was closed at the end of 1962, and production transferred to Plumstead; whilst 1962 also saw Francis-Barnett production transferred to the James factory in Greet, Birmingham.

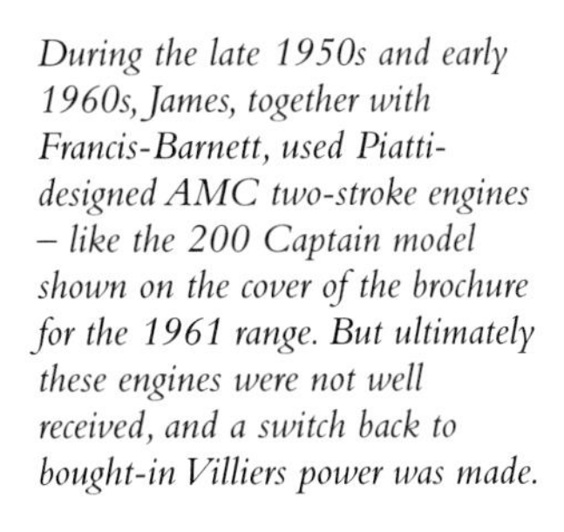
During the late 1950s and early 1960s, James, together with Francis-Barnett, used Piatti-designed AMC two-stroke engines – like the 200 Captain model shown on the cover of the brochure for the 1961 range. But ultimately these engines were not well received, and a switch back to bought-in Villiers power was made.

A 1963 AJS 646cc 31 CSR Sports Twin – also available as the Matchless G12 CSR.

These moves were supposed to save money, but what it did was to destroy sales ... loyal customers of all these brand names could see the whole project for what it really was – blatant badge engineering! The result was that the entire AMC Group simply got itself in to an ever larger financial hole – and the introduction of exotic-sounding model names simply added to the problems.

Another problem had been the saga of the Piatti-designed, AMC two-stroke engines for the James and Francis-Barnett machines. This had proved a costly failure, and a return was made to the use of bought-in Villiers power units. During the Piatti-engine era (late 1950s, early 1960s) a small capacity two-stroke was sold in North America as the Matchless Apache; few were sold...

By the end of 1962, with sales declining ever quicker, AMC appointed a new chairman, Sir Norman J. Hulbert MP; upon taking office he had the temerity to proclaim that they were 'on the way to recovery' – when, of course, things were going from bad to worse. Sadly the honourable gentleman was probably paid a consider able amount of money – money that AMC could ill afford – to give what was, after all, misleading information to interested parties such as shareholders and the press.

By the end of 1964 the entire AMC empire seemed to be heading for the rocks. *Motor Cycling's* Bob Holliday commented: 'The range for 1965 look as though someone had taken a collection of AMC, Jubilee and Featherbed frames, AJS, Matchless and Norton engines and, with name plates for all three marques, shaken them up with a giant hat to produce some twenty-two varieties of single- and twin-cylinder ohv motorcycles.'

In August 1966, Associated Motor Cycles had reached the point of no return: with its financial state becoming worse by the hour, the directors decided to quit. The official receiver was therefore appointed to take over the ailing empire – in fact it was the creditors, including the group's banks, who instigated this. In September 1966, terms were agreed for the takeover of AMC by Manganese Bronze, headed by Denis Poore. The new owners decided to merge the AMC motorcycle concern into the former Villiers Engineering Company, under the name of Norton Matchless Ltd. Norton-Matchless was ultimately a sub-company of Norton Villiers (NV).

Ex-AMC man Wally Wyatt, when interviewed during the early 1980s, said: 'AMC got what they deserved. They designed no new models and installed no new plant or machinery at a time when they were making more money than any other motorcycle firm in the world.' And the author has to agree: quite simply the death knell for the group began back in the mid-1950s, when it turned away from the Collier priorities of sound, innovative engineering, sporting successes, and money being ploughed back into investment in new models.

8 Twins

Royal Enfield, then Norton, and finally AMC launched brand new five-hundred vertical twins within weeks of each other during late October and early November 1948. The announcement from Associated Motor Cycles Ltd of its new Matchless (and AJS) vertical twins came as an eve-of-show surprise for the London Earls Court exhibition, opened on 18 November 1948 by Field Marshal the Viscount Montgomery of Alamein. Lord Montgomery was welcomed by George H.B. Wilson, President of the Manufacturers' Union. The Field Marshal was then escorted to a number of stands, including that of Matchless. He praised the contribution made by the motorcycle industry to the British export drive – and certainly at that time, the need for foreign trade took priority over the home market. In fact the new AMC twins were not available to British buyers until some time later, all initial production being earmarked for export.

The G9 Super Clubman

The new Matchless model was listed as the G9 Super Clubman, and *The Motor Cycle* had this to

AMC finally got the parallel-twin bandwagon rolling (if one discounts the AJS Porcupine racer) over a decade after Triumph had launched its Speed Twin, with the Matchless G9 and AJS Model 20 machines towards the end of 1948 (a 1952 G9 is shown). But unlike all its contemporaries, the AMC design featured a third, central main bearing. It also featured separate heads and barrels, plus gear-driven camshafts fore and aft.

The 1950 G9

Engine:	Air-cooled, ohv twin with vertical cylinders; separate alloy heads; separate cast-iron barrels; three main bearings (one central); one-piece crankshaft with split big ends and Hiduminium RR56 con-rods; gear-driven camshafts fore and aft; coil valve springs; separate rocker boxes (four)
Bore:	66mm
Stroke:	72.8mm
Displacement:	498cc
Compression ratio:	7:1; 1956–58, 7.8:1; 1959 onwards, 8:1
Lubrication:	Dry sump, twin gear-oil pumps
Ignition:	Magdyno, Lucas
Carburettor:	Amal 76 1in
Primary drive:	Chain
Final drive:	Chain
Gearbox:	Four-speed foot-change, Burman CP type; 1952–56 Burman B52; 1957 onwards, AMC
Frame:	Two-part with single front down-tube, branching into twin tubes under engine; single top (tank) tube
Front suspension:	AMC Teledraulic oil-damped forks
Rear suspension:	Swinging arm, with oil-damped twin shock absorbers
Front brake:	7in SLS drum, single-sided; 7in full-width 1954 onwards
Rear brake:	7in SLS drum, single-sided; 7in full-width 1954 onwards
Tyres:	Front 3.25 × 19; rear 3.50 × 19

General Specifications

Wheelbase:	55.2in (1,402mm)
Ground clearance:	5.5in (140mm)
Seat height:	30in (762mm)
Fuel tank capacity:	3gal (14ltr); 1954, 3.75gal (17ltr); 1959, 4.25gal (19ltr)
Dry weight:	394lb (179kg)
Maximum power;	29bhp @ 6,800rpm; 1956, 30.5bhp
Top speed:	87mph (140km/h)

1949 MATCHLESS PROGRAMME

HOME PRICES

		£	s.	d.	Purchase Tax £	s.	d.
Model 49/G3L	350 c.c. O.H.V. Single - -	112	0	0	30	4	10
Model 49/G3LS	As above with Teledraulic rear suspension - - - -	128	0	0	34	11	2
Model 49/G3LC	350 c.c. Competition Model -	117	0	0	31	11	10
	Lighting Extra - - -	7	10	0	2	0	6
Model 49/G80	500 c.c. O.H.V. Single - -	122	0	0	32	18	10
Model 49/G80S	As above with Teledraulic rear suspension - - - -	138	0	0	37	5	2
Model 49/G80C	500 c.c. Competition Model -	127	0	0	34	5	10
	Lighting extra - - -	7	10	0	2	0	6
Model 49/G9	500 c.c. Twin with Teledraulic rear suspension - - -	167	0	0	45	1	10

Illuminated Trip Speedometer, £4 0s. 0d. Purchase Tax £1 1s. 8d.

27/10/48

The 1949 Matchless programme, issued on 27 October 1948, showing the new G9 twin at £167, plus £45 1s 10d purchase tax.

say about it in their show report issue dated 25 November 1948:

> Chief interest centred in the extremely clean power unit, with its three-bearing crankshaft, separate cylinder barrels, aluminium-alloy heads and totally enclosed valve gear. Even the push-rod tunnels could not be seen without going down on all fours. A somewhat racy appearance is given by the integral Dunlopillo upholstery in place of a normal saddle [in other words, the Matchless had a one-piece dual seat, whereas the AJS version came with a single spring saddle and separate pillion pad]; there is ample room for a passenger (pillion footrests are fitted), or for getting down to it. There were whispers that the fleetness of the model is in keeping with such looks. Next to the engine, the Teledraulic rear suspension claimed a lion's share of attention.

The New Engine

A heavy-duty cast iron was used for the crankshaft of the new engine. This was a one-piece casting including the bobweights between the outer main bearings and the big-end bearings, and the flywheels between the big ends and the main bearing in the middle. This use of a centre bearing was unique amongst British ohv twins of the era. The outer mains were of the journal roller type, and the shafts measured 1⅜in (34mm) diameter at the journals. In the middle there was a

Vandervell shell white-metal bearing of 1⅝in (40mm) by 1¼in (32mm) wide. Bearings for the bid-ends were of similar type and diameter but were 1 5/16in (33mm) wide.

Location of the crankshaft was effected by the central bearing. This was a split bearing and was carried by a light alloy diaphragm plate bolted to the driving-side half of the crankcase; the plate was also spigoted into both halves of the crankcase, and thus could not be seen when the crankcase was assembled. To allow for crankcase expansion the outer roller bearings were not shouldered and therefore permitted lateral movement of the case relative to the crankshaft.

Light alloy – RR56 – was employed for the connecting rods. These were particularly robust in the area of the big-end eyes, and were polished to remove surface scratches (thus decreasing the possibility of premature breakage).

An unusual type of fixing for the bearing-cap retaining studs was used. Steel rods, which formed trunnions, were pressed into the con-rods. Into these screwed the big-end cap studs, and thus the cutaway necessary to accommodate the head of the usual form of retaining bolt – sometimes a source of weakness – was avoided.

There were no separate small-end bushes; instead the con-rods operated directly on the gudgeon pins. Each small-end eye was provided with four holes – two at the top and two at the bottom – for lubrication purposes.

Pistons were of the split-skirt, wire-wound variety, and had already proved their worth in the AMC single-cylinder engines. Each piston featured two compression rings and one slotted scraper ring. The piston crown was domed and had flats to clear the valves. Of ¾in (19mm) diameter, the gudgeon pin was tapered at the ends and retained by spring circlips. With bore and stroke dimensions of 66 × 72.8mm respectively, the five-hundred twin engine was slightly long stroke and displaced 498cc.

The cylinders were separate cast-iron castings and were sunk to a depth of approximately 2½in (63mm) in the crankcase mouths. And except for the segment below the cap of the middle crankshaft bearing, the diaphragm plate separated the crankcase into two compartments.

Cylinder heads were in light alloy, and again were separate castings. These castings included the inlet and exhaust valve spring wells and supports for the rocker spindles. A quartet of studs screwed into the crankcase to retain each cylinder head and barrel; on these studs were fitted chromium-plated, domed retaining nuts, and below them, waisted distance pieces. This waisting was provided so that airflow was not impeded. Bolted to the two cylinder heads above the exhaust ports was a flat head-steady, described by the AMC launch technical bulletin as a 'tie-plate'. Between each cylinder – which had a spigot – and its head was a gasket.

Each combustion chamber was hemispherical in shape and had shrunk-in valve seats. The iron inlet valve guide and a bronze guide for the exhaust were a press fit in their bosses, and were prevented from being forced too far by spring circlips. Cylinder-head finning was conventional except at the crown, between the valve spring wells, where the fins were of diagonal shape from the outside at the front to the inside at the rear. The valves featured semi-tulip heads and hardened stem ends to resist wear from contact with the rockers. Inlet and exhaust valves were in silchrome and KE965 steel respectively, and their dimensions were inlet 9/32in (7mm) diameter stem, 1⅜in (35mm) diameter head; exhaust 5/16in (8mm) diameter stem, 1¼in (31mm) diameter head. Each valve was equipped with a pair of inner and outer springs, concentric in shape, with split collets seating in a groove in the stem retaining the valve spring collar.

The rockers were one-piece forgings, and were each filled with a pair of ⅝in (16mm) long, phosphor-bronze bushes; the tips of the rockers bore directly on the valve stems, and the integral ball-ends were hardened. Rocker spindles were ½in (13mm) in diameter, and were mounted eccentrically in the supports in the cylinder head. This eccentric mounting was to provide rocker clearance adjustment, and followed the practice adopted on the AJS 7R three-fifty ohc single-cylinder racing engine. Each spindle had a wide, flat, circular head with a segment ground back, and a small clamp-bolt located in the inner rocker support bore on this segment and held the spindle when the correct rocker setting had been obtained.

Each rocker assembly had its own light-alloy cover, and there was a sealing washer between the cover face and the face round the valve spring well; four bolts, with extended heads for accessibility, clamped down the cover and thus ensured an oil-tight joint.

The inlet ports of the two cylinder heads were joined by a light-alloy manifold on which was fitted the single Amal Type 76 1in (25mm) carburettor. The exhaust pipes were a push-fit into the exhaust ports.

The Timing Gear

The timing gear was described by *The Motor Cycle* as 'noteworthy', long life and quietness in operation having been a priority in the designer's mind. Spur gears were employed with teeth of $\frac{9}{16}$in (14mm) width. Above the half-time pinion on the crankshaft was an idler pinion; this meshed with the inlet and exhaust camshaft pinions. The inlet camshaft pinion drove a Lucas flange-fitting magneto, which has manual timing control and a cut-out. The exhaust camshaft pinion drove a 3in (75mm) diameter Lucas dynamo at $1\frac{1}{3}$ engine speed. The dynamo was retained in a cradle formed in the crankcase casting by a clamping band, and also by screws from the timing chest into the end cover.

Of $\frac{13}{16}$in (20mm) diameter at the bearing journals, the one-piece forged camshafts each ran in three $\frac{5}{8}$in (16mm) long phosphor-bronze bushes. Two bushes were placed between the pinion and the cams, and the third bush was at the end remote from the pinion. The cams operated single-arm followers that were mounted direct on steel spindles; these spindles located in each half of the crankcase and acted as dowels. Formed in the followers were cups to take the ball ends of the pushrods.

The Lubrication System

Twin gear pumps were used for the lubrication system. These were bolted to the crankcase inside the timing chest, by way of an alloy plate. One pump was for supply, and the other for the return feed. The mounting plate also provided an outer support for the idler pinion. The oil pumps were driven by tongues mating with slots in the ends of the two camshafts, the exhaust cam operating the supply sump and the inlet cam the return.

From a $\frac{1}{2}$gal (2ltr) tank next to the seat tube, oil was transferred by a flexible pipe to a banjo union on the crankcase and then to the supply pump. In the crankcase casting was a spring-loaded ball valve to prevent overloading of the pump gears. In excess of a pre-determined pressure the valve opened and allowed oil to pass back into the feed line. From the pump the lubricant went via a filter chamber positioned laterally in the front of the crankcase casting.

The oil filter featured a fabric element and was provided with a spring-loaded relief valve to ensure that the element would be bypassed should it become choked. Access to this filter element was gained by removing a cap on the off-side (right) of the crankcase. Within the filter chamber cap there was another non-return ball valve to prevent oil draining from the tank into the crankcase when the engine was not running.

From the filter chamber the oil-way in the crankcase split into two. The main outlet conveying lubrication oil by means of a diaphragm plate to the crankshaft central bearing, and thereafter via the crankshaft to the big-end bearings. Then from the big ends, the oil was flung to the small ends, the pistons and the cylinder bores, plus the crankcase bearings. The small outlet led to a ported distributor at the end of the exhaust camshaft. This was located in the near-side (left) of the crankcase, and its boss was sealed by a detachable chromium-plated cap. This distributor directed oil to the upper and lower grooves round the deep spigots of the cylinder barrels.

Passages within the cylinder head and barrel castings led oil from the upper grooves in the inner rocker spindle in each rocker box. Again they split two ways, one along the centre of the rocker spindle with an outlet between the two bushes, the other directing or, more correctly, squirting oil into the pushrod-end cup in which the rocker ball-end was seated. Surplus oil lubricated the valve guide and then drained down the

ABOVE: *'The Machine that sets the Fashion to the World.' By the late 1920s Matchless motorcycles were to be found all around the world.*

RIGHT: *Panoramic view for the front cover of the 1928 Matchless range, showing one of the Plumstead factory's popular ohv singles.*

BELOW: *Built in the years immediately following the First World War, the Model H was a luxurious sidecar outfit, powered by a JAP V-Twin engine and featuring a swinging-arm frame.*

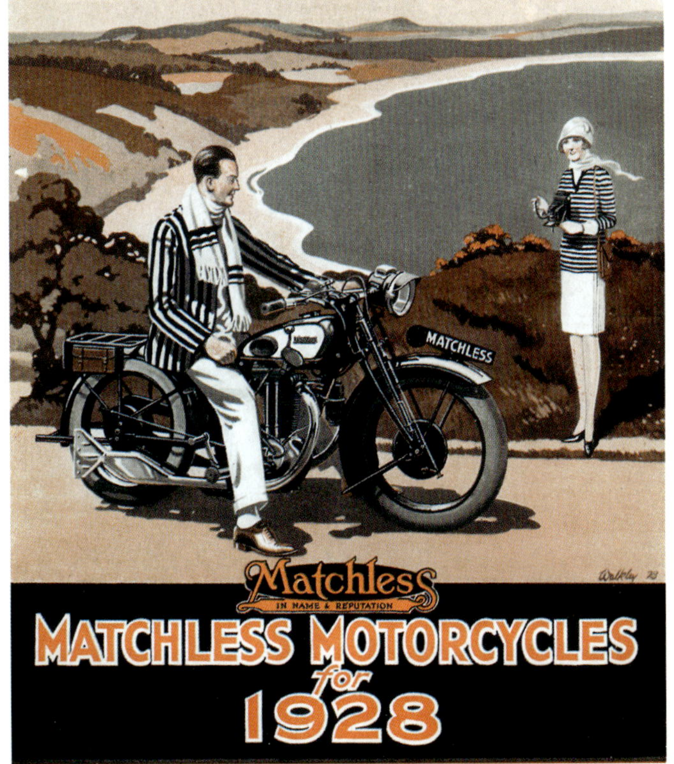

ABOVE LEFT: November 1948 advertisement telling enthusiasts to see the 1949 models on Stand 61 of the London Earls Court Show.

ABOVE RIGHT: 1951 Matchless G9 Super Clubman, with 498cc ohv twin-cylinder engine and Burman four-speed foot-change gearbox.

LEFT: A 1949 advertisement for Matchless, when virtually every newly produced British bike went for export.

August 1953 G80S/G3LS … telling potential customers that they could 'explore the by-ways of the countryside or traverse the highways of the world'.

BELOW: During the 1950s, heavyweight 500cc four-stroke singles like this Matchless G80CS ruled the world of off-road racing.

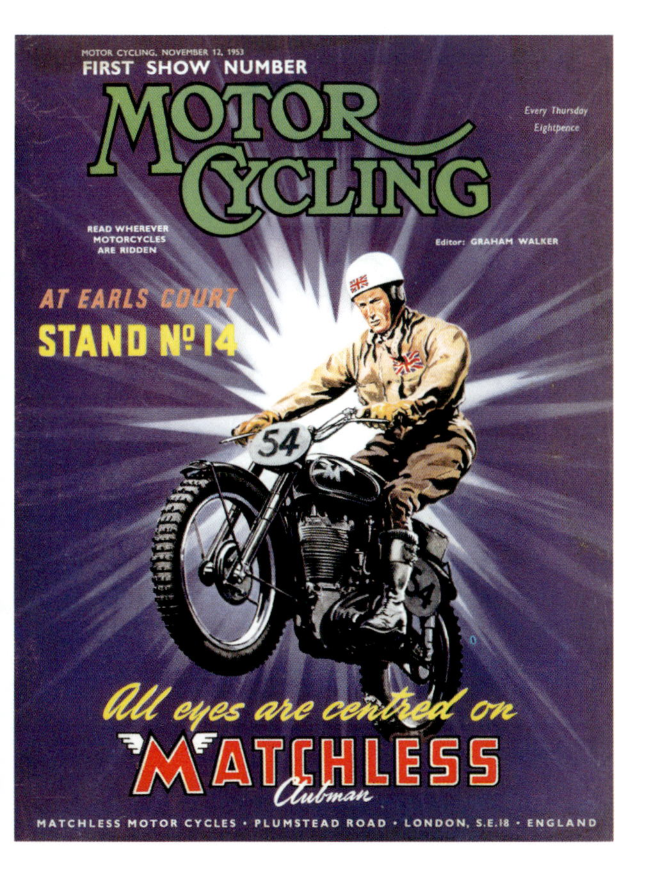

Developed from the G9 roadster twin, the G45 racer ran from 1952 through to 1957; the prototype had made its winning debut in the 1951 Senior Manx Grand Prix.

A 1954 model G9 twin with new, full-width alloy front hub.

November 1954 Matchless advert showing features of the recently announced 1955 model range.

The 1961 Matchless range, with a quartet of representative models, clockwise from the top left: G5 three-fifty lightweight single, G80CS Scrambler, G12 six-fifty twin in police guise, and G50 road racer.

The colourful Matchless logo.

A 1961 G12 with 646cc (72 × 79.3mm) air-cooled, ohv, twin-cylinder engine and single Amal Monobloc carburettor.

ABOVE: *A Matchless G50 (7) and its older brother, the AJS 7R (16).*

LEFT: *The G50 used a 496cc (90 × 78mm) sohc engine. Drive to the overhead cam was by chain. Other details included a four-speed AMC gearbox, Lucas racing magneto and Amal GP carburettor.*

The latest G12 six-fifty twin from the front cover of the 1962 Matchless range brochure.

G80 CS Scrambler from the early 1960s; a race-winner in the right hands.

Joe Dunphy with the G12 CSR he rode in the 1964 Thruxton 500-mile endurance race, the last to be held on that circuit for a number of years.

By the mid-1960s AMC was fully engaged in trying to cut costs by standardizing parts. This meant Norton hubs and Roadholder forks for this 1964 G12 twin.

During the 1980s the Matchless G50 (and its Seeley-framed counterpart) became the top bike in classic racing.

One of the Harris Matchless G80s built in Devon during the late 1980s, and powered by an Austrian Rotax engine.

pushrod tunnel in the cylinder head and barrel castings into the camshaft chamber.

From the lower grooves in the cylinder barrel spigots the oil was directed to the camshaft chambers, and the supply was enough to enable the camshafts to operate in an oil bath.

After circulating under pressure from the supply pump, the lubricating oil drained down to the base of the crankcase, whereafter it was drawn by the return pump through a cast-in pipe and forced back to the tank.

In the drive side of the crankcase and operated by the inlet camshaft was a mechanical release valve. A cap similar to the one that sealed the oil distributor was screwed into the crankcase wall. The release pipe led back to the oil tank.

The Gearbox

A separate Burman four-speed gearbox, with a five-spring multi-plate clutch and positive stop foot-change mechanism, was specified for the new twin. In addition a cam-type engine shaft shock absorber was fitted; primary drive was by a single chain and enclosed in the already well-known AMC pressed-steel oil-bath case.

Frame Design

The new twins were the first of AMC's production motorcycles to feature a spring frame as standard equipment. In laying out this new chassis, its designers retained the steering head, front down-tube, top tube and saddle tube of the existing rigid frame already in use on the single-cylinder line. In addition, the famous AMC Teledraulic and, except for a small detail, the brakes were also identical with those employed on the singles. The exception was that on the twin-cylinder models a long front-brake torque arm was fitted in place of bolts attaching the shoe plate to the fork leg.

For the spring frame (as AMC liked to describe their swinging-arm chassis), the twin cradle tubes that passed under the engine and gearbox were attached by a transverse bolt – the cradle tubes being gusseted for additional strength at this point – to the base of a light alloy bridge casting, which extended from the bottom of the seat tube and curved round the rear of the gearbox.

The cradle tubes extended beyond the transverse bolt and provided anchorages for the pillion footrests and silencers.

A 1in (25mm)-diameter steel tube acted as the swinging-arm pivot point, and the twin AMC 'Candlestick' suspension unit provided both comfort and road-holding abilities. The pivot tube operated on sintered bronze bushes 1in (25mm) long. Lubrication was achieved very simply by filling the tube with oil on assembly. The tube featured end plates which in effect sealed the oil reservoir, the oil feeding round the ends of the tube to the moving surfaces, between the inner ends of the fork eyes and the bridge casting of the swinging-arm fork casting with felt sealing washers.

The rear wheel spindle was of a larger diameter than the one employed with the rigid frame; another difference was that the adjustment was carried out by cams on the spindle bearing against projections on the swinging-arm lugs.

Based on the type already fitted to the AJS 7R racing model, the rear shock-absorber design, nicknamed the 'Candlestick', contained a coil spring and a hydraulic damping device. These units were rubber-bushed at the top and bottom. AMC sources stated that total movement at the wheel spindle was 3in (75mm).

Ancilliary Equipment

Other details of the new twins' specification included:

- centre and side stands;
- headlamp with latest Lucas fixed-focus bulb;
- pair of elongated toolboxes;
- 19in wheels; 3.25 front and 3.50 rear section tyres;
- 3gal (14ltr) fuel tank with twin taps;
- megaphone-shape silencers.

The differences as compared to the AJS version were the fuel tank size, the timing cover shape and the seating arrangements. The Matchless version was also more expensive: launch prices in November 1948 (including British purchase tax) were the Matchless G9 Super Clubman £212 1s 10d, and the AJS Model 20 Spring Twin £209 11s.

Philip Walker's Design

At the time amongst current parallel-twin motorcycle engines, P.A. Walker's unit was unique in having a three-bearing crankshaft, and unusual in using cast iron as the shaft material. The obvious attraction of cast iron was that a fairly complicated design could be cast, where it could probably not be forged – but what else induced him to employ cast iron? His answer was as follows:

> Having decided that we wanted a three-bearing crankshaft with integral flywheels, the selection of a cast shaft was economically inevitable – machining allowances on a steel stamping of the size required would be colossal as compared with those on a cast shaft and, in addition, a great deal of metal would have to be machined off the flywheels to obtain the correct crankshaft balance. In the case of a cast shaft, this material can be cored away in the casting. The high-grade alloy iron used for cast crankshafts provides an excellent bearing surface without heat treatment. Further, the less complicated production processes and easier machining of the cast shaft are economic virtues, which far outweigh any possible advantages that could be obtained from the higher tensile values of a steel shaft in this application.

Another question levelled at Walker concerned the central (third) bearing, as thus: 'The middle bearing, one assumes, ensures almost complete rigidity of the crankshaft assembly. Does experience show that the middle bearing, in fact, takes any appreciable load? If the answer is no, then is the middle bearing an advantage, since a slightly longer shaft is necessary?' Philip Walker's answer was as follows:

> Owing to the inherent rigidity of the crankshaft design, the centre main bearing is not heavily loaded, but it does, of course, take its fair share of the load. In view of the necessity for ample space between the cylinder barrels to ensure adequate cooling, the use of a centre main bearing does not, in fact, increase the overall length of the crankshaft. A most important advantage of the use of a centre main bearing is the opportunity it provides to feed oil to a point centrally between the two big-end throws and thus ensure equal oil supply in each. In addition, it provides a perfect means of end location of the crankshaft.

Model Range Development in the Fifties

When the 1950 model range was announced in mid-October 1949, the G9 twin remained unchanged, except for detail modification shared with the single-cylinder roadster machines: the rear brake pedal and the mudguards were redesigned, and the rear brake hub was made wider.

Almost a year later, in September 1950, there were quite significant changes for the whole 1951 range, including the G9 Super Clubman twin. On all touring and competition Matchless models there was a new clutch, its design based largely on racing experience, and developed from the AJS 7R.

Another more visible change was the introduction of new, fatter rear suspension units; these were soon dubbed the 'Jampot' type. Again, these had benefited from the company's participation in sporting events, but this time motocross rather than road racing. AMC claimed that the new shocks 'permit slightly less fork arm movement than has been the case heretofore, but this definitely avoids all tendency towards "bottoming" when the machine is used on really rough country.'

For the 1951 range, AMC gave chaincase sealing a revision. The long-established V-section rubber band used by the company gave way to what AMC described as a 'mushroom' section sealing band, this – at least in theory – forming a gasket between each half of the chaincase, and fitting into the light alloy retaining strap. However, both this seal design and an improved seal for 1953 still proved prone to leakage, and it was only an entirely new aluminium case several years later that came near to solving the problem.

Also new for 1951 was an entirely redesigned front suspension. Again, AMC sources claimed improvement over what had gone before: '[this] gives complete freedom from oil leaks, the loading

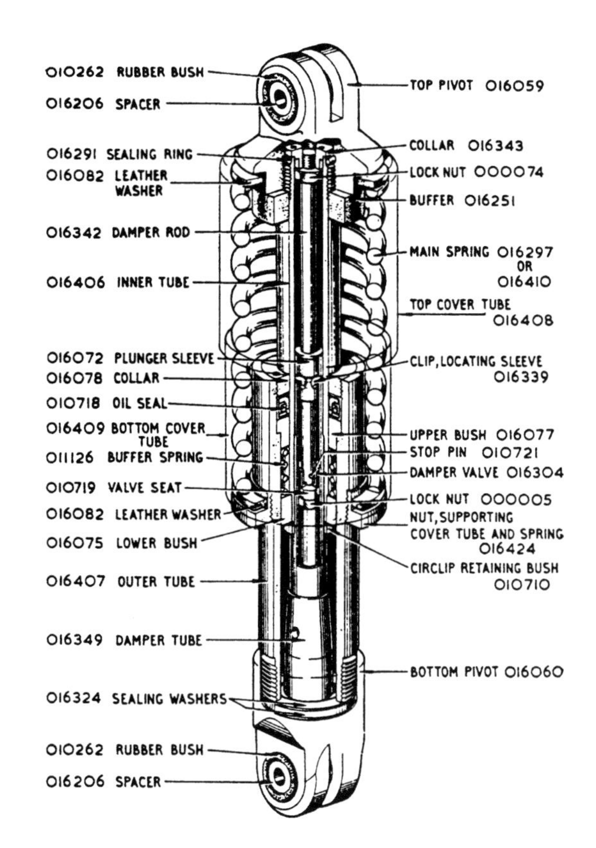

AMC-made 'Jampot' rear shock absorbers introduced for the 1951 season, which replaced the 'Candlestick' type originally fitted to the early twins.

on the hydraulic seals on the forks having been considerably reduced.' The company were also able to point out that one of *Motor Cycling*'s staff members had recently completed a 900-mile (1,500km) Continental Europe test, during which the journal had 'found that the manufacturers' claims with regard to these components (including the forks and rear shock absorbers) are fully justified.'

The new front fork sliders featured recessed drain plugs. This was a departure from a decade of established practice, and was dictated largely by the requirements of the Australian importers, following damage sustained by several owners to one or other of the existing drain plugs when parking their machines against the unusually high kerbs existing in some parts of that vast country!

There was now the inclusion of an air filter, and to accommodate this component the frame of the G9 (and its AJS equivalent) had been slightly altered. The magneto cut-out, since the twins' introduction at the 1948 London Show, had been handlebar mounted, and this now took the form of a simple push-button situated on the Lucas magneto contact-breaker cover.

In the words of AMC: 'With a view to making the range yet more attractive, a considerable number of minor "cleaning-up" innovations have been carried out.' For example there was a provision on the twin for longer centre-stand legs, giving higher lift – important for tyre maintenance. On all the swinging-arm frame models, the rear mudguard joints were now shrouded to prevent water and mud, flung up by the rear wheel, trickling through on to the outer side of the mudguard. All models now had a flexible horn mounting, since the older, rigid type of horn bracket tended to break. Improved production methods employed by AMC were responsible for the use of a forged-steel steering crown member instead of the fabricated component previously used.

December 1952 advertisement for the Matchless G9 twin.

A G9 with sidecar being raced in Rhodesia during the 1950s. The importers at that time were M&S Motorcycles of Union Avenue, Salisbury.

In addition, *Motor Cycling* was able to report in their 21 September issue: 'Particular good news for those who aspire to owning either the luxurious Matchless G9 Super Clubman twin or the AJS counterpart, the Spring Twin, is that both these models will definitely become available on the home market in 1951 – that is to say, from now onwards.'

When the 1952 range was announced in late September 1951 there was another raft of changes. All models, including the G9 twin, were given the new Burman B52 gearbox, also a clutch access cap in the primary chaincase, an alloy front brake plate, and a malleable iron top fork crown. There was also an underslung pilot light, flexible mounted voltage-control box, positive earth and colour-coded wiring. The only 'twins-only' innovation that year was the introduction of an engine breather in the crankshaft drive end.

Improvements for 1953

The policy of year-by-year improvements continued apace, and when the 1953 range was announced in mid-September 1952 there was another 'host of detail alterations' (*The Motor Cycle*). Strangely, the standardization of the dual seat (AMC called them 'twin seats') across the range of the road-going swinging-arm models was the most noticeable of the 1953 model-year features. This seat was similar to, though not the same as, the seat that had made its debut on the Matchless G9 Super Clubman in 1948, the 1953 seat being narrower, now measuring 11in (280mm) across the top. The length remained the same at 24in (608mm), and the general seat construction was unchanged. Red piping was employed on the edging of the Matchless seat, and blue for AJS models.

Otherwise, a cursory glance might have led one to believe that both the Matchless and the AJS machines were unchanged. That, however, was far from being the case, because although it was true that there were no major changes and no new models, there were numerous detail refinements – these including the twin-cylinder bikes.

Although still single-sided – and single leading shoe – the front brake had been modified to provide increased stopping power. There was very little that was different in the appearance of the newly revised brake compared to the one it replaced. The shoe plate had been moved anticlockwise through a number of degrees, whilst the cam lever had been turned relative to the camshaft, so that the lever projected forwards instead of to the rear; the cable stop had also been moved to the front of the fork. The new position of the cam lever provided maximum mechanical efficiency on the leading shoe instead of the trailing shoe, and thus superior stopping ability.

Also provided was (*The Motor Cycle*) 'a simple, thief-proof lock' – an indication that even in the early 1950s, motorcycle security was something of a problem. For this, the lower steering-head lug was drilled vertically in the vicinity of the nearside (left) tank stop.

For 1953, all AMC models were given a new primary chaincase sealing band. This new component was an endless, synthetic rubber moulding, wider than the one it replaced. AMC sources claimed that 'frequent removal and replacement of the band will in no way impair the oil lightness of the chain case'...though in practice, once it had been disturbed its sealing abilities were never quite as good as when it was new.

A new Lucas rear lamp, the Diacon, was introduced on all roadster models. This was manufactured in moulded plastic, the lens being oblong in shape with a white section underneath. It had been designed not only to provide more light at the rear, but also to permit a stop-light to be incorporated, the latter available as a cost option.

Other modifications that applied to all models were the incorporation of a short length of flexible tubing in the fuel pipe, and an alteration to the top covers of the fork legs. The covers to which the headlamp brackets were welded, were now free to pivot on the main fork tubes, and a tight fit was achieved by the insertion of a rubber washer at the base of each cover tube. This alteration had been made merely so that the headlamp brackets could be turned through 90 degrees when the machines were packed for export, meaning that the motorcycle was less likely to get damaged in transit. So that there was no unsightly gap when the fork was fully extended, the slider extension tube had been lengthened. Allen screws instead of studs were used to clamp the fork stanchions in the lower steering-head lug.

Another modification was that the rear mudguard was fully detachable. Previously, both the mudguard and its hinged extension had been dipped in the enamelling bath together, but occasionally this resulted in a series of 'runs' in the vicinity of the hinge and rivets. Thereafter both sections of the guard were dipped separately. To remove the detachable portion, four 5⁄16in BSF bolts had to be slackened off; these screws mated up with captive nuts in welded pockets, which were, in turn, welded to a mild steel bridgepiece on the underside of the guard. The bolt holes in the detachable guard were slotted to facilitate removal.

Another feature introduced across the range of AMC machines for 1953 was the fitment of a chromium-plated piston ring in the top groove. The company said it had 'carried out extensive tests which showed that the use of a chromium-plated ring reduced cylinder-bore wear by two-thirds'.

Engines of the Matchless G9 and AJS Spring Twin were now of a slightly different external appearance. The rocker-box covers were now retained by only two studs, instead of the four fitted previously, and the pair of cylinder-head steady tubes employed previously had been superseded by a triangular, 1⁄8in (3mm) thick, mild steel plate. This plate was joined to a pair of extensions on the cylinder head, and a lug brazed to the front down-tube of the frame.

The cam followers were now slightly longer, achieved by moving the follower fulcrums further away from the cams. The reason was to improve the angle between the cam and follower, and thus lengthen the life of the follower.

Finally, there was the provision of a small, neoprene rubber sealing ring in the carburettor joint face of the inlet manifold. This was needed because of service experience where AMC had discovered that the carburettor joint face of their twin-cylinder engine could become distorted after even a very low mileage. AMC said the basis of this was that 'the carburettor actively bends as a result of torque reversals in the engine, and the joint face, as a result, becomes slightly concave'. So the AMC engineering team solved the problem with what, in effect, was an 'O' ring. This idea was later taken up by Amal and introduced into their carburettor design.

Changes for the 1954 Range

A year later, when the 1954 range was announced in September 1953, the big news was the introduction of a full width, light alloy, die-cast front brake hub (sand-cast hubs, fully machined, were used on the initial batch of machines to avoid production delays). A feature of this hub was the use of straight spokes, which because they were inherently stronger than the angled variety, enabled a slight reduction in gauge size.

The flanged, 7in (178mm) diameter cast-iron brake drum was shrunk on to the hub shell and bolted through the flange. Waterproofing of the brake was achieved by incorporating, on that side of the hub, a conical face on the inside of the spoke flange. The conical face acted as a water flinger; in addition there was a step between the braking surface of the drum and the shell, which further helped to keep water out.

At the same time a new cast-aluminium brake plate was adopted, of slightly domed exterior and with a grease nipple for the cam spindle. The shoes themselves, and their operating mechanism and anchorage, were largely as on the existing single-sided brake. A light alloy disc with concentric corrugations closed the offside (right) side of the hub.

Only one modification to the twin-cylinder engine was introduced for the 1954 model year: the oil holes in the big-end journals were repositioned to eliminate any build-up of sludge in the oilways. Therefore de-sludging of the crankshaft at 20,000 mile (32,000km) intervals, which AMC had formally advised, was no longer needed.

On all models, including the G9 twin, the bottom front engine mounting bolt, which also connected the cradle to the front down-tube, had been increased in diameter from 5/16in to 3/8in (9mm) in the interests of rigidity.

For the 1954 season the G9 five-hundred twin was given a new full-width front hub, twin pilot lights, modified oil tank and other, smaller changes. The sign says 'Win this bike for only £1, 1953 Matchless G9 500cc'; which overlooks that AMC (together with the rest of the industry) went from the end of the previous season (usually October to October in other words).

A new fuel tank with a capacity of 3¾gal (17ltr) was now fitted to all 500cc models; this meant that for the first time the Matchless and AJS twins both shared the same tank.

In order to improve the accessibility of the oil filter, the filter element was now located in the outer half of the tank. Another modification, also made for the purpose of accessibility, was to move the voltage regulator unit to a position between the seat stays under the saddle; this meant that the air filter could be changed much more easily.

As has already been mentioned, on the twins the horn was rubber-mounted from a lug on the front down-tube to which the cylinder-head steady stays were bolted; this lug had now been redesigned.

There were a couple of changes made to the electrics, which were applicable to all models: a new dip switch (much easier to operate than before) was introduced, and the underslung pilot light was abandoned in favour of a pair of small lamps, one on each side mounted on the outside of the headlamp supports. In addition, the leads that emerged from the dynamo were enclosed in a rubber sheath, giving increased protection and a much neater appearance.

The AMC development team had also improved access to the clutch, so that the primary chaincase outer half did not have to be removed first. A domed cover that embraced the entire clutch and was held on by eight screws, replaced the small inspection cover panel. In addition the clutch was now lined with a new friction material that AMC sources claimed provided superior grip when oily, rather than dry, but didn't suffer from the usual 'sticking' problems that were evident with cork-lined plates running in oil. As a result of the improved frictional qualities, it had been possible to reduce the number of plates without increasing the chances of suffering clutch slip.

With the relaxation of nickel restrictions, chromium plating was reintroduced for the wheel rims; the wheels had enamelled centres, with silver lining for Matchless machines and gold for AJS models. The list price of the G9 twin in September 1953 was £240 including UK taxes.

The 1955 Model Year

When the 1955 model year range was announced in early September 1954, *The Motor Cycle* called it 'evolutionary development'. And although there were no new models or any really startling changes, there were, nonetheless, numerous refinements to the ten-strong Matchless range, which included two twin-cylinder machines: the G9 roadster and the G45 racer.

There is no doubt that the G45 racer assisted development of its touring brother, the G9, and for the 1955 version there were detail modifications to the 498cc twin-cylinder engine. These included improved lubrication at the pushrod end of the overhead rockers: in the top of the rocker arm was a groove that was fed with oil via an oilway leading from the bore of the plain rocker bearing to the inboard end of the groove. The oil was carried to the outer end of this groove by centrifugal force, and then ran over the rocker end into the pushrod cup. This copied what was already used on the G45 unit.

A shallower and more attractive cap nut was now fitted over the oil-filter element in the front of the crankcase, whilst there was an improved exhaust pipe lower mounting specified. The former double-cranked brackets from the header pipes to the front engine plates had been replaced by tubular pillar nuts that connected the pipes to the forward cradle bolt.

Several modifications were introduced that were common to all engines. Formerly, air filters (still an optional extra) had been of different types on singles and twins, but now one type was adopted across the entire range. And surprisingly, in that it had been announced in the press only a week earlier, the new Amal Monobloc carburettor was fitted as standard equipment; on the G9 this was a 1in (25mm) 376 instrument with, as originally supplied (for the UK market), a 220 main jet and a number 4 slide.

The lubrication system had been tidied up on the entire range, including the G9, by repositioning the main feed and return pipes below the oil tank. Previously those pipes when viewed from the offside (right) of the motorcycle, lay side by side, but in the revised layout one pipe sat in front of the other.

Following the success enjoyed by the full-width hub fitted to the front of 1954 models, for 1955 AMC introduced this type to the rear as well. However, the hub design for both wheels was, as *The Motor Cycle* said, 'greatly improved in appearance' by a reduction in width, achieved by increasing dishing on the brake shoe plate and end cover, and by providing the die-cast hub shell with a more barrel-like appearance. This latter feature had been achieved by making the middle cooling fins deeper than the outer fins. The rear hub did not, however, embody the brake drum, which was still in unit with the rear sprocket. On the spring-frame models (which of course included the G9 twin), the hub was quickly detachable, in which form it featured a pull-out spindle.

The front mudguard on all the AMC roadsters for 1955 had been redesigned following feedback from owners and the factory testers who had complained about a problem that much of the water and road filth thrown back on to the machine came via the front mudguard stays. The new mudguard, therefore, had no stays except at the very bottom. *The Motor Cycle* described the new mudguard thus: 'It is undoubtedly a good-looking guard, and is claimed to be as effective as a heavily valanced component.'

To provide adequate rigidity, the mudguard extensions attached to the fork legs were radiused into the mudguard and had a stiffening bridge member spot-welded in position.

The front fork stanchion tube diameter had been increased from 1⅛in (28mm) to 1¼in (30mm). The reason for this change was not to improve handling, but to provide greater resistance to damage in the event of an accident. The upper covers, between the steering head yokes, were tapered to make up the larger diameter spring covers; and the welded-on headlamp brackets, instead of providing a triangular form, now had a horizontal top edge.

Both the upper and lower fork yokes had been redesigned, the lower one now a forging clamped to the fork tubes by means of socket-head screws; the speedometer cable passed through a rubber-grommeted hole in the web of the yoke.

The overall height of the steering head was reduced, the steering column having been reduced, whilst the handlebar shape had also been altered to provide increased tank clearance for the riders' fingers on full lock.

The rear 'Jampot' shock absorbers had been modified, so that the bottom spring abutment was no longer screwed to the slider, and was now a shell moulding located by a circlip. An internal modification to the damper assembly had eliminated problems surrounding the damper fluid experienced in the original set-up when under extreme conditions.

The frame now had a hole for an air filter tube, pressed steel lugs for pillion rests, and there was a deeper chain guard together with a simplified oil tank and battery carrier mounting. Yet another change was a deeper headlamp shell, carrying the speedometer.

Show Time

At Earls Court in November 1954 there was 'a show within a show' (*The Motor Cycle*) on the Matchless stand: it featured a special display of engine units that the marque had used, with one dating back to 1902. Amongst the famous power units – undoubtedly viewed by some of the older show-goers with a certain degree of nostalgia – were a 1931 600cc overhead camshaft Silver Hawk V-four, and a 1930 400cc side-valve Silver Arrow narrow-angle V-twin. But so that visitors could see how much progress had been made, a 1912 1,000cc single-speed V-twin (a complete bike) was displayed alongside a 1955 498cc G9 Super Clubman vertical twin. *The Motor Cycle* observed: 'In its latest form, the Super Clubman is certainly a very sleek model with its full-width, light alloy hubs, well tailored dual seat, pivoted rear fork, rear springing and chromium-plated fuel tank distinctively panelled in Aldwych red.' In line with tradition, the Matchless stand was easily noticeable, for it was dominated by a huge winged 'M', a gigantic replica of the Matchless fuel-tank motif.

The Matchless G11

Two six-hundred twins – which were identical with the existing 498cc models except for tank finish and engine displacement – were announced by AMC in early September 1955. The newcomers were the Matchless G11 and the AJS Model 30, and they were developed in response to the demand for increased power from AMC's chief export markets, notably the USA, and also from the sidecar enthusiast at home who required greater pulling power than was available from a five-hundred. Also, as *The Motor Cycle* pointed out:

> For the solo rider in Britain, too, whether he requires extra speed or not, there are advantages accruing from the use of increased capacity. Improved torque means better low-speed pulling; and reduced engine wear and tear is likely to be achieved since the power unit, for most of its life, is operating comfortably within its limits.

Displacing 592cc, the extra engine capacity had been achieved by increasing the bore size of the engine from 66mm of the five-hundred to 72mm, the stroke in each case being 72.8mm. This meant that the new six-hundred engine was almost square. Engine modifications to the latest 498cc G9, and incorporated also of course on the new 592cc G11, were wider oil scraper rings and the replacement of the oil tank fabric filter by a crankcase magnetic filter. Thanks to improving supplies of higher octane fuels, the compression ratio of the G9 had been raised from 7:1 to 7.8:1; the ratio for the new six-hundred G11 was 7.5:1.

There was also a new frame (also employed on the latest singles), featuring a vertical, instead of diagonal seat tube. AMC also claimed that lateral rigidity had been improved by locating the swinging-arm pivot in a malleable iron lug clamped between the cradle tubes and brazed to the lower end of the seat tube; previously the pivot spindle had been carried in a light alloy casting linking the seat tube with the rear of the cradle.

In general terms the mixed brazed and bolted-up construction of the frame had not changed, but by minor changes to the rear subframe, the horizontal line of the fuel-tank base was now continued through to the rear of the motorcycle, thus 'enhancing the general appearance' (*The Motor Cycle*).

The 1956 G11

Engine:	Air-cooled, ohv twin with vertical cylinders, separate alloy heads; separate cast-iron barrels; three main bearings (one central); one-piece crankshaft with split big ends and Hiduminium RR56 con-rods; gear-driven camshafts fore and aft; coil valve springs; separate rocker boxes (four)
Bore:	72mm
Stroke:	72.8mm
Displacement:	593cc
Compression ratio:	7.5:1
Lubrication:	Dry sump, twin gear-oil pumps
Ignition:	Magdyno, Lucas
Carburettor:	Amal Monobloc 376 1in
Primary drive:	Chain
Final drive:	Chain
Gearbox:	Four-speed foot-change, Burman B52 type; 1957 onwards, AMC
Frame:	Two-part with single front down-tube, branching into twin tubes under engine; single top (tank) tube
Front suspension:	AMC Teledraulic oil-damped forks
Rear suspension:	Swinging-arm, with oil-damped twin shock absorbers
Front brake:	7in SLS full-width alloy drum
Rear brake:	7in SLS full-width alloy drum
Tyres:	Front 3.25 × 19; rear 3.50 × 19

General Specifications

Wheelbase:	55.2in (1,402mm)
Ground clearance:	5.5in (140mm)
Seat height:	31.5in (800mm)
Fuel tank capacity:	3.75gal (19ltr)
Dry weight:	394lb (179kg)
Maximum power:	33bhp @ 6,800rpm
Top speed:	92mph (148km/h)

1956 Super Clubman G9 with new frame with vertical seat tube, long thin oil tank on offside, toolbox on nearside to match, and engine with higher compression ratio. This was the last year of Burman gearbox and 'Jampot' rear shocks.

BELOW: 1956 also saw the introduction of the new G11 six-hundred twin; 593cc (72 × 72.8mm), 33bhp at 6,800rpm and a top speed of almost 100mph (160km/h).

Design Changes for 1956

The AMC development team had also set about strengthening the fabricated sidecar attachment brackets on each side of the rear subframe (on all roadster models). These brackets, which also supported the silencers and pillion footrests, were previously fillet-welded to the subframe tubes, but this had led to a number of owners experiencing distortion glitches. This problem had been tackled by using a one-piece pressing on each side of the machine, each of these new brackets being wrapped round the tube and brazed to it, and the two meeting edges being subsequently welded together.

A distinctive feature between the 1955 and 1956 models of the roadgoing AMC range was the introduction of a much longer and thinner oil tank. There was also an increase in capacity, from 4 to 5½ pints (2 to 3 litres). A new toolbox on the nearside (left) matched the new oil-tank design; the two were bridged at the front by a detachable cover. If the optional (at extra cost) air filter was fitted, it was concealed behind this cover. Because of the higher oil temperature of the twins, a shield was mounted to the face of the oil tank, separated from it by a ¼in (6mm) air gap.

Featuring a lid hinged at its lower edge, the new toolbox housed the battery in its forward end; this was secured by a quick-release rubber strap, and was separated from the tool compartment by a bulkhead. At the upper rear section of the toolbox was located the automatic voltage-control assembly; this sat in what *The Motor Cycle* described as 'an anti-vibration, sponge-rubber nest', and was in fact taken from a similar layout adopted for the factory's International Six Days Trial models.

The horn was now concealed under the dual seat. The length of the seat had been increased by 2½in (62mm), in order to 'provide additional accommodation for adults of above-average stature' (AMC press release).

Another change for the 1956 model year machines, both twins and singles, concerned the primary chain adjuster. Although perfectly accessible before, the development team felt it was 'rather unsightly', and moved it to an equally accessible new home between the gearbox plates, where it was neatly concealed by a snap-on cover.

Whilst the full-width alloy hubs with their straight spokes, and the internals of the brakes remained unchanged, there were changes to the brake-operating mechanism. In order to achieve 'a cleaner appearance' (*The Motor Cycle*), the front brake had, in effect, been rotated through 180 degrees so that the cam lever now lay above the wheel spindle and aft of the fork leg. At the rear, the brake adjuster had been transferred to the forward end of the operating rod so that it was accessible from the saddle.

The offside (left) of the machines was enhanced by a polished aluminium rear brake shoe plate that replaced the previous back plate. In addition, a modified rear brake pedal was fitted; this featured a straight shank, whilst the shorter arm was inclined at approximately the same angle as the subframe tube. The cotter-type retention of the pedal to its spindle and the concealed return spring, introduced the previous year, were still employed, but the adjustable stop was now clamped between the pedal spindle and the frame.

Minor detail modifications had been made to the Teledraulic front forks, including attention to the wheel-retaining cups at the lower ends of the sliders and to the fork top cap nuts. There were also now holes on either side of the top yoke for cables to pass through. Another detail improvement, this time concerning the electrical equipment, was the introduction of a Lucas combined horn button and dip switch.

To distinguish between the five-hundred and six-hundred twins, the fuel tank of the larger model had chromium-plated side panels. These were fixed to the tank by two screws retaining a plastic badge; two more screws held the knee-grip plates in position. Plastic beading round the edge of the panel sealed the gap between it and the side of the tank. Colours of beading and tank enamel were very well blended – giving what *The Motor Cycle* said was a 'most attractive' overall impact. The 592cc G11 had a dark red tank with black beading, whereas the 498cc G9 was enamelled black, with the beading in red. The lining was silver, with plastic tank badges.

The major news of 1956 was the arrival of a new 'in-house' AMC-built gearbox; this was announced in May of that year, and was thereafter incorporated on all models for the 1957 season. When reviewing the AMC range in their 27 September 1956 issue, *The Motor Cycle* had this to say:

> Tourists, racing men, trials riders and scramblers can all find models to whet the appetite in the AJS and Matchless ranges, which are, of course, basically similar. All models have pivoted-fork rear springing and telescopic front forks. The roadsters – comprising singles of 347 and 498cc and parallel twins of 498 and 592cc – are renowned for their comfort, high-quality finish and mechanical quietness.

Improved Engine Design

Although the general performance of the Matchless twins had always been good, the demand of potential buyers for more speed and acceleration led to the introduction of modified inlet and exhaust cams on its twin-cylinder models.

The desire to eliminate oil leakage had been responsible for a slight modification to the end cap of the pressure oil filter situated in the nearside (left) crankcase; this cap was now manufactured as a one-piece assembly instead of two, thus eliminating a joint that had been subject to oil pressure. Though the spring retaining the filter element was different from that for the by-pass ball-valve, it had been possible with the old ball-cap to interchange them – with disastrous results. The end-cap modification made the interchange impossible. Finally, neoprene push-on oil pipes were adopted, which meant that threaded unions became a thing of the past.

Frame Design Changes

In adopting Girling rear shock absorbers, AMC became one of the last manufacturers to buy in, rather than make their own, in this field. Incorporating a three-position adjustment for load, these new units were similar to those fitted to several other marques of motorcycle, but the upper and lower attachments were specially made for the Plumstead models.

At the base of each shock-absorber assembly was a rubber-bushed, cast-alloy yoke. The top fixing point took the form of a single eye containing a rubber sleeve. As the AMC shocks embodied yokes at both ends, the plain upper attachment ears originally welded to the frame loops had been superseded by box-section lugs. Thus the new shock absorbers were not interchangeable with the old. Another departure from conventional Girling practice was the use of polished alloy for the split collets which retained the upper spring shroud.

To provide additional frame strength for sidecar work on both the twins and the singles, the bolt that clamped the rear frame loops to the top of the seat tube was increased in diameter to ⅝in (16mm). Also the attachment point was moved forwards slightly so that the lug on the mainframe member was formed integrally with the rear tank support lug (before, two separate lugs were employed).

In mid-1956 the front-fork damping was altered so that on both shock and recoil movements the hydraulic control was now more progressive in operation; AMC claimed that this eliminated front-end pitching. To prevent the possibility of chatter occurring after an extensive mileage had been covered, and to provide an additional degree of resilience in the transmission, a considerable alteration had been made to the five-pin drive of the QD rear wheel on all the roadster models. Previously the driving (and braking) torque had been transmitted to the solid pins bolted in the full-width, light-alloy hub by their engaging with five holes drilled in the cast-iron assembly, which doubled up as brake drum and chain sprocket. The radius at which the pins were disposed from the hub axis had been doubled, whilst the pins themselves were hollow and of much larger diameter than previously, each pin being rubber sleeved externally. In the brake-drum casting the holes the pins engaged with took the form of tubular bosses some ⅞in (22mm) long, connected by an annular rib.

A year earlier the toolbox, battery and voltage-control regulator had been grouped together in a long box, which matched the equally extended oil tank on the other side of the machine. But this had presented a problem, because when attached to a sidecar (on the British side!) the hinged toolbox lid could not be opened fully, because it was too close to the upper rear sidecar mounting connection. To overcome this problem, the lid was no longer hinged to the box, and instead, two ears were formed at the lower edge of the lid, which engaged with slots in the box. So now the lid could be completely detached despite its close proximity to a sidecar connection.

A black moulded-rubber strap replaced the endless red rubber band that had held the battery in place on the 1956 models; for 1957 the lower end of the strap carried a metal peg which hooked into slots in the battery platform.

On the twins, a separate cover was attached to the side of the oil tank to match the toolbox lid. Both cover and lid had a trio of horizontal ribs embossed on them to minimize the possible effects of chafing by a pillion passenger's riding gear and also as a styling ploy.

The ongoing saga of preventing oil leakage from the primary chaincase led to a number of modifications carried out on the rear portion of the pressed steel case. First, the edge of the hole through which the engine shaft protruded was turned outward, and a composite cork washer was placed between the crankcase and chaincase at that point. Next, a sliding oil thrower, consisting of two dished plates riveted together one on each side of the slotted hole in the case, was located on the gearbox mainshaft and moved backwards or forwards with the gearbox during primary chain adjustment. The singles had additional changes in the search to improve oil tightness in this area (*see* Chapter 6).

The shielding of the final drive chain had also been improved by extending the chainguard further downward to the rear of the drive sprocket to cover the chain where it ran on to the gearbox sprocket.

Innovations for the 1958 Model Year

When the 1958 range was announced in mid-September 1957, the main innovation was a newly designed primary chaincase across the range. All used an aluminium, two-piece affair, but the twins featured a different version to the

Reproduction from the 1957 Matchless brochure showing various views of London with G9 and G11 models.

one found on the singles – the main difference was that a bulge on the crankshaft axis was less pronounced, since there was no generator to be accommodated.

The two halves of the chaincase were polished and held together by a total of fourteen screws. There were also two flush-fitting plugs in the outer half. One of these threaded plugs was for checking chain tension and filling the case with oil; the other provided access to the clutch adjuster in the centre of the pressure plate.

Introduced the previous year, the AMC gearbox was retained, but the gearchange action had been made lighter by the fitment of a lower-rate selector spring; this modification applied not only to the roadster twins, but also to the singles and the competition models.

There were two more small alterations applicable to both the twins and the singles: the first a ½in (13mm) reduction in seat height (as a result of shortening the shock-absorber length); and chromium plating of the middle of the wheel rims in addition to the side. Incidentally, it is worth noting that AMC had their own plating vats at the giant Plumstead works.

New Models for 1958: the G11 CS and the G11 CSR

Apart from the list of minor alterations and the introduction of the aluminium chaincase, the twins were unaltered. However, there were two new twin-cylinder models for the 1958 season: the G11 CS, a scrambler (*see* Chapter 10); and the G11 CSR, introduced in January 1958. Basically, the CSR was similar to the CS scrambler, announced the previous September and exported to North America, Scandinavia and other markets.

Located in a modified motocross-type frame, the GSR had a tuned engine with 8.5:1 compression pistons, and a siamezed exhaust header pipe that terminated in a single silencer on the offside (right) of the machine. It used the same 3¾gal (17ltr) fuel tank of the standard G11 roadster, with chromium-plated side panels. The covers of the front fork and the rear shock absorbers were also chromium plated.

The 1958 G11 CSR

Engine:	Air-cooled ohv twin with vertical cylinders, separate alloy heads; separate cast-iron barrels; three main bearings (one central); one-piece crankshaft with split big ends and Hiduminium RR56 con-rods; gear-driven camshafts fore and aft; coil valve springs; separate rocker boxes (four)
Bore:	72mm
Stroke:	72.8mm
Displacement:	593cc
Compression ratio:	8.5:1
Lubrication:	Dry sump, twin gear-oil pumps
Ignition:	Magdyno, Lucas
Carburettor:	Amal Monobloc 376 1⅟₁₆in
Primary drive:	Chain
Final drive:	Chain
Gearbox:	Four-speed foot-change, AMC
Frame:	Two-part with single front down-tube, branching into twin tubes under engine; single top (tank) tube
Front suspension:	AMC Teledraulic oil-damped forks
Rear suspension:	Swinging-arm, with oil-damped twin Girling shock absorbers
Front brake:	7in SLS full-width alloy drum
Rear brake:	7in SLS full-width alloy drum
Tyres:	Front 3.25 × 19; rear 3.50 × 19

General Specifications

Wheelbase:	55.2in (1,402mm)
Ground clearance:	5.5in (140mm)
Seat height:	31in (787mm)
Fuel tank capacity:	3.75gal (17ltr)
Dry weight:	381lb (173kg)
Maximum power:	37bhp @ 6,800rpm
Top speed:	100mph (160km/h)

The handlebar was of conventional roadster shape, and the standard wheels – with full-width alloy hubs – were equipped with 3.25 × 19 and 3.50 × 19 front and rear tyres respectively. Polished aluminium mudguards were specified, as was the competition-pattern dual seat. Lighting

For 1958 only, Matchless offered the 593cc (72 × 72.8mm) G11 CSR sport model with siamezed pipes, alloy mudguards, tuned engine and competition dual seat. A touring version, the G11, was available from 1956 until the end of 1958. The alloy chaincase arrived for 1958.

equipment was of the quickly detachable variety.

The price of the G11 CSR in January 1958 was £299 8s, including British purchase tax; the basic (export) price was £240. In April 1958 journalist and former racer Vic Willoughby rode one of the G11 CSRs at the MIRA testing track, near Nuneaton, Warwickshire, putting on no fewer than 102.9 miles (175.4km) in a single hour, thus proving the bike's sporting potential.

Bigger Bikes for 1959

When the 1959 range was announced in September 1958 the most significant change was that the range of twins had been extended from three to four (or eight, if the AJS versions were included), whilst the use of a longer-stroke crankshaft

The 1959 G12

Engine:	Air-cooled, ohv twin with vertical cylinders, separate alloy heads; separate cast-iron barrels; three main bearings (one central), one-piece crankshaft with split big ends and Hiduminium RR56 con-rods; gear-driven camshafts fore and aft; coil valve springs; separate rocker boxes (four)
Bore:	72mm
Stroke:	79.3mm
Displacement:	646cc
Compression ratio:	7.5:1
Lubrication:	Dry sump, twin gear-oil pumps
Ignition:	Magdyno, Lucas 6-volt; 1959 onwards, coil/alternator; 1964 onwards, 12-volt
Carburettor:	Amal Monobloc 389 1⅛in
Primary drive:	Chain
Final drive:	Chain
Gearbox:	Four-speed foot-change, AMC
Frame:	Two-part with single front down-tube, branching into twin tubes under engine; single top (tank) tube; 1960 onwards, duplex cradle frame
Front suspension:	AMC Teledraulic oil-damped forks
Rear suspension:	Swinging-arm, with oil-damped twin Girling shock absorbers
Front brake:	7in SLS full-width alloy drum
Rear brake:	7in SLS full-width alloy drum
Tyres:	Front 3.25 × 19; rear 3.50 × 19; 1963 onwards, 18in

General Specifications

Wheelbase:	55.2in (1,402mm)
Ground clearance:	5.5in (140mm)
Seat height:	31in (787mm)
Fuel tank capacity:	4.25 gal (19ltr); 1964 onwards, 4gal (18ltr)
Dry weight:	396lb (180kg); 1964 onwards, 403lb (183kg)
Maximum power:	356bhp @ 6,600rpm
Top speed:	98mph (158km/h)

1959 G9 De Luxe, with AMC gearbox and coil ignition with alternator and distributor (note the head steady and chrome tank side panels).

had increased the displacement of the larger versions from 592cc to 646cc; the model code changed from G11 to G12. In fact they were not strictly new, because a few examples had been sent to the USA over the preceding months. The 646cc engine closely followed the pattern of its predecessors, the only external difference being that the cylinder barrels were longer and sported an extra fin.

With the existing cylinder centres the limit on bore size had, at 72mm, been reached on the six-hundred version, so the required capacity increase had been achieved by lengthening the stroke from 72.8 to 79.3mm, the increase in cylinder-barrel length making it practicable to employ the existing connecting rods and pistons. The size of the single Amal Monobloc carburettor had been increased from 1$\frac{1}{16}$in (27mm) to 1$\frac{1}{8}$in (28mm) for the new six-fifty.

There were Standard and De Luxe versions of the 646cc G12, both using a compression ratio of 7.5:1, whereas the sporting versions had 8.5:1. Power output had been further increased on the CSR (and the CS) by a modification to the shape of the inlet tract; AMC's chief development engineer, Jack Williams, had been responsible for this.

Following its successful use on the 347cc and 498cc roadster singles, a Lucas RM15 alternator was fitted to 1959 Standard twins (in both 498cc and 646cc forms), but a separate magneto and dynamo continued to be specified on the remaining twins. Installation of the generator was exactly as on the singles, with the rotor keyed to the drive's main shaft, and the stator located by a spigot in a bulge in the outer half of the primary chaincase. The distributor took the place of the magneto behind the cylinders.

Another feature of the 1959 model-year twins (except the CS scrambles version) was a new,

John Clark displays his winning trophy, following a concourse display in Lincolnshire; c. 1985. The motorcycle is a 1959 G9 De Luxe, but with AJS-type silencers instead of Matchless megaphones.

Nice 1959 G9 De Luxe; the last year of the single down-tube frame and this design of dual seat.

larger, 4¼gal (19ltr) fuel tank, replacing the previous 3¾gal (17ltr) one previously fitted. The new tank also differed in construction from the others, in that the welded seam was on the centreline of the motorcycle, and not along its bottom edges. Oil-tank capacity was 4pt (2ltr), except in the CSR (and CS), which had a 5pt (3ltr) tank.

Although a black tank was usual on the Standard twins, chromium-plated side panels – included in the specification of the De Luxe twins – were available at extra cost. Also the G9 and G12 models had an alternative finish: the mudguards, oil tank and toolbox were in Arctic white (instead of black), with the choice of an Arctic white tank with chrome panels, or a two-colour white-over-red tank. A chromium-plated strip separated the two tank colours where applicable.

Major Changes for 1960

When the annual round of updates was announced towards the end of 1959, it was seen that there were quite major changes for the twin-cylinder family of Matchless (and AJS) models. Chief amongst these, and shared with the heavyweight singles (*see* Chapter 6), was the introduction of a full cradle frame. Duplex front down-tubes were taken back to pass beneath the engine and gearbox. A single 1½in (38mm) diameter, twelve-gauge top tube and a vertical seat tube completed the main frame, that was built on the time-honoured principle of malleable iron lugs brazed into position. There were substantial cast lugs forming the steering head and rear fork pivot housing. The rear subframe was bolted to lugs situated just below the rear of the gearbox and the nose of the dual seat.

AMC claimed that greater rigidity of the new frame, plus an increase in the front fork trail, provided improved steering and handling over the outgoing single front down-tube frame. Previously only found on the new semi-unit ohv two-fifty single, a three-point fuel-tank mounting was a feature of the new frame, there being two mountings at the front and one at the rear.

LEFT: A G12 CSR at Snetterton race c. mid-1980s. Still providing everyday transport with a sporting touch.

BELOW LEFT: The G12 CSR six-fifty with siamezed pipes, alloy guards and duplex frame was an attractive, cobby bike. It was offered from the end of 1958, through to the middle of 1966.

In 1960 a new cylinder head was introduced, with an additional fin and three small diagonal fins each side on the underside next to the exhaust port. This is a G12 CSR six-fifty.

On all models except the two-fifties and the new lightweight three-fifties, the gearbox internal ratios had been changed to provide more even spacing, and in particular reduce the gap between third and top. Bottom was now slightly higher, at 2.56:1 (formerly 2.67:1), second remained unchanged at 1.77, and third was raised to 1.22 (formerly 1.33). Top gear provided direct internal drive at 1:1. However, to special order, the previous ratio could be specified.

The 1960 G12 CSR

Engine:	Air-cooled ohv twin with vertical cylinders, separate alloy heads; separate cast-iron barrels; three main bearings (one central); one-piece crankshaft with split big ends and Hiduminium RR56 con-rods; gear-driven camshafts fore and aft; coil valve springs; separate rocker boxes (four)
Bore:	72mm
Stroke:	79.3mm
Displacement:	646cc
Compression ratio:	8.5:1
Lubrication:	Dry sump, twin gear-oil pumps
Ignition:	Magdyno, Lucas 6-volt; 1962 onwards, alternator; 1964 onwards, 12-volt
Carburettor:	Amal Monobloc 389 1⅛in
Primary drive:	Chain
Final drive:	Chain
Gearbox:	Four-speed foot-change, AMC
Frame:	All-steel construction, brazed and bolted; single top (tank) tube, twin tube cradle, including front down-tubes
Front suspension:	Teledraulic two-way oil-damped forks
Rear suspension:	Swinging-arm, with oil-damped twin Girling shock absorbers
Front brake:	7in SLS full-width alloy drum
Rear brake:	7in SLS full-width alloy drum
Tyres:	Front 3.25 × 19; rear 3.50 × 19; 1964 onwards 18in

General Specifications

Wheelbase:	55.2in (1,402mm)
Ground clearance:	5.5in (140mm)
Seat height:	31.5in (800mm)
Fuel tank capacity:	4.25gal (19ltr); 1963 onwards, 4gal (18ltr)
Dry weight:	381lb (173kg); 1964 onwards, 390lb (177kg)
Maximum power:	42bhp @ 6,600rpm
Top speed:	106mph (170km/h)

The cylinder head of all the twin-cylinder models had been redesigned. Thus the combustion chamber shape was now hemispherical, and flat-top pistons with small recesses for the valves were used – but the compression ratios were unchanged. The inlet tract could be best described as an arc between the carburettor and inlet valve. The object of this design, said chief development organizer Jack Williams, 'was to promote swirl in the gases' and another effect 'was that the valve stem and protruding portion of the valve guide are at one side of the tract where they offer less restriction to gas flow'.

A couple of external differences on the cylinder heads of the 1960 model year twins were thicker lugs at the front for mounting of the head steady, and an additional fin. Cast into the underside of the extra fin were three small short fins disposed diagonally to the direction of airflow; this was incorporated by Jack Williams to improve cooling in the region of the exhaust port.

In conjunction with the new shape of the combustion chamber and inlet port, in the twin the valve included angle had been reduced to 40 degrees. In addition, the twin's bolted-on induction manifolds had also been modified to suit the redesigned ports.

Yet another change was that two-rate valve springs (the coil type was still used) were now featured on the twins, instead of the previous single-rate type. The former spring-loaded felt oil filter was superseded for 1960 by a type using wire gauze of two mesh sizes. A spring-loaded pressure-release valve was now fitted on the twins, this being located inside the front of the timing chest; oil released from this flowed into the timing chest, and then drained off into the crankcase.

A new Lucas 12-amp hour battery (still 6 volts) of a more compact design – still retained by a rubber strap in the combined battery and toolbox –

Another G12 CSR shot from the 1980s – together with a friend's 1979 Moto Guzzi Le Mans II V-twin.

G12 CSR controls and instrumentation, with choke and manual advance levers, steering damper knob, Smith's speedometer and ammeter in headlamp shell.

This is an immaculate 1960 G12 six-fifty Matchless with Watsonian sidecar as seen in the mid-1980s. Features included 'dustbin' fairing, 15in wheels, Gold Star-type silencer with siamezed exhaust and rear carrier.

was now featured on all Matchless models, except the two-fifty and new lightweight three-fifty. There was also a new, more compact headlamp (which still had the speedometer). Yet another innovation common to the heavyweight singles and twins was a two-level dual seat, designed to provide additional comfort for the pillion passenger without making the rider's seating position over-high.

Model Range Improvements in the Sixties

After the major changes of the previous autumn, very little was done in 1961, just detail improvements, mainly to the engines, and providing new colour schemes.

The main change to the parallel twins (except the axing of the G12CS scrambler) was to the lubrication system. Previously, oil from the rocker gear drained into the camshaft tunnels and thereafter, by way of the timing chest, to the crankcase. This new arrangement permitted oil from the exhaust camshaft tunnel to drain direct into the nearside (left) of the crankcase, ensuring a more even distribution. Oil returning from the inlet camshaft tunnel alone had proved adequate for timing-gear lubrication.

On the high-performance G12 CSR (also known as the 'Sports Twin'), the siamezed exhaust pipe had been redesigned so that it now ran below, instead of inside, the offside (right) footrest hanger. This change had been dictated by a modified footrest assembly. Previously the footrest brackets clamped directly to the frame tubes, but this meant that no height adjustment could be provided. There was now a square rod, to which the rests were secured, placed transversely at the rear of the engine, thus providing a choice of positions.

On the Standard and De Luxe G9 and G12 models, the deeply valenced front and rear mudguards had been shortened; also tyre clearance at the leading edge of the front guard had been increased.

There were badges for both larger tanks, whilst some Matchless models had a two-tone paint finish, with Cardinal red and Artic white. Those machines fitted with the chromium-plated tank panels had an overall finish of red for the tank.

The prices of the 1960 twins in late August 1959 were as follows (all including UK purchase tax):

498cc	G9	Standard	£275 12s 7d
646cc	G12	Standard	£280 9s 1d
646cc	G12	De Luxe	£291 6s 2d
646cc	G12	CSR	£302 15s 5d

A feature of the 1962 range – announced in September 1961 – was that every model on the AMC range (except for the Matchless G50 and AJS 7R racing machines) was given a name as well as a catalogue code. In addition the last of the 498cc twins, the G9 Standard, was discontinued at the same time, leaving only the 646cc G12 and G12CSR; the De Luxe version of the six-fifty was no longer listed separately, though it could

A 1961 G12 De Luxe, similar to the standard G12 of that year, but with magneto ignition (instead of coil), detachable chromium-plated tank panels, and a quickly detachable rear wheel incorporating shock-absorbing rubber-sleeved driving pins.

The standard 1961 G12 could be identified by the coil ignition with dynamo and alternator and revised tank cosmetics (with chrome-plated panels); otherwise it shared the same engine tune and running gear as that year's De Luxe version.

still be obtained by specifying magneto ignition and QD rear wheel when ordering. The G12 was known as the Majestic, whilst the CSR was now the Monarch.

But as far as any modifications or innovations, *The Motor Cycle* reported in their 14 September 1961 issue: 'Most noticeable of the modifications common to all these models (referring to *all* AMC's roadsters) are the new petrol tank motifs'. Less apparent, but of far more everyday use to potential buyers, were the following:

- softer rubber tank mounts;
- modified oil tank;
- stronger kickstart return spring;
- extension on centre stand;
- battery reverted to original size;
- new-pattern Lucas horn: smaller, lighter and louder;
- combined ignition/light switch.

In addition, the poundage of the front fork springs on the standard twins was increased to bring it in line with the CSR version. On the sportster twin the pillion footrests were now carried on brackets extending back from the subframe (as on the standard twins) instead of being brazed direct to the subframe. This, AMC claimed, made the mountings stronger and better placed.

In an attempt to counter flagging sales (the UK market having peaked in 1959), AMC dropped prices across the range: on 14 September 1961 when the 1962 model-year list was announced, the twins were as follows: the G12 Majestic £262 6s, and the G12CSR Monarch £289 15s. During 1961, falling sales (and, of course, profits) had seen shareholders discontent. This led at the end of July to an extraordinary general meeting in London attended by around 150 shareholders. It was proposed that the joint managing directors A.A. Sugar and J.F. Kelleher should be removed from office, but this motion was defeated. The same meeting also rejected proposals to appoint three new directors.

Many who attended the meeting voiced complaints concerning the sales policy of the AMC group. They urged a more energetic programme of expansion, allied to an extension of the company's activities to other fields of manufacture. This was in the same week that the British government put up purchase tax from 25 to 27½ per cent. In addition, other taxes, including that on petrol, rose steeply, whilst interest rates also rose.

At the end of August 1961, AMC sales director Jock West resigned from the AMC board.

The official stance at the time was that Jock had 'a divergence of opinion with his co-directors'. Actually, for once this was an accurate statement when someone quit, rather than the more usual 'whitewash'. Jock West's main reason for leaving was the failed policies of another board member, Donald Heather; for example, Heather had authorized the James scooter project, which Jock had been against from the start, and which proved a costly financial failure.

As *The Motor Cycle* commented upon his resignation: 'Jock is probably motor cycling's most notable road racer turned businessman.' In the late 1930s he had been with AFN, the British BMW importers; he had competed in several classic runs, including winning the Ulster Grand Prix and finishing runner-up to Georg Meier in the 1939 Senior TT. After the war he had ridden in the AJS works team. During his sixteen years with AMC (he had been sales manager from 1945 until he joined the board) he had travelled widely in search of exports, and was well known all around the world. During the 1950s he had also spent a considerable amount of time helping the James factory in Greet, Birmingham, build back their sales (James being a member of AMC at the time).

Jock West soon found a new post first with Glanfield Lawrence, and later with BMW Concessionaires as the latter's sales chief, a post he was to hold for several years until his eventual retirement. And there is no doubt that, in West, AMC had lost the services of its most 'hands-on' board member, someone who understood the product he was selling and the industry he served. Thereafter the group was, like the *Titanic*, doomed!

Jock West's position at AMC was taken by W.J. (Bill) Smith, who until then had been general sales manager at Norton (also part of AMC). Bill Smith took over his duties as home and export sales manager for AJS and Matchless from the 1 October 1961. A Scot, Smith had ridden as a member of the OK Supreme team in pre-war days, and later became one of Scotland's most outstanding trials and scrambles riders.

During 1961 AMC had also considered moving its manufacturing base to a new factory at the Isle of Sheppey, Kent. However, this project was abandoned in mid-October that year. At the time the reasons given were primarily 'the possibility of labour shortage'. But the existing workforce was not keen on the idea and finding skilled workers appeared out of the question. But what it did show was that AMC were looking at ways of 'downsizing' its business.

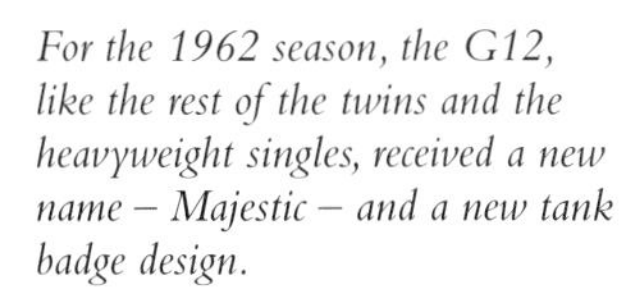

For the 1962 season, the G12, like the rest of the twins and the heavyweight singles, received a new name – Majestic – and a new tank badge design.

Police version of the 1962 G12 Majestic six-fifty, with all-white paint job, screen, mirrors, carrier, siren, radio equipment, single seat and front crashbars. Note the AJS-type silencers.

A Year of Streamlining: 1962

Nineteen sixty-two was a year of streamlining for the AMC group. First it was announced that Norton's Bracebridge Street, Birmingham, was to close its doors at the end of the year, with production being transferred to Plumstead. Then when the Matchless (and AJS) model ranges for the 1963 season were announced at the end of September 1962, the number of models had been significantly reduced: there were now eight Matchless models listed, including the two remaining twins – the 646cc G12 Majestic and G12 CSR Monarch. Yet at the beginning of November 1962 the price of some of the Matchless models had been increased, the Majestic six-fifty tourer to £276 18s, and the Monarch sportster to £306.

1963 Styling Revisions

There were considerable changes to the appearance of the 1963 Matchless range, including the big twins. The Majestic was affected most, with some of the revisions also appearing on the latest CSR Monarch. First, wheel diameter had been reduced by 1in (25mm) to 18in (450mm), though tyre sections remained unaltered; and the steering-head angle was taken back 1 degree to restore the original fork trail.

The appearance of the aluminium full-width hub had been revised (*The Motor Cycle*); this had been achieved by tapering the sides and reducing the number of circumferential ribs from seven to five. The diameter of the brake drums was still 7in (18mm), but shoe width had increased by ¼in (6mm) to 1⅛in (28mm). A new cast-alloy brake-shoe plate was internally ribbed. The front and rear mudguards now had reduced radius to suit the smaller wheels, the makers having changed blade section from C to D and incorporated a rib along the middle.

The bolted-on rear sub-frame had been shortened. This, claimed AMC, had brought a double benefit, rigidity being increased, whilst the suspension units now sloped forward slightly.

There were also small changes to the swinging arm: the brazed-on wheel spindle lugs were now steel plates rather than the previous malleable-iron castings, whilst two tiny cross-tubes were set into the nearside (left) fork arm to accept fixing bolts for a rear chaincase. This new fitment was of conventional design, comprising upper and lower steel pressings. The front end of the case was overlapped by a pressed-steel sprocket cover, meaning that no section of the final drive chain was left exposed.

The contours of both the oil tank (on the offside) and matching battery/toolbox (on the nearside) had been totally revised, with an entirely new, more rounded style. Knee recesses with stuck-on rubber grips reduced fuel-tank width between the rider's thighs. The tank filler cap had moved to the centre line, whilst a single two-level tap replaced the previous two separate tap assemblies. The dual seat had been narrowed at the rear and the depth reduced at the front. In concert with the smaller wheel size, this dropped the seat height by 1½in (38mm).

In an attempt to satisfy the anti-noise brigade, an entirely new type of silencer was introduced. This is best described as being 'cigar'-shaped and although considerably quieter than the type it replaced, somehow it didn't look as eyecatching (in the author's opinion it was blob-like). The size of the number-plate holder was increased, to accommodate seven-digit registration numbers. The rear light was also bigger, and there was a new stop-light switch with an enclosed spring to tidy up appearance.

The only engine change to the twins for the 1963 season was that the width of the oil-pump gears had been doubled, to step up the circulation rate.

Of all the changes and modification described above, the CSR Monarch had only the new fuel tanks, silencer and oil-pump gears. For endurance racers the factory offered a speed kit for the CSR, comprising twin 389 1⅛in carburettors, 10.25:1 pistons and high-lift camshafts.

Optional at no extra cost on the G12 Majestic (when ordered on a new bike) were sidecar suspension and gearing, and siamezed exhaust system. The factory also listed the following as cost options for the G12 Majestic:

- two-tone colour finish £4 8s 2d;
- air filter £2 6s 2d;
- rear carrier £3 16s 6d;
- pannier set £9 5s 3d;
- steering damper £1 4s;
- safety bars £5 12s 6d;
- steering lock 2s;
- rear chaincase. Price to be announced;
- magneto ignition £10 1s 7d;
- high-compression (8.5:1) pistons £1 12s 10d.

For the G12 CSR Monarch cost options were listed thus:

- headlong cowl (with rev counter) £18 18s; or without rev counter £7 4s;
- rev counter separately £11 15s;
- dpeed kit (h.c. pistons, twin carbs, special cams) to be announced.

The 1964 Model Year – and Rising Debts

The need to cut costs to counter a rising burden of debt – and the fact that Nortons, as well as AJS and Matchless models, were all being produced in the same Plumstead facilities – led to a standardization across the range.

A publicity photograph from sidecar manufacturers Watsonian in 1964, showing a Matchless G12 Majestic, with siamezed CSR-type exhaust and a Watsonian double adult chair.

ABOVE: By 1964 the 650 CSR – now known as the Monarch – was but a pale shadow of what it had been before. Instead of the rakish, cobby sportster, there was a much heavier-looking motorcycle adorned by an excess of chrome plate. A speed kit comprising twin carburettors, high-compression pistons and special camshafts was offered at additional cost.

RIGHT: The 646cc Matchless engine of the 1964 G12 Majestic; this machine has siamezed exhaust.

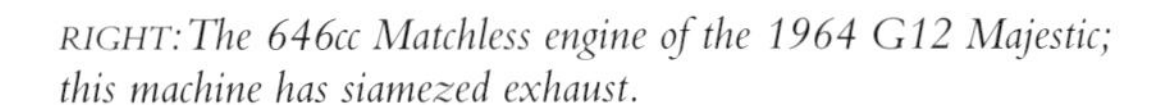

Also from the 1964 model year all the twins were fitted with Norton forks and hubs, whilst there were now 12-volt electrics with two sets of contact breaker points. This G12 Majestic has been given non-standard alloy guards, fork gaiters and is missing the small rubber knee grips for the fuel tank.

Introduction of the G15 model, with the 745cc (73 × 89mm) Norton Atlas engine in a 650 G12 Majestic frame; it arrived for the 1965 model year.

The main change for the 1964 model year was the use of Norton front forks and brake hubs, in place of the previously used AMC components; this meant the famous 'Roadholder' forks and the adoption of the alloy, full-width hub assemblies of 8in (203mm) front and 7in (178mm) rear respectively. However, the duplex G12 frame was retained, although to allow fit of the Roadholders, the frame had to be slightly modified.

Twelve-volt electrics (together with two sets of contact-breaker points) were adopted for both the touring G12 and its more sporting brother the CSR. The latter now received 18in wheels, the altered subframe and gearing, and the rounded oil tank and toolbox, as the Standard model had received a year before.

Then towards the end of 1964 came the G15 (also marketed as the AJS Model 33). This made use of the Norton 745cc (73 × 89mm) Atlas engine. Running on a compression ratio of 7.6:1, maximum power output was 49bhp at 6,400 rpm. This retained the AMC duplex frame, but of course employed the Norton forks and hubs. A prototype of this machine had been first seen back in 1963, and as fellow author Roy Bacon was to recall: 'The Norton engine went back as long as the AMC, and was just as well stretched, old and rather overdeveloped.'

Actually this move did Matchless (and AJS) sales no good at all; in fact it lost them sales. The fact was, Norton fans would buy the Atlas as a true Bracebridge Street-derived model with its Featherbed race-derived chassis, whilst AMC enthusiasts preferred AMC engines – even if this meant having a six-fifty instead of a seven-fifty. Quite frankly by now the ailing AMC group had all but lost their battle for survival.

The G15 CSR

Following hot on the heels of the standard G15 came the G15 CSR. Launched at the Earls Court Show in late 1964, this came with all the extras desired by the contemporary café racer brigade – this coming from a firm who only a few months before had decried British youth and had said it had 'no intensions of pandering to the tearaway culture of the café racer'. But AMC had been forced to eat humble pie after experiencing falling sales and huge balance-sheet losses.

But although the G15 CSR might have looked the part, with its masses of chrome and polished alloy, low handlebars, swept-back exhausts, matching speedometer and rev counter, fork gaiters, rear set footrests and controls and much more, it didn't attract buyers in any real number. And certainly not enough to help the once great Associated Motor Cycles, now in terminal decline.

During 1965, the Matchless G15 CSR was joined by an AJS version, the 33 CSR. And as a

Launched at the Earls Court Show in November 1964, the G15 CSR came with all the café racer goodies, including clip-ons, swept-back exhaust, rearsets and much more.

The 1965 G15 CSR

Engine:	Air-cooled Norton ohv twin with vertical cylinders, one-piece cylinder head, one-piece barrel, plain bearing big-ends, coil valve springs
Bore:	73mm
Stroke:	89mm
Displacement:	745cc
Compression ratio:	7.6:1
Lubrication:	Norton gear pump
Ignition:	Battery/coil
Carburettor:	Pair Amal Monoblocs 389 1⅛in
Primary drive:	Chain
Final drive:	Chain
Gearbox:	Four-speed foot-change, AMC
Frame:	Duplex
Front suspension:	Norton Roadholder forks
Rear suspension:	Swinging-arm Girling shocks
Front brake:	8in SLS full-width alloy drum
Rear brake:	7in SLS full-width alloy drum
Tyres:	Front 3.25 × 18; rear 3.50 × 18

General Specifications

Wheelbase:	56.5in (1435mm)
Ground clearance:	5.5in (140mm)
Seat height:	33in (838mm)
Fuel tank capacity:	4gal (21ltr)
Dry weight:	398lb (181kg)
Maximum power:	49bhp @ 6,400rpm
Top speed:	110mph (170kph)

sign of just *how* bad things were, the only real change to the twins was the introduction of triangular tank badges! It was very much a case of clutching at straws. There was also an enduro version (mainly for the American importers Berliner of New Jersey). Even then the resultant machine, the G15 CS, was later built as the Norton N15 simply by changing tank badges.

As recorded elsewhere, late in 1966 the official receiver was called as bankruptcy loomed. Earlier the same year the final G12 six-fifties had been built, and with their passing, the genuine Matchless twins, which had begun back in 1948 with the G9 five-hundred, came to an end.

The firm survived into 1967 as Norton-Matchless, thanks to Manganese Bronze boss Denis Poore. The AJS version of the Norton-powered twin survived until the middle of that year. The Atlas engine saw changes to its lubrication system, whilst the CSR models reverted to 19in wheels.

The G15 CS and CSR models ran into 1968, together with the touring G15, the latter now labelled as the Mark II and fitted with capacitor ignition; this system was adopted by the CSR as well. All three struggled on into 1969, but were finally axed by Poore and his management team, this decision being influenced by the huge success enjoyed by the new Norton Commando model.

And so the Matchless twin at last left the scene.

9 The G45

The racing history of Matchless is unusual because it is split into two defined periods: the years prior to the outbreak of World War I (*see* Chapter 1), and the years post-World War II. For the three decades between the two there was virtually complete inactivity.

In the very early days of the company the Matchless name was often in the headlines thanks to the exploits of the Collier brothers Charlie and Harry, who not only designed the bikes, but rode them too, in true pioneering fashion. Together the brothers formed an almost unbeatable combination, riding together or singly in the major racing events of the day. It was a Matchless ridden by Charlie Collier that was victorious in the very first Isle of Man TT in 1907.

After World War I the marque withdrew its support from racing until the late 1940s, apart from just one occasion in 1923 when an overhead camshaft, single cylinder, three-fifty Matchless made a brief and unsuccessful appearance. Initially after the war the company focused on specially prepared G80 ohv singles (*see* Chapter 6) ridden in short-circuit races and hillclimbs by the likes of Les Graham and Mick Featherstone (badged as either AJS or Matchless).

First Competition Races for the G9 Twin

As discussed in Chapter 8, the AMC ohv parallel twin had arrived in late 1948 as the 498cc (66 × 72.8mm) Matchless G9 and its AJS brother, the Model 20. The newcomer was powered by an entirely new engine, that followed the basic layout of the traditional British vertical twin with its

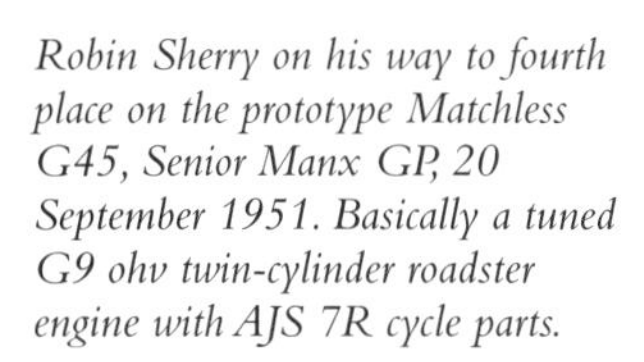

Robin Sherry on his way to fourth place on the prototype Matchless G45, Senior Manx GP, 20 September 1951. Basically a tuned G9 ohv twin-cylinder roadster engine with AJS 7R cycle parts.

pistons moving together as dictated by the magneto ignition, which at that time was seen as mandatory. But in several other respects the AMC design was unusual – and in one in particular it was unique: unlike all its contemporaries it featured a third, central main bearing between the two crank throws. In addition the engine had separate cylinder heads and barrels, plus gear-driven camshafts fore and aft.

The first competition debut of the new twin, at least in road racing, was in June 1951, when for the first time the Matchless G9 (and its AJS brother) were entered for the Senior Clubmans TT in the Isle of Man. Apart from polished ports and 'extra careful assembly' – blueprinting – the engine remained standard, as did the carburettors, but flexible twin fuel pipes replaced the original single copper line. Competition-weight mudguards of light alloy were fitted in place of the normal (heavy!) steel assemblies, and the lighting equipment was removed.

To prevent oil leakage, a neat circular plate covered the hole in the timing cover, through which the dynamo shaft normally passed. The rear frame loops had been modified and lugged to provide folding/rearset footrests, together with a competition-type kickstart lever, the latter with a folding pedal. The gear pedal itself had been moved through 190 degrees on its shaft, and therefore now pointed to the rear. Starting procedure was to fold up the offside (right) footrest, operate the kickstarter, fold the pedal forward and lower the footrest.

Open exhaust pipes were employed, with no megaphones, with the carburettor jetted up accordingly. Tests showed that the stock exhaust-pipe length with the silencers removed was the most suitable.

In total, six Matchless G9s and four AJS twins were entered for the race. All were equipped with the larger, AJS-type fuel tanks to enable their riders to complete the course on one filling. And it was the Matchless machines that were by far the most successful in the 1951 Senior Clubman's TT, finishing 7th, 14th, 21st and 27th. By far their best effort was Scunthorpe clubman R.A. Rowbottom, who averaged 76.88mph (123.7km/h) as compared to the Norton International winning machine's speed of 79.70mph (128.24km/h).

On the 31 August 1951 the *Snaefell*, one of the Isle of Man's steam packet ferries, lay alongside the landing stage at Liverpool docks; she was due to sail at 3.30pm. Already there was ample evidence that the Manx Motor Cycle Club's annual races were in the offing, and amongst the assembled throng was Robin Sherry, who had been a front runner in the Junior Manx Grand Prix a year earlier until trouble had put him out on the last lap. This year Sherry had a 7R AJS and a Matchless twin for the Senior event. In their practice-week report *The Motor Cycle* set the scene:

> Douglas, Saturday September 1. There is glorious sunshine and a crystal-clear day. The deep blue of the sea is relieved by white horses whipped by a fresh breeze. Spirits are high. A fortnight of this kind of weather would be just the thing.
>
> Sherry's Matchless for the Senior really looks something. It is an experimental vertical twin with massively finned light-alloy cylinder barrels and heads on a Super Clubman (G9) crankcase. The carburettor is an Amal TT type, with separate float chamber mounted on the seat tube. Short in length, the exhaust pipes are fitted with stubby megaphones. This unit is housed in a 7R frame, with 7R gearbox and an all-round chain guard. Front fork, and the separate, clipped-on handlebars are as seen on the works 7Rs last June (at the TT), and so, substantially, are the wheel and brakes.

So was this a works entry? Strictly speaking these were not allowed by the Manx Motor Cycle Club's rules.

Riding with the number 41, Sherry was right up with the leaders from the very start, and at the end of lap one was in third spot, having averaged a very respectable 84.93mph (136.65km/h) from a standing start. On the second lap, still third, the Matchless rider went round at 85.48mph (137.54km/h). But the race was held in gale-force winds, and the Matchless twin slowed towards the end of lap three when one of the rocker pillars broke, causing a considerable amount of unwanted vibration. Even so, Sherry – who had won the Junior Manx a couple of days earlier on an AJS 7R single – still managed to finish fourth, which in the circumstances was an excellent achievement, with a race average of 83.71mph (134.69km/h).

More development of the machine took place over the winter, and in early March 1952 came news that it was to be ridden in the TT by Ernie Ring of New South Wales; he had been chosen as a member of the Australian team, the others being Ken Kavanagh and Tony McAlpine (both on Nortons). Unfortunately Ring crashed on lap five of the seven-lap, 264.11-mile (424.95km) race, causing his retirement. The Australian rider also rode this machine on the Continent and at Boreham.

The same machine was next entered for the Manx GP in September 1952, this time ridden by D.K. (Derek) Farrant, who, like Sherry a year before, would ride an AJS 7R in the Junior race. Ernie Ring, its previous rider, was on the island, together with AMC service manager Fred Neill, to look after the machinery. The race was a huge success for Matchless, and in its 18 September 1952 issue *The Motor Cycle* ran the headline 'Amazing Senior Manx Grand Prix'; the report continued:

> Both race and lap were shattered last Thursday when the Senior Manx Grand Prix was won, in perfect weather, by D.K. Farrant, riding the now famous 498cc Matchless twin at an average speed of 88.65mph [142.64km/h] for the six laps [226½ miles/364.5km] of the Isle of Man TT circuit.

During the course of his ride Farrant broke the lap record four times, his final circuit, in 25min 15.8sec, representing a speed of 89.64mph (144.23km/h).

The G45 Goes On Sale

Towards the end of October 1952 AMC announced that it was to offer for sale limited numbers of the Manx GP-winning machine, to be known as the G45, together with racing conversion kits for the G9 Clubman (and AJS Model 20 Spring Twin) roadster models. These latter kits would include camshafts, twin carburettors, hi-compression pistons, rear footrests, rear brake pedal, sparking plugs and exhaust-pipe clips. Optional extras were rev counters and megaphones.

Technical Details

The G45 (the 45 refers to its original planned output of 45bhp) was the work of H.J. (Ike) Hatch. Apart from the cylinder heads and barrels (still separate units), the engine closely resembled the stock Matchless (and AJS) roadster twins announced in late 1948. And in fact, the G45 shared the same 66 × 72.8mm bore and stroke dimensions, giving a displacement of 498cc.

To cope with the increased power, the crankshaft was no longer of cast iron; instead, it was

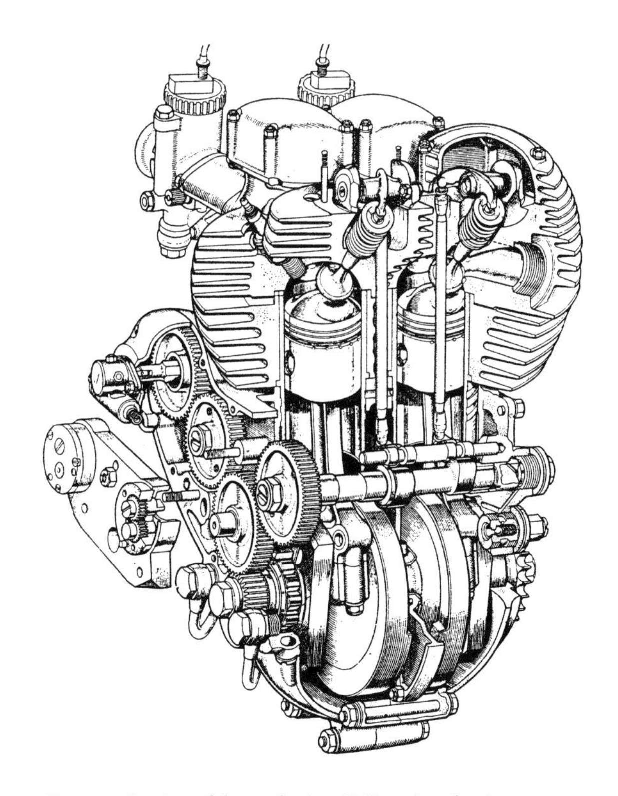

Cutaway drawing of the production G45 engine, showing gear-driven cams, double oil pumps, coil-valve springs and massive crank flywheels.

now an alloy steel forging with shrunk-on flywheel rims. The plain central main bearing was slightly narrower than hitherto, but the other mains, of roller pattern, and the light alloy connecting rods were standard G9/Model 20 components.

The high compression (9.4:1), die-cast pistons featured solid skirts and carried two compression rings and a slotted scraper ring. The wire winding on the G9/Model 20 pistons was not retained for racing, since mechanical noise was not important.

Delivering 26gal (120ltr) per hour at 7,000rpm, the standard oil pump had been found adequate for G45 requirements. The camshafts, however, were revised: of case-hardened steel, these provided inlet and exhaust valve timings of –70 degrees +50 degrees, and –50 degrees +68 degrees respectively. This meant that in conjunction with roller-type followers and special overhead rockers, they provided more overlap and quicker valve opening and closing than the series-production roadster units. (For comparison, the standard engine figures are –35 degrees +65 degrees, and –65 degrees +35 degrees.) Similarly, cold 'touring' tappet clearances had been increased to .006in inlet and .010in exhaust.

Bearing on the cams were roller-type followers, each roller having its own needle bearing mounted on a hollow, hardened steel pin. Thrust was transmitted by light alloy tubular pushrods of $\frac{3}{8}$in (9mm) outside diameter, each having a hardened steel ball at the lower end, and a hardened steel cup at the top. Pushrod diameter had been increased slightly to cope with the higher state of the engine tune. Bronze-bushed rockers provided diagonal, straight-line operation (rather than angled, as on the roadsters) between pushrod and valve stem. The adjustment of valve clearance was affected by eccentrically mounted rocker spindles, as on the standard engine.

Aluminium alloy was used for both the cylinder heads and barrels, the latter assemblies comprising deeply finned, alloy muffs with shrunk-in iron liners. A G45 cylinder-head characteristic was its deep finning. The heads were fitted with bronze exhaust and austenitic iron inlet shrunk-in valve seats and bronze valve guides, each head being secured by four thru-studs, similar to those of the standard engine.

Triple helical valve springs were employed, each having a two-rate winding to minimize surge. Inlet valve diameter was $1\frac{17}{32}$in, and that of the exhaust valve $1\frac{13}{32}$in – both larger than the roadster power unit. The rockers bore directly on the valve stems, and these were Stellite-tipped.

Electron magnesium alloy was used for the rocker covers, the finning on the exhaust covers being largely responsible, together with the twin carburettors, for the different appearance of the G45 engine as compared to the G9. The covers were retained by studs and nuts, whereas the stock engine had bolts that screwed into the head. Twin Amal TT carburettors were fitted to the early 1953 and 1954 G45s. Of $1\frac{3}{16}$in, these had 340 main jets as standard. Later (from the 1955 model year), the TTs were replaced by the new GP instruments, but of $1\frac{3}{32}$in and having 240 main jets.

A racing close-ratio Burman 7R50 four-speed gearbox was specified, together with the 7R-type dry clutch and single primary chain. The engine-shaft shock absorber of the roadster twins was replaced by a series of rubber blocks in the clutch centre. The gearbox of the Smiths magnetic rev counter was driven from the nearside (left) end of the exhaust camshaft, and not from the magneto pinion as on the original prototype machine.

As regards the cycle parts, both the fuel and oil tanks were of light alloy, and had capacities of 6gal (27ltr) and 1gal (4.5ltr) respectively. Frame, suspension and brakes were virtually identical to the 1953 AJS 7R, as were the rest of the cycle parts, including features such as the fuel-tank mounting and the chain lubrication system. The tyres were an exception, these being 3.00 at the front and 3.50 at the rear. To ensure that the exhaust header pipes cleared the frame, the port angle was wider than on the roadster engine.

When announced at the London Earls Court Show in November 1952 the G45 was listed at £376 18s 10d; however, by April 1953 this price had dropped to £356 9s 2d.

Racing Success in 1953

Several of the new G45s were entered for the 1953 Isle of Man TT; however, in the Senior race that year there were only thirty-six finishers (of over 100 starters). The Matchless finishers were H.A. Pearce, ninth; M. Templeton, fourteenth; and P.H. Carter, twenty-fourth. However, several G45s retired, for a number of different reasons; these included bikes ridden by G.A. Murphy; D.K. Farrant; A. Wheeler; J.H. Cooper; L.T. Simpson; H. Clark; M.P. O'Rourke; E. Ring and T. McEwan.

Better results came later that year, first at the ACU Championship held at Blandford Camp on August Bank Holiday Monday, when D.K. Farrant took his G45 to victory – to gain, in effect, the British 500cc title for 1953. Then the following month, in September, Derek Ennett took his G45 to third place in the Senior Manx Grand Prix, behind the Manx Nortons of winner Denis Parkinson and runner-up R.G. Keeler. Ennett averaged 86.52mph (139.21km/h), as compared to Parkinson's 89.68mph (144.3km/h).

Modifications for 1954

In the light of experiences gained during the 1953 season with the production G45, several modifications were introduced to the model's engine. Though externally unchanged, the cylinder head was now of 'Y' alloy, whilst the cross-section of the rocker posts had been slightly increased. The forged rockers, which were polished all over, now incorporated a small oilway and a longitudinal groove on top to improve lubrication of the pushrod cups. Previously plain bored, the rocker bushes incorporated an internal, oil-spreading annulus in which there was an oilway that mated up with the one in the rocker.

Some problems had been encountered in 1953 through valve-spring breakages, and for 1954 a new type of spring was fitted. Two other alterations to the valve gear were the fitting of heavier section upper collars, and the addition of a groove half-way round each collet. The purpose of the groove was to provide the collet with a degree of resilience, so that it seated firmly in the

The G45 sidecar outfit of Fritz Staschel in the 1954 German Grand Prix. Note the sidecar wheel was hydraulically operated from the rear brake control.

Twin Amal GP carbs, racing magneto, exhaust-cam driven rev counter gearbox and exposed clutch.

The 1954 G45

Engine:	Air-cooled ohv twin with vertical cylinders; separate alloy heads, separate alloy barrels with cast-iron liners; three main bearings (one central); one-piece forged crankshaft with split big ends; gear-driven camshafts fore and aft; coil valve springs.
Bore:	66mm
Stroke:	72.8mm
Displacement:	498cc
Compression ratio:	9.4:1; from May 1954, 10:1
Lubrication:	Dry sump; twin gear-oil pumps
Ignition:	Magneto
Carburettor:	2 × Amal TT 1 3/16in; 1955 onwards, 2 × Amal GP 1 3/32in
Primary drive:	Chain
Final drive:	Chain
Gearbox:	Four-speed foot-change, close-ratio Burman 7R50 type
Frame:	Duplex, all-welded construction
Front suspension:	AMC Teledraulic forks
Rear suspension:	Swinging arm, with twin AMC 'Jampot' shock absorbers
Front brake:	Conical magnesium hub, 2LS
Rear brake:	Conical magnesium hub, 2LS
Tyres:	Front 3.00 × 19; rear 3.50 × 19

General Specifications

Wheelbase:	55.5in (1,410mm)
Ground clearance:	6in (152mm)
Seat height:	31.5in (800mm)
Fuel tank capacity:	6gal (27ltr)
Dry weight:	320lb (145kg)
Maximum power:	48bhp @ 7,200rpm; 1957, 52 bhp @ 7,400rpm
Top speed:	128mph (206km/h)

collar and thus gripped the valve more securely (very occasionally a valve had dropped in on the 1953 production batch of G45s, both exhaust and inlet).

A slightly convex curvature had been given to the exhaust valve head, in place of the flat head previously employed. To provide an increased bearing area in the cam followers, a larger number of smaller diameter, longer rollers were now employed in the follower spindle bearings.

Owing to the non-availability of forgings, the 1953 G45 crankshafts were machined from the solid. But for the 1954 batch the shafts were forgings, though they were almost identical in appearance with their predecessors. Lateral movement of the drive and timing-side main bearings in their housings was prevented by the locking of each outer race into the housing boss by means of two washers. Each washer had a flat milled on its periphery, and corresponding flats were ground on the outer race. The locking washers were recessed into the boss and secured by set-screws. There was also a new oil-thrower ring on the driving-side mainshaft to minimize oil leakage past the main bearing.

In addition to the improvements catalogued above, several more minor modifications were carried out to the 1954 G45 engine. AMC claimed a power output in excess of 48bhp at 7,200rpm using premium-grade pump fuel. In other respects the 1954 G45 was virtually unchanged. As on the AJS 7R, however, ventilation holes were featured at the front of the primary chain guard, whilst at the rear of the guard there was now a drain pipe for excess oil. The gearchange had been improved by means of a modification to the pedal linkage.

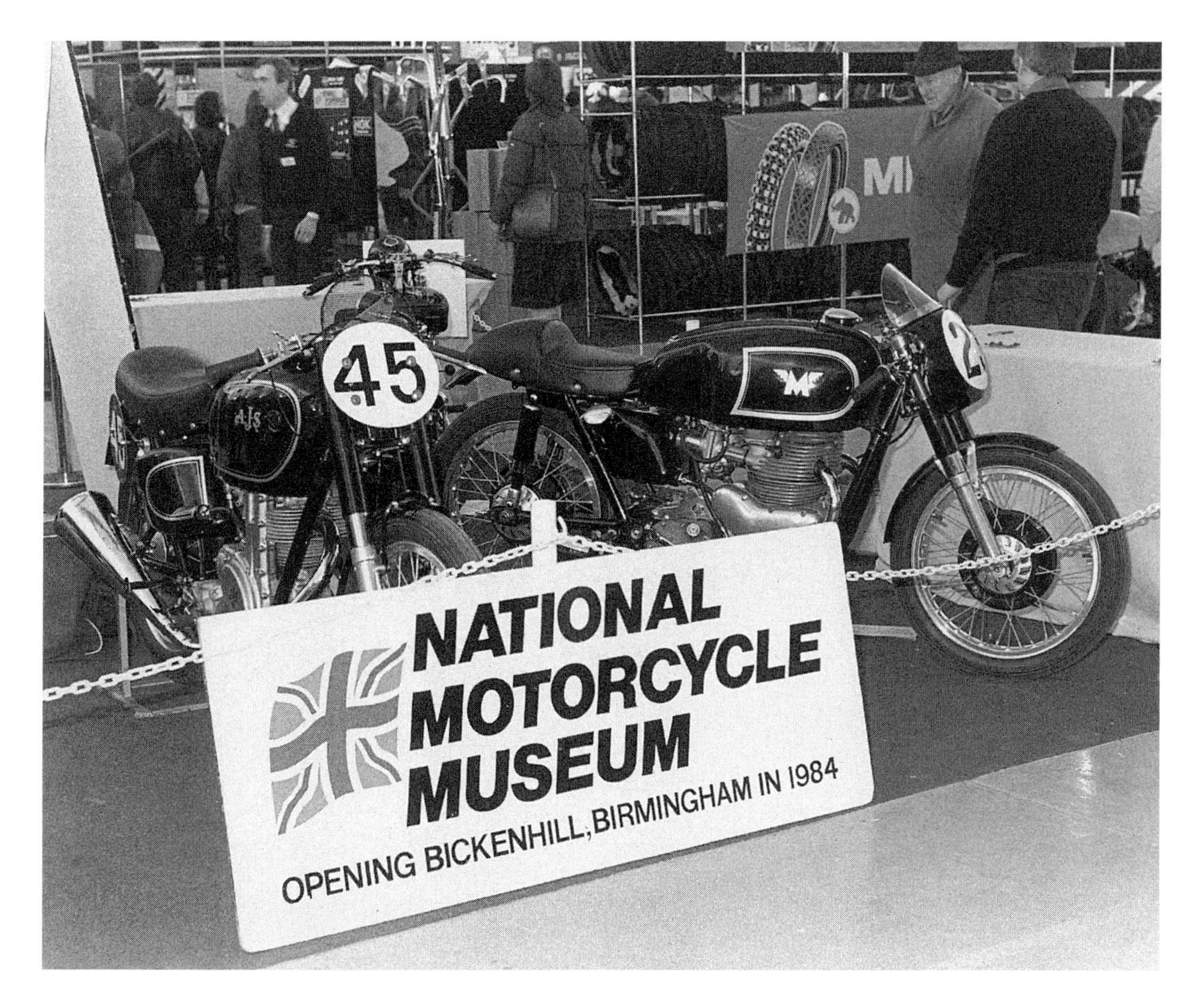

The Road Racing Show at Alexandra Palace, London in the early 1980s, an early AJS 7R and a G45 on display, advertising the future opening of the National Motorcycle Museum. Sadly, in September 2003, hundreds of the museum's collection of bikes were destroyed in a massive fire.

Racing Success in 1954

On 28 August 1954, with a G45 equipped with a streamlined cowling, New Zealander John Dale (manager of his country's race team in the 1953 Isle of Man TT), recorded an average of 118.42mph (190.53km/h) over the flying mile in speed trials held on Muriwai Beach, near Auckland. In fact several G45s were exported to both New Zealand and Australia during the period 1953 through to 1957.

The Manx Grand Prix in September 1954 once again proved a happy hunting ground for G45 competitors. Run for the most part in truly awful conditions, Derek Ennett was the leader for the first two laps of the race on his Matchless twin, before being forced out towards the end of the race. His problems had begun early in the race when on the second lap (together with gale-force winds); as *The Motor Cycle* reported, 'his endeavours were ill-fated; his machine was over-geared for the day, and at Windy Corner one cylinder of his tired engine became inoperative. He coasted disconsolately into the pits.' Even so, a G45 rider was still on the rostrum at the finish:

ABOVE: *Future Suzuki teamster Frank Perris (65) with his works-supported G45 at Ibsley, 1955.*

LEFT: *Previously unpublished photograph of Peter Tester with his ex Geoff Monty G45, c. mid-1950s.*

In the 1955 Manx Grand Prix G45 twins took three of the top five places, with David Christian taking third position.

G.R. Dunlop finished third, having averaged 80.23mph (129.09km/h). Other Matchless riders in the top twelve finishers were B.J. Thompson seventh, and Eddie Crooks twelfth.

Continued Production in 1955

At the end of the year it was announced that both G45 and AJS 7R production would continue; for the 1955 model year the only change, for both bikes, was a twin-feed primary-chain oiler.

Former race rider and now journalist Vic Willoughby tested a G45 for the first time for *The Motor Cycle*, and reported his findings in their 16 June 1955 issue. This was the Reynolds-Earles pivoted fork model, ridden in that year's Senior TT by K.W. Swallow. Even though the main purpose of the outing was to assess the new front fork (which was entirely a private venture and nothing to do with the Plumstead factory), Willoughby had this to say of the G45's performance:

> For a standard production racer the G45 was fast. It was geared at 4.4 to 1 on top, and made no fuss about going up to 7,000 and 6,700rpm in opposite directions on a level stretch of road. The former engine speed represents 124mph (200km/h). The inevitable megaphonitis disappeared at 4,200rpm and I formed the impression that skilful use of the gearbox was desirable to obtain the best road performance.

Changes for 1956

In line with AMC's policy of continual year-by-year detail improvement, the G45 (together with the AJS 7R single) received a number of changes, albeit of a relatively minor nature, for the 1956 season.

- Rotating magnet magneto.
- Ventilation of both brakes.
- Minor alterations to the frame, fuel- and oil-tanks (to provide a more compact riding position). The tubular loop supporting the seat was no longer inclined upwards at the rear, thus providing a lower seat height. The seat was also shallower than before. A reduction in the width of the oil tank and of the rear section of the fuel tank enabled the rider to tuck his legs in more closely. The frame was now ½in (13mm) narrower across the footrest mounting, the footrests having

been moved further forwards, whilst the gear pedal operated directly, without the linkage used the previous year.

- The twin-feed primary-chain oiler now incorporated a control cock and an air release.
- The rear mudguard was shortened.
- New bracket for the front number plate, incorporating a flexible mounting for the magnetic rev counter.
- Straight clip-on handlebar, replacing the earlier swan-neck type.
- Front brake lever now embodied a self-locking knurled cable adjuster.

LEFT: *1956 factory brochure showing the G45 as it was that year…*

BELOW: *…compared to the 1957 model seen here. It is worth noting that the G45 always had a Burman rather than an AMC gearbox.*

ABOVE: *G45 in action during the British Championship meeting at Thruxton, August 1958.*

RIGHT: *T.P. Foldwell/P.M. Knocker with their G45 outfit during the 1958 Sidecar TT, held over the shorter Clypse circuit.*

Racing Success in New Zealand

G45s took the first four places in the twenty-third annual New Zealand TT, held over a 6-mile (10km) circuit at Mangere, Auckland on Saturday, 9 February 1957. The race distance was 102 miles (164km), and it was Matchless machinery, under the direction of manager John Dale, which stayed the distance; Norton had a poor day, with not one Manx model finishing the full distance! The race winner was G.A. (Peter) Murphy, who also won the 500cc Rotorua GP in January 1958 and the New Zealand Senior TT for the second year running later that same month.

The G45's Final Year

The only change for 1957 was to install Girling rear shock absorbers in place of AMC's own 'Jampot' units; this was the final year of G45 production.

The final years of the G45 saw really very little major change at all. The engine was generally reliable except for the early valve problems already described, and a series of broken push-rods, especially on the exhaust side. The real Achilles heel of the design was its narrow power band, which meant that only the most gifted of riders were able to get the best from it. When this did happen, however, the G45 was able to exceed

LEFT: Clubman Colin Hampshieff during a Wednesday afternoon practice session at Brands Hatch during the late 1950s.

BELOW: Classic racer Ken Clark's G45 at Snetterton, 22 September 1985.

all expectations for what was, after all, just a souped-up road-based engine in 7R cycle parts.

Also, after designer Ike Hatch's untimely death in 1954, the factory largely lost interest in the design. It was finally superseded by the single-cylinder G50 during the 1958 season. And the biggest question is why it took owners AMC so long to make this move – a decade after the three-fifty 7R had been launched – because the G50 was in reality a bigger bore version of the 7R, with very few other changes. Its full story is related in Chapter 11.

10 Dirt Bikes

New for the 1936 season, the Model 36/G80C (Competition) was intended for use in both trials and scrambles. Based on the existing 500 'Clubman', the G80C not only had a tuned engine, but modifications to the cycle parts for off-road work…

…there was also a three-fifty version, Model 36/G3C, that was identical except for the engine size. But it was not until the post-Second World War period that Matchless machines really set the dirt bike world alight.

The post-war Matchless – read AMC – competition bikes had their origins firmly set in the WD (War Department) tele-forked Matchless G3/L model. In fact because of the virtual ban on home-market sales of any of their bikes in the first few months of peace – everything having to go for export to balance the books of Great Britain Ltd – the majority of Matchless machinery used in trials and scrambles of the day at home were in fact converted wartime bikes rather than newly built examples. As for the factory-built, over-the-counter competition machinery, this was prized indeed, even though in reality the G3C of 1946 was very much a road model, less lighting equipment. *The Motor Cycle* in their 14 March 1946 issue carried an article under the following heading: 'A Small Number of Special Trials Mounts in Production'; these would consist of fifty AJS and fifty Matchless machines, thirty of each being three-fifties, the remaining twenty five-hundreds.

The official factory line was that 'The special competition models will not be catalogued, but will be sold to trials enthusiasts on the recommendations of local AMC agents.' This was also a way of getting round the 'export-only' agreement.

The general layout of these models came as the result of works experience, notably by George Rowley who had carried out a number of tests over the British Experts Trial course and on location in Wales. One of the alterations from standard roadster specification was a special steering-head angle for the frame, together with revised trail. *The Motor Cycle* described these machines as 'particularly cobby in their competition form', their features including a low-level exhaust system with the header pipe tucked in close to the timing chest, and the silencer upswept. At the time AMC also claimed that specially selected engines were being fitted, the gear ratios for the 350cc being 6.13, 7.93, 12.91 and 19.58:1, and for the 500cc 5.49, 7.1, 11.55 and 17.52:1. Other details of the specification included:

- folding kickstarter;
- 2.75 × 21 front; 4.00 × 19 rear tyres, with two security bolts per wheel;
- extra heavy spokes for front wheel;
- butted spokes;
- painted duralumin mudguards with tubular stays;
- all unnecessary lugs removed from frame;
- duplicated (spare) clutch and throttle cables;
- optional (extra cost) lighting equipment;
- 7in (178mm) ground clearance.

Because of what was referred to as 'the slipper-shaped lug' at the bottom of the front down-tube (a cradle frame was employed), no crankcase undershield had been deemed necessary.

Of course the specification also included many of the production roadster's basic components, such as Teledraulic front forks, rigid frame, single sprung saddle, Burman gearbox and clutch, and ohv engine with iron head and barrel. That these competition models were only for the selected few was clearly underlined in *The Motor Cycle* of 7 November 1946:

> A limited number of competition models, both Matchless and AJS, are being manufactured. The factory insists on knowing the name and past competition record of the prospective purchaser of one of these machines. The underlying reason is that otherwise some might find their way into the hands of ordinary road users, and since the number of machines is limited, various good trials riders might possibly have to go without.

As for prices, the three-fifty competition model cost £111 plus (in the UK) £29 19s 5d purchase tax; and the 500cc version £121, plus £32 13s 5d tax. Speedometers and lighting equipment were cost options.

Things were very different across the Atlantic, where in the first two years after the end of the conflict large numbers of Matchless motorcycles were sent. In fact the Stateside market in the USA and Canada was so large that in 1947 the share capital of AMC had doubled – and it was the competition-based models that proved particularly popular. This was most seen in California, where the handling, traction and reliability of Matchless (and AJS) machines was highly rated for all forms of off-road sport including desert racing, green lanes or scrambles. The importer for Matchless machines in the USA at that time was the Indian Sales Corporation of Springfield, Massachusetts, but for California there was a special arrangement for that state by Cooper Motors of Los Angeles.

Back in Britain there was news in February 1947 that one of the South-East Centre riders in post-war events, B.H.M. (Hugh) Viney, had joined the competition department of Associated Motor Cycles. Viney was to ride AJS machines in all the major trials and would be a member of the AJS team with George Rowley and A.R. Foster. Nominated riders of Matchless machines for the 1947 season were Colin Edge, L.A. (Artie) Ratcliffe, A.W. Burnard and M. Laidlaw. One has to remember that development of the Matchless and AJS competition models ran very much in tandem in the post-war era.

Another important factor to take into consideration when following the development of the

The 1947 G3 LC

Engine:	Air-cooled, ohv single with vertical cylinder; iron head and barrel; vertically split aluminium crankcases; fully enclosed valve gear; coil valve springs; built-up crankshaft; roller big end; gear-driven cams
Bore:	69mm
Stroke:	93mm
Displacement:	348cc
Compression ratio:	6.3:1
Lubrication:	Dry sump, two-start oil pump
Ignition:	Magneto
Carburettor:	Amal Type 76 1in
Primary drive:	Chain
Final drive:	Chain
Gearbox:	Four-speed, foot-change, Burman wide ratio
Frame:	Diamond type with single front down-tube
Front suspension:	AMC Teledraulic forks
Rear suspension:	Rigid
Front brake:	5.5in, SLS drum, single-sided
Rear brake:	5.5in, SLS drum, single-sided
Tyres:	Front 2.75 × 21; rear 4.00 × 19

General Specifications

Wheelbase:	53in (1,346mm)
Ground clearance:	6.5in (165mm)
Seat height:	32.5in (825mm)
Fuel tank capacity:	3gal (13.5ltr)
Dry weight:	300lb (136kg)
Maximum power:	16bhp @ 5,600rpm
Top speed:	65mph (105km/h)

The 1947 G80 C

Engine:	Air-cooled, ohv single with vertical cylinder; iron head and barrel; vertically split aluminium crankcases; fully enclosed valve gear; coil valve springs; built-up crankshaft; roller-bearing big end; gear-driven cams
Bore:	82.5mm
Stroke:	93mm
Displacement:	497cc
Compression ratio:	5.9:1
Lubrication:	Dry sump, two-start oil pump
Ignition:	Magneto, Lucas
Carburettor:	Amal Type 89 1⅟₃₂in
Primary drive:	Chain
Final drive:	Chain
Gearbox:	Four-speed, foot-change, Burman
Frame:	Diamond type with single front down-tube
Front suspension:	AMC Teledraulic forks
Rear suspension:	Rigid
Front brake:	5.5in, SLS drum, single-sided
Rear brake:	5.5in, SLS drum, single-sided
Tyres:	Front 2.75 × 21; rear 4.00 × 19

General Specifications

Wheelbase:	53in (1,346mm)
Ground clearance:	6.5in (165mm)
Seat height:	32.5in (825mm)
Fuel tank capacity:	3gal (13.5ltr)
Dry weight:	307lb (139kg)
Maximum power:	23bhp @ 5,400rpm
Top speed:	70mph (113km/h)

competition models is that the majority of changes which were made each year were the same as those carried out to the single-cylinder roadsters. When the 1948 models were announced in October 1947 it was seen that the competition bikes had the new brakes adopted by the roadsters (*see* Chapter 6) and other improvements, together with a special short wheelbase frame which measured 52 ⁵⁄₁₆in (140mm) with the real wheel spindle in the mid-position, a reduction of 1⅛in (28mm). *The Motor Cycle* in their show report dated 4 December 1947 reported: 'So popular are the competition models that the factory will be unable to accept orders for probably at least a year.'

Changes into the Fifties

As covered in Chapter 6, the changes to the ohv singles for the 1949 model year included redesigned cylinder heads, hairpin instead of coil valve springs, and redesigned frames. Those changes only applicable to the competition models were a separate and thus detachable crankcase undershield, and an improved carburettor intake shield. In that year, 1948, Hugh Viney had won the Scottish Six Days – albeit riding an AJS rather than a Matchless – so the AMC competition bikes were basking in their own special ray of sunshine at the Earls Court Show in November. The G3C and G80C models retained their rigid frames, even though the 1948 London Show had heralded the arrival of the new spring (swinging-arm) frame, which was standard on the new G9 twin and an optional extra on the series-production roadsters.

As an indication of the size of AMC at that time, no fewer than 1,000 employees plus their wives attended the annual party at the Woolwich Town Hall in January 1949. Amongst the guests were the Mayor and Mayoress of Woolwich.

For fans of the AMC competition models, the big news for 1950 was the introduction of alloy engines. As *Motor Cycling* said in their 13 October 1949 issue:

> The four competition models, 347 and 498cc 'Ajay' and Matchless of similar capacities, strike a new note in the programme. These machines have alloy barrels with cast-in iron liners (and alloy cylinder heads) making for lightness – both competition models in the region of 300lb (136kg).

Other new features for the competition bikes that year were the introduction of a Lucas Wader magneto, five-spring clutch and front brake torque arm.

At this time American preferences were beginning to influence competition models, and had led to what Stateside enthusiasts referred to as 'chopped jobs'; AMC had responded by providing a shorter wheelbase and a specification that *Motor Cycling* described as 'abbreviated to purely sporting requirements'. As offered, the competition models were equipped with tyres of 'suitable size for trials or scrambles' and a speedometer and bulb horn, but without lighting, the latter being an extra £9 10s inclusive of the dreaded UK purchase tax. And in place of the 2¾gal (12.5ltr) fuel tank then found on the roadster singles, they had a peanut-shaped 2gal (9ltr) tank attached to the frame by improved quick-release bolts. The saddle was raised to 32½in (825mm), and in place of the normal toolbox was a smaller tubular container with a quick-release cap located beneath the saddle. The aluminium mudguards were now left unpainted and were polished.

ISDT Success

In the 1950 ISDT held in Wales, the AMC competition models showed up well, AJS and Matchless riders winning the following medals:

FIM Gold Medals:

W.H.J. Peacock	347cc	Matchless sidecar
E. Usher	347cc	Matchless
B.H.M. Viney	347cc	AJS
B. Stonebridge	347cc	Matchless
A.B.N. Taylor	347cc	AJS

In February 1954, Matchless machines finished first, second and third in the legendary American Big Bear Run. Of 489 starters, only forty-two finished!

Basically a 1950 rigid-frame Matchless Competition model, but with a later full-width hub and tank decals instead of badges.

D.M. Murdoch	498cc	AJS
T.H. Wortley	347cc	AJS
A.W. Burnard	347cc	AJS
T. Hawkins	347cc	AJS
S.E. Cunningham	498cc	AJS

FIM Silver Medals:

H. Kelly	498cc	AJS
A.F. Philip	347cc	AJS
R. Mason	498cc	Matchless
D.J. Ratcliffe	347cc	Matchless

FIM Bronze Medals:

F.E. Woodward	347cc	Matchless sidecar
J.F. Kentish	498cc	Matchless
W.A. Roberts	498cc	AJS

In other words, no fewer than seventeen of the sixty-three medal winners were AMC (Matchless or AJS) mounted. Also Hugh Viney was a member of the winning International Trophy team, whilst Ed Usher was a member of the equally victorious International Silver Vase squad.

Designated Trials and Scrambles Bikes

For the first time, the 1951 AMC model range saw the works produce different bikes for trials (coded C) and scrambles (coded CS). Essentially the competition bikes were still made in what AMC termed 'limited quantities', being built in two batches, one in the autumn and one in the spring. The new spring-frame models for scrambles (or for the ISDT) were manufactured with a

A 1951 advertisement for the new G80 CS model with all-alloy engine, swinging-arm frame and Burman BA gearbox. A works model ridden by Brian Stonebridge enjoyed considerable success in major scrambles events that year.

silencer as standard, with a straight-through (open) pipe as an option. The trials version was largely as before, in other words with a rigid frame. And also as before, various improvements (including revision to the Teledraulic front forks) were incorporated.

The 1952 Model Year

There was a new Burman-made gearbox for the 1952 model year. Based on the racing AJS 7R unit, it was manufactured in three other guises: the B52 standard (roadster), the B52 close (scrambles, etc.), and the B52 trials (wide, for trials). (The B52 Burman gearbox is fully described in Chapter 6, *see* page 63.)

Another major change, found on all 1952 Matchless singles, entailed repositioning the magneto forward of the cylinder, as on AJS models, and providing a new timing case; this was to make it easier to inspect and remove the dynamo for the roadsters.

A particularly practical modification for both the competition models and the roadster was the provision of a circular inspection cover, held in place by three screws, for the primary chaincase.

The Belgian star Auguste Mingels, the second winner of the European Motocross Championship title in 1953; here riding a G80 CS Matchless.

From then on until the end of 1953, virtually no real development occurred on the competition models, except those changes introduced across the single-cylinder range.

A Raft of Changes for 1954

All models, including the competition bikes for the 1954 model year, had received a full-width alloy front hub with straight spokes. The off-road models were given internal gearbox changes, improved gearbox-to-chaincase seal, an altered oil-filler cap, and an alloy fuel tank; the rigid-frame models had an all-welded front frame, whilst the spring frame had new rear shocks and a dual seat.

The spring roadster singles and competition bikes had a larger timing mainshaft, lighter flywheels and a modified oil tank. And these improvements proved their worth when in May 1954, A.L. (Artie) Ratcliffe won the Scottish Six Days Trial on his works GB/LC.

There was little change for 1955, except for a full-width rear hub, and, on the scrambler only, a TT carburettor.

ABOVE: A 1956 G80 CS scrambler with integral pushrod tunnels in the cylinder barrel; also Amal Monobloc carb, road-type frame, full-width hubs and 'Jampot' rear shock absorbers.

RIGHT: A 1956 Model G3/LC three-fifty trials, with short-wheelbase frame, 'Jampot' rear shocks and full-width alloy hubs.

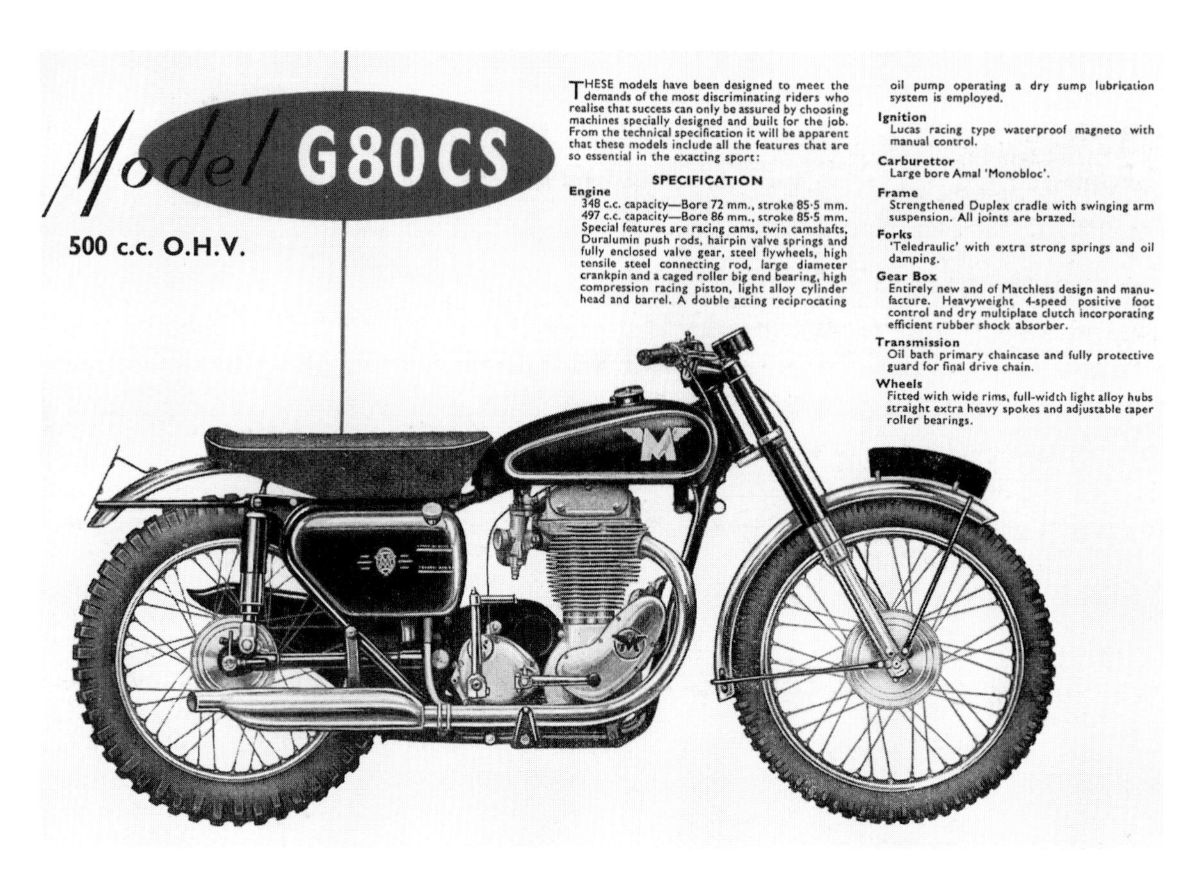

Model G80 CS

500 c.c. O.H.V.

THESE models have been designed to meet the demands of the most discriminating riders who realise that success can only be assured by choosing machines specially designed and built for the job. From the technical specification it will be apparent that these models include all the features that are so essential in the exacting sport:

SPECIFICATION

Engine
348 c.c. capacity—Bore 72 mm., stroke 85·5 mm.
497 c.c. capacity—Bore 86 mm., stroke 85·5 mm.
Special features are racing cams, twin camshafts, Duralumin push rods, hairpin valve springs and fully enclosed valve gear, steel flywheels, high tensile steel connecting rod, large diameter crankpin and a caged roller big end bearing, high compression racing piston, light alloy cylinder head and barrel. A double acting reciprocating oil pump operating a dry sump lubrication system is employed.

Ignition
Lucas racing type waterproof magneto with manual control.

Carburettor
Large bore Amal 'Monobloc'.

Frame
Strengthened Duplex cradle with swinging arm suspension. All joints are brazed.

Forks
'Teledraulic' with extra strong springs and oil damping.

Gear Box
Entirely new and of Matchless design and manufacture. Heavyweight 4-speed positive foot control and dry multiplate clutch incorporating efficient rubber shock absorber.

Transmission
Oil bath primary chaincase and fully protective guard for final drive chain.

Wheels
Fitted with wide rims, full-width light alloy hubs straight extra heavy spokes and adjustable taper roller bearings.

ABOVE AND OPPOSITE: Reproduced from the 1957 Matchless catalogue, the G80 CS (497cc) and G3/LCS (348cc) dirt-bike racers.

A New 350 Trials Machine

For the 1956 season AMC introduced a new 347cc trials machine with a swinging-arm frame. This frame, together with the roadster and the scrambler models, was new, with a vertical seat tube (explained in detail in Chapters 6 and 8). Another component shared by both on- and off-road models was the new alloy full-width rear hub assembly. (It should be noted that the trials model was only offered as a three-fifty, whereas the scrambler came in both engine sizes.) However, the roadster and trials frames were not identical, the main portion of the latter being somewhat similar to that introduced for the 1954 rigid-frame competition models, of welded construction with a single tube forming the front down and top members, and a wrap-round gusset plate at the steering head. But like the latest roadster frame, the main tube now extended back under the seat, to link up with the pivot lug.

Although the pivot lugs of the roadster and trials frames bore a resemblance to one another, there was an important difference: the pivot axis of the roadster frame was offset ½in (13mm) to the rear of the seat-tube centreline, whereas that of the competition frame was offset ahead by the same amount, thus providing a 1in (25mm) difference in wheelbase.

The 1956 Matchless competition model prices list (as at 15 September 1955) were as follows: for the 347cc G3/LC, £212 8s; for the 347cc G3/LCS, £218 8s; and for the 498cc G80/CS, £235 4s. Lighting was £9 18s extra. All prices included British purchase tax.

Improvements for 1957

For the 1957 season the Matchless scrambler engines were modified for increased power. Both engine sizes featured modified inlet ports and larger inlet valves. The choke size of the Amal

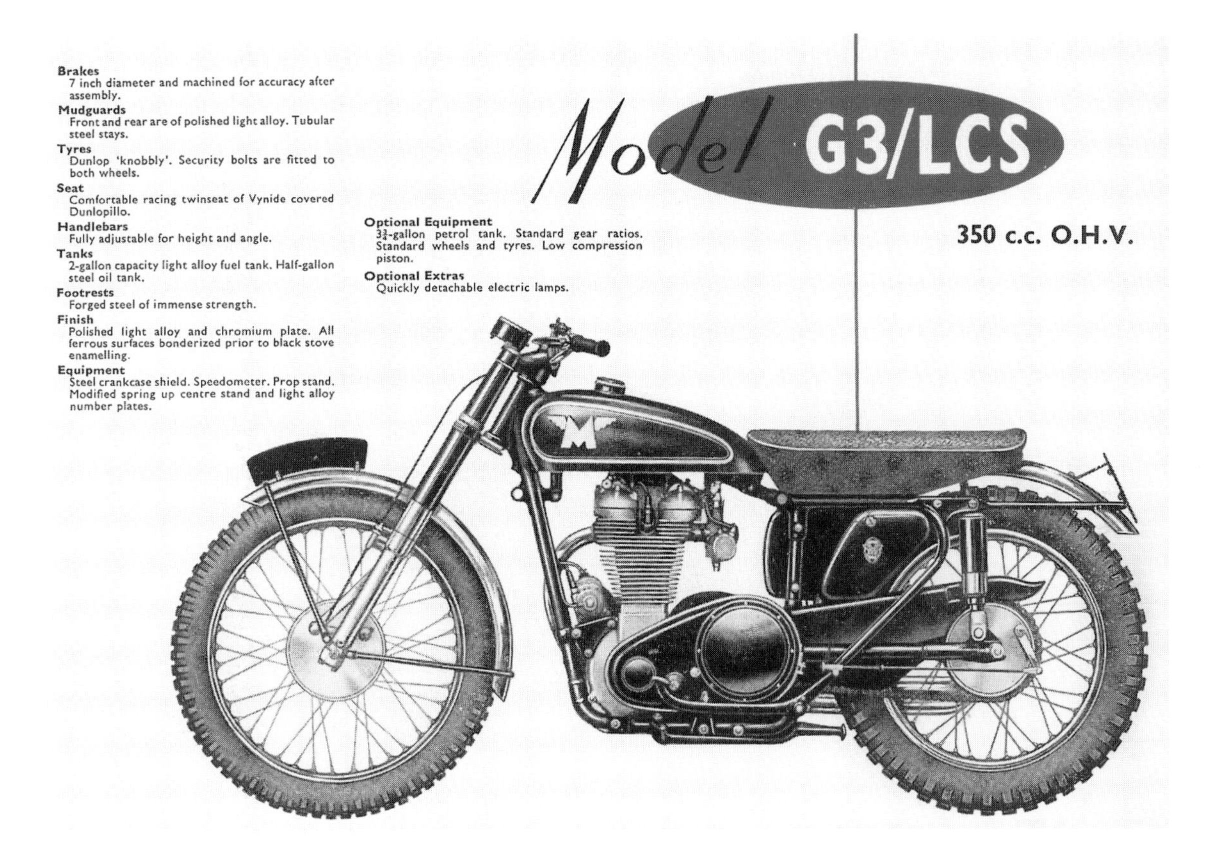

Monobloc carburettor on the 348cc unit had been increased by 1/16in (1.5mm) to 1⅛in (28mm). On the 497cc engine the carburettor bore remained at 1³⁄16in (29mm).

Note that both the three-fifty and five-hundred scramblers now had revised bore and stroke dimension, hence the change from 347 to 348cc and 498 to 497cc; thus the 348cc became 72 × 85.5mm (formerly 69 × 93mm), and the 497cc became 86 × 85.5mm (formerly 82.5 × 93mm). The trials and roadsters singles engine size/bore and stroke dimensions remained as before.

For 1957 the Matchless G3 LC (and AJS Model 16 MC) trials model was the only machine in the range to utilize a welded frame. In addition, the integral structure comprising the duplex engine cradle and the rear frame loops was raised considerably, with the result that ground clearance (with the bike unladen) was increased from 7in (178mm) to 10in (254mm). The altered sweep of the tubes permitted the exhaust pipe to be tucked in more closely, with the result that it was no longer necessary to employ an exaggerated outward crank for the kickstarter pedal. The trials engine, unlike the scrambler type, remained unchanged from the previous year.

Like the roadsters, the dirt bikes received an AMC-developed gearbox (and clutch) for the 1957 model year. And there is no doubt that this move came as a major commercial shock to AMC's former supplier, the Birmingham-based Burman concern. This new gearbox (still a four-speeder) employed a Norton-type clutch with shock absorber. Yet another change was a switch from AMC's own 'Jampot' rear shock absorbers, to bought-in Girling ones.

More Developments for 1958

Although coil ignition with an alternator was adopted for the 1958 model year single-cylinder roadsters, the competition bikes remained faithful to the magneto. Meanwhile, the AMC gearbox change had been lightened by use of a lower-rate selector spring (this applied to both the competition models and roadsters). The

ABOVE: More G80 CS action, this time leading a Greeves Hawkstone.

LEFT: The little known twin cylinder G11 CS scrambler: it was only built for a few months from late 1957 until August the following year.

The 1957 G80 CS

Engine:	Air-cooled, ohv single with vertical cylinder; alloy head and barrel; vertically split aluminium crankcases; fully enclosed valve gear; coil valve springs; built-up crankshaft; roller-bearing big end; gear-driven cams; integral pushrod tunnels in barrel
Bore:	86mm
Stroke:	85.5mm
Displacement:	497cc
Compression ratio:	8.7:1
Lubrication:	Dry sump, two-start oil pump
Ignition:	Magneto, Lucas
Carburettor:	Amal Monobloc 389 1$\frac{3}{16}$in
Primary drive:	Chain
Final drive:	Chain
Gearbox:	Four-speed, foot-change, AMC
Frame:	All-steel construction, full cradle with single front down-tube
Front suspension:	AMC Teledraulic forks
Rear suspension:	Swinging arm with twin Girling shock absorbers
Front brake:	7in, SLS drum, aluminium full-width
Rear brake:	7in, SLS drum, aluminium full-width
Tyres:	Front 3.00 × 21; rear 4.00 × 19

General Specifications

Wheelbase:	55.2in (1,402mm)
Ground clearance:	6.5in (165mm)
Seat height:	32.5in (825mm)
Fuel tank capacity:	2gal (9ltr)
Dry weight:	324lb (147kg)
Maximum power:	33bhp @ 6,200rpm
Top speed:	80mph (129km/h)

scramblers were given a new seat and wider mudguards, whilst the oil tank was set more inwards; there were also quickly detachable lights, similar to the trial models.

In response to the demand for its CS (scrambler models) in the USA, Matchless also introduced twin-cylinder scrambler models for 1958, powered by the 498cc (66 × 72.8mm) G9 and the new 592cc (72 × 72.8mm) G11 ohv parallel-twin power units. These new twins featured the single-cylinder scrambler frame, full-width brake hubs, 2gal (9ltr) fuel tank, siamezed exhaust pipes, speedo on the fork crown, old-type headlamp shell, scrambler handlebars, knobbly tyres (3.00 × 21 front and 4.00 × 19 rear), competition (alloy) mudguards and QD lights. Prices as at 12 September 1957 were as follows:

- 347cc G3LC trials, £243 5s 3d;
- 348cc G3LCS scrambler, £250 14s 11d;
- 497cc G80CS scrambler, £271 19s 1d;
- 498cc G9CS scrambler, £288 15s 11d;
- 592cc G11CS scrambler, £299 8s 0d.

All prices included British purchase tax.

An Updated Trials Model for 1959

As with its predecessors, the 1959 model-year Matchless and AJS 347cc trials mounts had a power unit similar to the roadster three-fifties, but with a lower compression ratio, softer cam profile, a light-alloy cylinder barrel and magneto ignition. But in other areas the machine had been considerably updated.

The wheelbase was considerably shortened by no less than 1¼in (32mm) to 52¼in (1,327mm) by the simple expedient of fitting a rear fork of different design. The previous type resembled that of the roadsters, in having a massive malleable casting at the swinging-arm pivot with a bridge member ahead of the wheel. It had been replaced by an unbridged fork which, as on the new two-fifty roadster (*see* Chapter 12), had one arm integral with the pivot spindle and the other clamped and cottered thereto. This modified construction had contributed significantly to the total weight-saving of around 25lb (11kg), whilst a further reduction came from discarding the malleable cast fork ends in favour of trapped ends to the tubes forming the arms.

The rear subframe was also new, being of much lighter construction, again based on the two-fifty design. The diagonal struts bracing the horizontal tubes were bolted to the seat tube above the fork-pivot lug, and the long, Girling

A 1959 G3 C, with new frame, long inclined Girling rear shocks, revised rear fork and small single-sided brakes. It was based closely on the works model.

rear-suspension legs were inclined forwards by a considerable degree. Since these tubes were shorter, it had been possible to employ smaller-diameter material without sacrificing strength.

Of welded construction, with gussets at the steering head, the main frame was as before, but the Teledraulic front fork had been lightened by means of smaller diameter stanchions, heat-treated to compensate for their reduced tube section. Further weight had been saved by using a small 2¾-pint (4ltr) oil tank and fabricated 5.5in (140mm)-diameter, single-sided hubs in place of the much larger roadster-type, full-width 7in (178mm) assemblies of the previous trials model.

This, then, was the definitive AMC trials mount, which the man in the street could buy, and which was to remain a highly effective mud-plugger from its introduction, and until the British four-stroke trials bikes were superseded by machines such as the Bultaco and Montesa two-strokes from the mid-1960s onwards.

A New Scrambler 250 for 1959

Also new for the 1959 season was a scrambler version of the new Matchless G2 (AJS Model 14) roadster (*see* Chapter 12). This 248.5cc (69.85 × 64.85mm) power unit gave every impression of being of unit-construction design, but actually the gearbox was a separate assembly. The AMC development team had embodied into the scrambler version (coded Matchless G2 CS/AJS 14CS) several changes to specification to make the machine suitable for its off-road racing role. For instance, the engine had its compression ratio raised to 10.5:1, it also had modified crank flywheels and a hotter camshaft. And higher grade steel was employed for some of the gear-box internals.

The only significant modification to the main frame was the use of heavier-gauge tubing for the front down-tube. The same rear subframe tubes as the roadster were employed, but to allow 19in wheels to replace the standard 17in,

The 1960 G3 C

Engine:	Air-cooled, ohv single with vertical cylinder; alloy head and barrel; vertically split aluminium crankcases; fully enclosed valve gear; hairpin valve springs; built-up crankshaft; roller-bearing big end; gear-driven cams
Bore:	69mm
Stroke:	93mm
Displacement:	348cc
Compression ratio:	6.5:1
Lubrication:	Dry sump, two-start oil pump
Ignition:	Magneto
Carburettor:	Amal Monobloc 376 1 1/16in
Primary drive:	Chain
Final drive:	Chain
Gearbox:	Four-speed, foot-change, AMC wide-ratio
Frame:	All-steel construction, full cradle with single front down-tube
Front suspension:	AMC Teledraulic forks
Rear suspension:	Swinging arm with twin Girling shock absorbers
Front brake:	5.5in, SLS drum, single-sided
Rear brake:	5.5in, SLS drum, single-sided
Tyres:	Front 2.75 × 21; rear 4.00 × 19

General Specifications

Wheelbase:	52.2in (1,326mm)
Ground clearance:	10in (254mm)
Seat height:	32.5in (825mm)
Fuel tank capacity:	2gal (9ltr)
Dry weight:	319lb (145kg)
Maximum power:	18bhp @ 5,750rpm
Top speed:	67mph (108km/h)

the horizontal tubes were canted upward, whilst the diagonal tubes were welded to them further forward. Extended Girling units were fitted to suit the altered triangulation. The more robust front fork was based on the Teledraulic assembly specified for the three-fifty trials model. Mudguards were of lightweight polished aluminium, and tyre sizes were 3.00 × 19 front, 3.50 × 19 rear. Other details of the two-fifty scrambler were its open exhaust, knobbly tyres, offset hubs, smaller seat, energy transfer ignition and competition handlebars. As for the bigger-engined scramblers, these continued into 1959 unchanged; nevertheless, later in that year the G3 LCS three-fifty and the G9 CS five-hundred twin were axed due to poor sales.

Like the latest roadsters (except the 250/350 lightweights), the surviving scrambler models – the five-hundred single and the six-fifty twin – gained a new frame for the 1960 season. This featured duplex front down-tubes, taken back to pass beneath the engine and gearbox. A single 1 3/4in (45mm) diameter, fourteen-gauge top tube (larger than the roadsters) combined with a vertical seat tube to complete the main frame. The rear subframe was bolted to lugs just below the rear of the gearbox and the front of the saddle. Previously found only on the two-fifty roadster, a three-point fuel-tank mounting was a feature of the new frame, there being two mountings at the front and one at the rear.

As with the roadster single-cylinder five-hundred, the G80 CS scrambler cylinder head had been redesigned, with the combustion chamber shape now hemispherical and featuring a flat-top piston with small recesses for the valves. Also on the five-hundred scrambler the oil tank had been relocated to the nearside (left) of the seat tube to enable a 1 3/8in (35mm) Amal GP carburettor to be fitted to the redesigned cylinder head. The oil tank's former home was now occupied by a comprehensive air filter.

Both the G80 CS and G12 CS scramblers were normally supplied stripped, 'ready to race'. If lights were required by the purchaser, these bikes could be supplied 'ex-works' with an AC generator in addition to the magneto. The battery was fitted on the offside (right) of the seat tube beneath the air filter.

The C2 CS two-fifty scrambler now had a larger inlet valve, whilst the gears had again been given added durability – also in the light of experience gained during the past season the gearbox internal ratios had been altered and included a higher bottom gear. The new internal ratios were: 3.24, 2.44, 1.56 and 1:1.

For trials enthusiasts the three-fifty G3 C (and AJS 16C) was retained with little change for 1960, the exceptions being a beefed-up support for the rear mudguard, and a modified pivot bearing which contained a small reservoir of oil.

Prices as at 1 October 1959 were as follows: for the 248cc G2 CS scrambler, £202 13s 0d; for the 347cc G3 C trials bike, £235 4s 5d; for the 497cc G80 CS scrambler, £265 7s 6d; and for the 646cc G12 CS scrambler, £287 1s 9d. All prices included UK purchase tax. However, only seven months later, more price increases were made, and AMC defended these rises thus: 'Higher labour costs following the shorter working week in the engineering industries have resulted in further price rises.' All this took effect on 2 May 1960, and was a clear indication of the industrial and financial problems that were to blight the remainder of Associated Motor Cycles' life.

When the 1961 model range was announced at the end of August 1960, the last of the scrambler twins, the six-fifty, was axed from the line-up.

Improvements into the Sixties

For the 1961 season AMC introduced additional engine changes to the two-fifty scrambler (the Matchless G2 CS and AJS 14CS), these being made in the light of experiences gained. Inlet valve size thus went up from $1\frac{1}{16}$in (27mm) to $1\frac{1}{8}$in (28mm), whilst the combustion chamber altered in shape because the increase in power thus achieved required a more robust crankpin – increased in diameter from $\frac{3}{4}$in (19mm) to $\frac{7}{8}$in (22mm) – and a stronger connecting rod.

There was a change from energy transfer ignition to battery/coil. This was done because the former system needed extreme accuracy when checking the ignition timing, something which was often difficult to achieve whilst working in the field. A Varley dry-cell battery was used to avoid spilling, 'should', as *The Motor Cycle* said, 'the machine fall in battle'.

Little change was seen on the larger competition singles that year, the trials three-fifties continuing

Matchless heavyweight mudplugger single (non-standard spec) at the Talmag Pre-65 Trial, c. 1981.

ABOVE: A G80 CS competitor leading the field, c. 1960.

RIGHT: A club rider with a G80 CS scrambler, 1961.

BELOW: The Matchless G2 CS two-fifty. This 1961 bike has coil ignition rather than the energy-transfer system of the earlier model.

The 1961 G2 CS

Engine:	Air-cooled, ohv single with vertical cylinder; alloy head; cast-iron barrel; vertically split aluminium crankcases; fully enclosed valve gear; hairpin valve springs; built-up crankshaft; single gear-driven camshaft; cross-over enclosed pushrods; roller-bearing big end
Bore:	69.85mm
Stroke:	64.85mm
Displacement:	248.5cc
Compression ratio:	10:1
Lubrication:	Dry sump, plunger worm pump
Ignition:	Coil; 1959–60, energy transfer
Carburettor:	N/A
Primary drive:	Duplex chain
Final drive:	Chain
Gearbox:	Four-speed, AMC, adjustable type, with improved materials and different ratios from roadsters
Frame:	All-steel construction, brazed and bolted; single main and front tubes; pressed steel under-channel in heavier gauge materials and modified sub-frame
Front suspension:	AMC Teledraulic forks; two-way oil-damped
Rear suspension:	Two-piece swinging arm, with oil-damped, adjustable, extra-long Girling shock absorbers
Front brake:	7in SLS drum
Rear brake:	5in SLS drum
Tyres:	Front 3.00 × 19; rear 3.50 × 19

General Specifications

Wheelbase:	54in (1,372mm)
Ground clearance:	7.2in (183mm)
Seat height:	32in (813mm)
Fuel tank capacity:	2.75gal (12.5ltr)
Dry weight:	321lb (146kg)
Maximum power:	22bhp @ 7,500rpm
Top speed:	75mph (121km/h)

October 1961 advertisement showing a G3 C trials model.

without change apart from a modified oil pump (introduced on all single-cylinder models that year); whilst for the scrambler five-hundreds, the inlet valve-guide circlip, as on the roadster versions, was also incorporated.

Competition Successes

Over the years the AMC trials three-fifty had proved its worth as both Matchless and AJS – the reality being that as the years had gone by, the two were, in effect, the same motorcycle except for their tank logos. And in May 1961 Gordon Jackson (riding an AJS-badged bike) scored a famous victory in the gruelling Scottish Six Days, only dropping a single point! The next best man was the legendary Sammy Miller and his equally famous Ariel with five marks lost, and third was Triumph works star Roy Peplow, with minus seventeen marks.

For 1962 the G80 CS was given the name Marksman; however, little else had changed.

The Matchless G80 CS engine (and AMC gearbox) were highly regarded, and this led to a number of specials. A particularly nice one was the Greeves-framed device built by the Australian Tim Gibbs in 1963.

The 1966 G85 CS

Engine:	Air-cooled, ohv single with vertical cylinder; alloy head and barrel; vertically split aluminium crankcases; fully enclosed valve gear; hairpin valve springs; built-up crankshaft; roller-bearing big end; gear-driven cams; integral pushrod tunnels in barrel
Bore:	86mm
Stroke:	85.5mm
Displacement:	497cc
Compression ratio:	12:1
Lubrication:	Dry sump, Norton gear-oil pump
Ignition:	Magneto
Carburettor:	Amal GP or 389 Monobloc
Primary drive:	Chain
Final drive:	Chain
Gearbox:	Four-speed, foot-change, AMC
Frame:	All-welded frame, duplex full cradle
Front suspension:	AMC Teledraulic forks
Rear suspension:	Swinging arm, with short Girling rear shock absorbers
Front brake:	7in AMC hub with fins machined off; SLS
Rear brake:	8.25in; AJS 7R conical hub; SLS
Tyres:	Front 3.00 × 21; rear 4.00 × 18

General Specifications

Wheelbase:	56.9in (1,445mm)
Ground clearance:	8.5in (216mm)
Seat height:	33in (838mm)
Fuel tank capacity:	2gal (9ltr) aluminium
Dry weight:	291lb (132kg)
Maximum power:	41bhp @ 6,500rpm
Top speed:	85mph (137km/h)

As with the roadster, the competition models were given names for the 1962 season: 'Maestro' for the 347cc G3 C trials, and 'Marksman' for the 497cc G80 CS scramblers. Otherwise there were no changes to the remaining two competition models. By now progress and fresh ideas were at a premium, with very little development taking place.

It was much the same a year later, with *The Motor Cycle* reporting in their 27 September 1962 issue: 'Justifiably unaltered is the 347cc trials machine (AJS Experts or Matchless Maestro), a replica of the mount that carried young Mick Andrews to victory in the Bemrose last March.' The 497cc scrambler (AJS Southerner or Matchless Marksman) now had the new front hub (also found on the roadsters) and a new, works-type, large, flat air filter. Optional was a 12:1 piston, also used by the factory team riders.

Prices as at 27 September 1962 were: £236 8s 0d for the 347cc G3 C Maestro trials bike; and £293 11s 7d for the 497cc G80 CS Marksman scrambler. Prices included UK taxes. The two-fifty G2 CS scrambler had been axed at the same time.

For the 1964 model year, the G80 CS scrambler was given a Norton oil pump (as had the roadster singles that year), whilst the G3 C trials mount was equipped with a fixed seat with a

Last of the line, the 1968 G85 CS; it was produced after the Manganese Bronze takeover of September 1966.

RIGHT: A 1965 G80 CS – the last year before it was replaced by the G85 CS; with duplex frame, full-width AMC alloy hubs, Amal GP carb and hi-level exhaust.

BELOW: A 1966 G85 CS being put through its paces. Now with central spark plug, 12:1 compression ratio, magnesium alloy rear hub (from the G50 road racer), and AMC front hub with the fins machined off.

fibre-glass base, a revised subframe and shorter Girling shock absorbers. Late that year the trials bike was axed from the range in the face of the rising tide of lighter, smaller capacity two-strokes.

The following year, 1965, saw no change whatsoever to the sole remaining competition model, the five-hundred scrambler single. Then for 1966 came the introduction of the much revised G85 CS, featuring a duplex fully welded frame, AMC front hub with the fins machined off, an AJS 7R rear hub, all-alloy engine (with 12:1 compression ratio and central plug), central (alloy) oil tank, and polished fuel tank with quick-action filler cap. The G85 CS was also only offered as a Matchless, even though versions with 'AJS' on their tanks were used by factory riders in the ISDT.

The End of the Line

With the entire AMC empire in tatters following the appointment of the official receiver in late 1966, the G85 CS was nevertheless developed further, with an improved oil pump for the 1967 model year. Dry weight was claimed as 291lb (132kg), with maximum power of 41bhp at 6,500rpm. The G85 CS was now the only model left in what had once been a huge range of Matchless (and AJS) machines. The last G85 CS was built in early 1969.

Matchless Motocross Successes

British Championships 500cc

1955	Dave Curtis	3rd
1956	Dave Curtis	2nd
1957	No contest; Suez Crisis	
1958	Dave Curtis	1st
1960	Dave Curtis	4th
1961	Dave Curtis	2nd
1963	Vic Eastwood	2nd
1964	Vic Eastwood	2nd
	Chris Horsfield	3rd

European Championships 500cc

1952	Auguste Mingels	2nd
	Marcel Cox	4th
	Brian Stonebridge	6th
1953	Auguste Mingels	1st
1956	Nic Jansen	3rd

World Championships 500cc

1959	Dave Curtis	3rd

Moto Cross Des Nations – Best individual performance

1952	Brian Stonebridge

Note: Several other placings/championships were gained using Matchless-engined Rickman Metisse machines.

The Rickman brothers, Don and Derek, built and raced a series of Metisse-framed motocrossers. A popular engine choice was the Matchless G80 CS ohv single.

11 The G50

Introduced towards the end of 1958, the 496cc (90 × 78mm) Matchless G50 was a truly beautiful looking motorcycle. It has always been a mystery why AMC didn't build what was, in effect, a bigger bore version of the AJS 7R years earlier.

The biggest mystery about the G50 was that it took AMC so long to introduce it; after all, it was virtually a larger bore AJS 7R, rather than a new bike. One of the reasons was that the 7R had been designed by Phil Walker, and the G45 – the G50's forerunner – by Ike Hatch. Another was that a big-bore 7R wasn't AMC's idea at all; instead, motocross star Bill Nillson built a five-hundred 7R to win the European (the precursor of the World title) Championship crown. Yet another was group politics, AMC viewing the 7R very much as an AJS in the early days after its 1948 launch – even though the group was happy enough to use a badge-engineering regime with its series-production roadsters. But whatever the reasons, the G50 didn't appear until 1958, a decade after the 7R.

Ike Hatch died in 1954, and it was his replacement Jack Williams who was responsible for the G50 project. There is no doubt that Williams was not keen on the G45, seeing it as an inferior design to its main rival, the double overhead camshaft Featherbed Manx Norton, in terms of both power output and handling.

Before going on to recount the story of the G50's development and racing successes, it is important to give details of the 7R's design features, as the majority were employed on the

Taken from the 1962 factory brochure.

The AMC Racing Gearbox

Introduced for the 1958 racing season, the AMC-made racing gearbox was fitted as original equipment not only to the Matchless G50, but also to the AJS 7R and Manx Norton models. Though based on the roadster gearbox already fitted to the over-250cc AMC bikes and Nortons, the gearbox differed in a number of respects, including the materials used, and the clutch and its method of operation.

Mainshaft and layshaft were supported at both ends in ball race bearings and were of En.355, an 85-ton steel containing nickel, chromium, manganese and molybdenum. This material was also employed for the gears. Layout for the gear cluster followed conventional practice, in that peg-type dogs were employed for the engagement of bottom gear, but otherwise normal block dogs were utilized. The floating gears (second on the mainshaft, bottom and third on the layshaft) ran on fully floating bronze bushes. Internal ratios were 1.78, 1.332, 1.1 and 1 to 1.

The positive-stop mechanism was of the type employing a spring-controlled double-ended pawl. Coaxial with the pedal shaft, the ratchet quadrant carried a peg that engaged with a knuckle joint at the right-hand end of a transverse rocker, the rocker pivot being mounted inside the front wall of the gearbox shell. At the other end of this rocker was a toothed quadrant engaging with a pinion on the cam plate.

The cam plate was of conventional two-track design, save that the lobes between the location notches were shallow, thus permitting the spring-loaded plunger to be supported as near as possible to its point, thereby minimizing tilting. The plunger housing was screwed into the bottom of the shell. A single transverse spindle carried the pair of selector forks.

Identical with that found on earlier Manx Nortons, the clutch was notable for featuring friction inserts in the sprocket, protruding on each side, and three tongued Ferodo RZL driving plates alternating with four steel-driven plates. Each steel plate had eight radial keyhole slots to prevent any tendency for the plate to become conical when hot. The cast-alloy pressure plate carried three springs of square-section wire and a central adjustable thrust pad.

Resembling that utilized on the AMC two-strokes, the clutch thrust mechanism was both well thought out and efficient. Integral with the operating lever was a spindle carried in a housing that was seated in the inner end cover and secured by a screw-in gland ring. The axis of the spindle was offset below that of the thrust rod and the housing, and in the middle of the spindle was a transverse groove of semicircular section.

Between the thrust-rod end and the spindle, in the bore of the housing, was a steel ball; it was located in the groove which, when the clutch was in the engaged position, was inclined to the vertical.

Actuation of the operating lever by the clutch cable rotated the spindle and caused the groove to act as a cam, moving the ball along the bore in the housing.

G50. The cycle parts consisted of a full double-cradle frame, modified AMC Teledraulic front forks, and twin rear shock absorber and swinging arm. In the braking department conical hubs were used, the front featuring two leading-shoe operations. But the centre of attraction was the engine, where to keep weight to a minimum, wide use was made of magnesium castings; these were finished in a highly distinctive gold-coloured, corrosion-inhibiting paint. Like the pre-war R7, the 7R had a capacity of 348cc (74 × 81mm), used a single overhead camshaft and hairpin valve springs, and as on the R7, the camshaft was driven by a Weller-tensioned chain. Otherwise the 1948 7R was largely a new design.

A whole series of year-by-year changes took place. For example, for the 1956 season Jack Williams changed the bore and stroke dimensions to 75.5 × 78mm respectively, giving a displacement of 349cc. And another major change was to an AMC gearbox for the 1958 season, together with a three-spring clutch.

The Prototype G50

Two G50 prototype machines appeared during the 1958 season. These were ridden by Peter Ferbache and the Australian Jack Ahearn, and right from the start it was clear to everyone that the 'new' G50 five-hundred was in fact a big brother of the already well-established 7R. Indeed, the stroke remained the same at 78mm, but the bore was enlarged to 90mm, giving a capacity of 496cc; this had the added advantage of turning the engine into a short-stroke type.

The only external difference between the two engines was that on the G50 outside plumbing was used for the pressure feed-pipe to the cam gear, and the fore and aft drains from the rocker boxes. Carburation was taken care of by a 1½in (38mm) Amal GP instrument. Valve sizes on these prototype machines were the same as the 7R, as was the part-sphere of the combustion space; the piston-crown hump was thus considerably smaller than the bore, so that squish was provided as the piston approached TDC (Top Dead Centre). During 1958 the engine was purely experimental, with AMC chief development engineer Jack Williams hard at work to perfect it so it would be ready to go on sale for the 1959 season. The idea of actually marketing the G50 had come from sales director and former racer Jock West.

Graham Walker reported on the new G50 in his article 'Talking Technically' in *Motor Cycling* dated 19 June 1958:

> The Wizards of Woolwich have produced a most promising 'Senior' model, weighing well under 300lb (136kg), developing some 49bhp at 6,800rpm on a compression ratio of 10 to 1, and, with a 1½in-bore carburettor, pulling an exceptionally high gear, quoted approximately 4 to 1. The attractions of such a flexible, easy-to-handle-and-maintain 'bigger banger' for private owners are pretty obvious, and the fact that Jack Ahearn got a silver replica (in the TT) at 88.71mph [142.73km/h] on its first outing, despite some gearbox trouble, augurs well for its subsequent progress.

No less a man than John Surtees (who had just become double 350/500cc World Champion), together with Bruce Main-Smith of *Motor Cycling*, was able to give the G50 a thorough testing at Brands Hatch in October 1958, with Jack Williams in attendance. As Main-Smith was to recall: 'When race chief Jack Williams bowled up with *both* of the two G50s currently in captivity, my day was made, in spite of the ominous weather forecast and the already rain-sodden track.' Bruce Main-Smith was able to ride both bikes, commenting:

> One had the earlier frame and is a slightly more peppy motor, the other a new frame, a much more tucked-in exhaust system, vastly improved seating arrangements, and other desirable mods. Since it is virtually a bored-out 7R, I expected similar characteristics, namely, freedom from temperament, clean acceleration with no trouble from megaphonitis, a throaty bellow from the one reverse-cone trumpet, and a smooth, vibration-free rate of progress.

Production Begins

When it entered production during the spring of 1959, the G50 had purpose-built casting, rather than reworked 7R components. This meant that instead of 49bhp at 7,000rpm of the prototypes, the production models gave 51bhp at 7,200rpm. There were also wider section 19in tyres – 3.00 front, 3.50 rear. And it was soon evident that in the G50, Matchless had a new winner. Although at the time vastly outnumbered by

The late Fred Neville winning on his G50: Brands Hatch, summer 1960.

Robin Dawson taking his G50 to eleventh position in the 1960 Senior Manx Grand Prix.

Norton machinery, the new AMC single made an extremely good impression at the Isle of Man in June 1959, with no fewer than four of the top thirteen machines being G50s. The best finish was Derek Powell, who came home fourth, averaging 82.87mph (133.34km/h) in what is generally seen as one of the most difficult races in TT history; *The Motor Cycle* summed it up simply as the 'Storm-Lashed Senior TT'. Alan Shepherd was seventh, George Catlin eighth, and Bill Smith thirteenth. Because of the terrible conditions, a mere twenty-two riders – just a quarter of the field – finished the race.

For the 1960 season, engine alterations to the G50 included closer adjustment to the vernier ignition timing, a stronger magneto strap, more rigid float chamber mounting brackets, and a larger 1⅞in (47mm) diameter inlet valve, replacing the original 1¾in (44mm) component.

Changes for the 1961 Season

When details of the 1961 G50 racers were announced at the beginning of April that year there were a number of changes, mainly to the cycle parts (these being shared with the 7R). All forty G50s scheduled for production had already been sold by the previous December, such was the demand. The price, including UK purchase tax, was £455 19s 3d.

A notable area of attention had been the front forks. The two springs formerly used in each telescopic-fork leg were replaced by a single multi-rate spring, and damping characteristics had been altered to match this spring. The fork oil seals were now double-lipped, the outer lips wiping and cleaning the fork stanchions to exclude dirt and grit. In addition the metal fork covers had been dropped in favour of rubber gaiters, for weight saving and greater cleanliness; the fork travel had also been increased.

The rear swinging-arm shock absorbers had been given improved damping characteristics, and were individually tested and matched in pairs by makers Girling. The front brake air-scoop now had more frontal area, but was a few grams lighter as a result of an improved production technique.

The 1961 G50

Engine:	Air-cooled, sohc single with vertical cylinder; alloy head and barrel; chain-driven cam with Weller tensioner; hairpin valve springs; roller-bearing big end
Bore:	90mm
Stroke:	78mm
Displacement:	496cc
Compression ratio:	10:1; 1960 10.7:1; 1962 11.2:1
Lubrication:	Dry sump; twin gear-oil pumps
Ignition:	Magneto
Carburettor:	Amal GP 1½in; 1962, Amal GP 1⅜in
Primary drive:	Chain
Final drive:	Chain
Gearbox:	Four-speed, foot-change, close-ratio AMC type
Frame:	Duplex, fully welded
Front suspension:	AMC Teledraulic forks
Rear suspension:	Swinging arm, with twin Girling shock absorbers
Front brake:	Conical magnesium hub, 2LS
Rear brake:	Conical magnesium hub, 5LS
Tyres:	Front 3.00 × 19; rear 3.40 × 19

General Specifications

Wheelbase:	55in (1,397mm)
Ground clearance:	6in (152mm)
Seat height:	31.5in (800mm)
Fuel tank capacity:	5.5gal (25ltr)
Dry weight:	300lb (136kg)
Maximum power:	48bhp @ 6,800rpm; 1960, 50bhp @ 7,200rpm; 1961, 51bhp @ 7,200rpm
Top speed:	130mph (209km/h)

The brake-shoe expander cam had an end-plate to locate the shoes on the cam. Another, albeit tiny, reduction in weight was the fitment of a smaller oil-tank filler cap.

A modification to the shape of the timing chest had enabled an exhaust pipe with an improved curve so that it could be tucked in closer. This change also resulted in positioning the megaphone further to the rear of the bike and out of the way of the rider's feet.

LEFT: Alan Shepherd enters the Promenade at Portstewart on his way to a comfortable victory in the 500cc class of the 1962 North West 200 in Northern Ireland.

BELOW: Alan Shepherd smiles after his successes in the 1962 North West 200: wins on his G50 and 7R (the latter in the 350cc race), and second spot on an Aermacchi in the 250cc event.

1962, Final Year of Production

The final year of production for both the G50 and the AJS 7R, at least by AMC, was 1962. The price of the G50 had now risen to £527 0s 9d (including taxes). Production of the 1962 models began in February that year, and there were several important changes to both the engine and cycle parts.

Improvements to the Engine

Crankcase breathing was now effected through a flat-type disc valve in the end of the hollow mainshaft. Operated entirely by the crankcase/atmospheric pressure differential, this valve was not driven in any way, and slightly improved crankcase breathing. Coinciding with this modification, the mainshaft had been shortened to bring in the chain-line closer to the bearing; this reduction in overhang also resulted in sundry other dimensional changes.

The light-alloy big-end cage was now forged, whereas previously it had been turned from a bar, and ran within the con-rod eye, instead of on the crankpin. Any danger of it bursting under centrifugal force was thus avoided. As before, the cage was slotted for a single row of 14½ × ¼in (368 × 6mm) rollers.

Although no changes were made to the bore and stroke of the engine, a very significant alteration was made to the top half of the engine. This consisted of a shim fitted underneath the cylinder barrel as a means of setting the combustion chamber squish clearance accurately. Sufficient clearance had been provided between the edge of the piston crown and the base of the cylinder head, when cold, to allow not only for the expansion caused by heat, but also for the cumulative effect of the microscopic distortions encountered

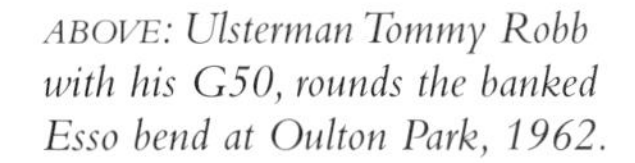

ABOVE: Ulsterman Tommy Robb with his G50, rounds the banked Esso bend at Oulton Park, 1962.

RIGHT: G50 action at Scarborough in 1962. Number 2 is essentially stock except for a one-off half fairing.

at high rotational speeds. With the engine hot and revving hard, this clearance must be as small as possible so that optimum squish effect is obtained. It must never be so small as to allow the piston to touch the head at any time. On the other hand, if it were too large, the turbulence that is caused by squish, and which improves combustion, would be reduced.

The degree of accuracy to which this shim permitted the squish gap to be set resulted in improved peak power, acceleration and reliability. In other words, it was a 'win-win' situation. This also enabled larger valves to be used in the 1962 G50 engine, both now being of 2in (50mm) diameter.

TOP: *Sidecar racer Owen Greenwood's Matchless G50-powered kneeler outfit at Silverstone in the spring of 1963. Note the near-horizontal layout of the engine.*

MIDDLE: *Mike Hailwood and the works four-cylinder MV(1) leads Alan Shepherd (7) riding a Tom Kirby G50 at the Race of the Year, Mallory Park, in September 1963.*

LEFT: *Kings Lynn rider John (George) Ward during the 1964 Senior Manx Grand Prix. A shortage of spares meant that he switched to a Royal Enfield GP5 two-fifty from 1965.*

South African star Paddy Driver posing for photographs on his Tom Kirby G50 at the Isle of Man TT, June 1964.

Bill Smith rode this G50 in the 1964 Senior TT.

Blackpool rider Derek Woodman at Bridge Corner during the 1964 Southern 100; he finished second in the 500cc race.

TOP: Bill Ivy (Kirby G50 Matchless) gets well down to it at the 500cc Dutch TT, Assen in June 1965.

ABOVE: The rider's eye view of the G50 controls.

RIGHT: Roger Hunter (helmet) and AMC works race mechanic Tom Mortimer (seated on a Kirby G50), 1965.

John Hartle (37) and Dave Croxford (14) at Oliver's Mount, Scarborough, in 1967; both are riding G50s.

ABOVE: The Rickman works in the spring of 1966. A complete G50-engined Metisse is shown, together with a part-assembled example and a number of frames.
LEFT: The Rickman Brothers, Don and Derek, of New Milton, Hampshire, long famous for their Metisse motocross machines, entered the road-racing arena in 1966. Their most success came using the Matchless G50 engine.

Jack Findlay (17) with the legendary McIntyre Matchless leads Chris Conn and Jack Ahearn (Nortons) during the Austrian GP in May 1966.

Australian Jack Findlay (McIntyre Matchless G50) finishing runner-up to MV World Champion Giacomo Agostini in the 1968 Czech GP at Brno.

Findlay working on the McIntyre Matchless in 1968.

ABOVE: Cadwell Park, Skegness & District Club team, c. 1971. Left to right: John Kirkby, 125 Yamaha (3); John Borsbery, G50 Seeley (26); Mal Wheeler, Seeley (27); Billy Hill, Aermacchi (18).

LEFT: Present owner of the Findlay machine is Northampton dealer Mick Hemmings, seen here at Scarborough, 22 September 2001.

Alan Barnett (Kirby G50/Metisse) coming up out of the Governor's Bridge dip during the 1969 Senior TT.

ABOVE: The Arter G50 Matchless as ridden by Peter Williams during the early 1970s to many victories. The initial design of the frame had been carried out by John Surtees (for an AJS 7R engine) back in the late 1950s.

LEFT: Peter Reynolds pilots his immaculate G50 around Brands Hatch, c. 1979.

A brace of Matchless racers in the National Motorcycle Museum, Birmingham, c. 1985. The machine in the foreground is a 1961 G50, the other a 1957 G45 twin.

The Cycle Parts

Several alterations were made to the cycle parts, resulting in a useful reduction in weight; these included a duralumin gearchange pedal, a rubber instead of a metal tank-strap, and the deletion of the fuel-tank breather. The method of mounting the gearbox was improved, in that it was now held in a pair of all-embracing alloy plates which, together with their mountings in the frame, changed the vibration frequency of the two bottom frame tubes. This change was mainly intended to benefit the smaller, higher revving 7R engine, but was also incorporated in the G50.

To minimize the effects of vibration further, the 7R's Amal GP2 carburettor was now flexibly mounted by an assembly of light alloy and rubber. However, the 1½in (38mm) GP2 carb of the G50 continued to be mounted rigidly. Both machines used the latest pattern Amal 'Matchbox' float chamber, suspended from a rubber mounting.

Other cycle-part alterations included attention to steering and brakes. Rigidity of the top front-fork yoke had been increased by a new head-stem nut that had a wedging action when tightened. Each brake shoe carried two pieces of friction lining of Ferodo AM4 material; those of the twin leading-shoe front brake were unchamfered to improve their cleaning effect on the drum, but to reduce the tendency to grab under relatively harsh foot operation, the front edge of the first section of the rear brake's leading shoe lining was conventionally chamfered. No less a man than Bob McIntyre voiced the opinion that 'the new G50 brakes are the equal of any that I've used before'.

A review of the latest G50 and 7R designs in the 7 February 1962 issue of *Motor Cycling* made

Today it is still possible to see the G50 in its original Matchless guise thanks to owners such as Eric Downey, whose 1961 machine is above.

this comment: 'They are now so highly developed that the designer's aims of increased power, speed and reliability must be rapidly becoming almost impossible to achieve.' But this question was never answered, as AMC ceased production; and although a few machines were subsequently built from spares, the 1962 changes were the last of those undertaken by Jack Williams and AMC.

Popular modern features can include belt drive for the primary transmission and a Czech Pal magneto in place of the original Lucas component.

In total, some 180 G50s were constructed before production ceased in 1962, plus fifty examples of the G50 CSR (*see* box); the latter was a street-legal version for the American market. The reason for the CSR's existence was simply to allow its pukka racing brother, the G50, to take part in AMA (American Motorcycle Association) events, stateside star Dick Mann becoming national champion aboard a G50 in 1963.

In Europe, the G50 continued winning races throughout the remainder of the 1960s. Peter Williams on the Tom Arter G50 was still winning into the early 1970s, and of course Colin Seeley (*see* Chapter 13) continued using the engine in his races. Then at the end of the 1970s and early 1980s the classic movement provided the venerable Matchless with a second life. And today, at the beginning of the twenty-first century, the G50 in both its Matchless and Seeley guises is still to be seen in considerable numbers.

12 Lightweight Singles

The Matchless G2

Launched at the Geneva Show in March 1958, the Matchless G2 and its twin brother the AJS Model 14 were the result of AMC's decision to return to the quarter-litre class for the first time in the post-World War II era. Previously the two marques had suffered in that newcomers to motorcycling usually had to purchase something else, rather smaller, as their first bike, and then, as a result of brand loyalty, would very often stick with the other make when choosing their next machine. In addition there was talk of new legislation restricting novices to small bikes, and AMC thus needed to supplement their existing James and Francis-Barnett two-stroke models. In any case, Matchless (and AJS) saw BSA, Royal Enfield and Triumph as their main competition.

And so it was that the range of 'Lightweight' singles was initiated, ultimately encompassing not only touring, sporting and competition two-fifties, but also a three-fifty version as well. At first sight the newcomer appeared to have followed the Continental by Europeans using unit construction. However, this was not in fact the case, as the gearbox was a separate assembly. The same could be said of the 'lightweight' tag, because at 325lb (147kg) the new two-fifty was anything but that. However, the description stuck – and in any case the three-fifty version was considerably lighter than the long-running G3 series.

Switzerland in early spring might have seemed a strange place to launch a new British motorcycle. As *The Motor Cycle*'s show report said: 'Around Geneva, as far as the eye could see, was draped a vast mantle of snow. Inside the *Palais des Expositions* man seemed to be challenging nature's spectacle with a glittering show of chromium plating and burnished aluminium.'

AMC's sales director Jock West had this to say at the Geneva launch: 'We have tried to achieve that indefinable modern appearance without resorting to the excessive bulk and extreme "one-ness" that costs money and often results in poor accessibility.'

Displacing 248.5cc, with bore and stroke dimensions of 69.85 × 64.85mm respectively, the actual crankshaft throw was 32.385mm; but the cylinder was offset 0.25in (0.6mm) forward of the crankshaft, thus giving a *dé saxé* effect. Although this set-up was rare on motorcycle engines, it was certainly not so in the car world. And there were two definite advantages: first, there was less piston slap and bore wear thanks to the movement of the piston across from the non-thrust to the thrust side of the cylinder bore at the top of the stroke, which was more gentle. This minimized 'slap', whilst the connecting-rod angularity at maximum combustion pressure was reduced. The other advantage was that there was better use of that portion of the power stroke, together with a small, but worthwhile, reduction in piston friction.

In designing their new two-fifty power unit, AMC engineers stated that 'the degree of offset used is not great, however, and the system was chosen not just for the benefits (stated above) but also because it fitted in with the general geometry of the engine.'

Engine Design

Although to the casual observer the new engine appeared radically different from existing AMC design techniques, in practice it followed familiar ground, with a built-up crankshaft and many of

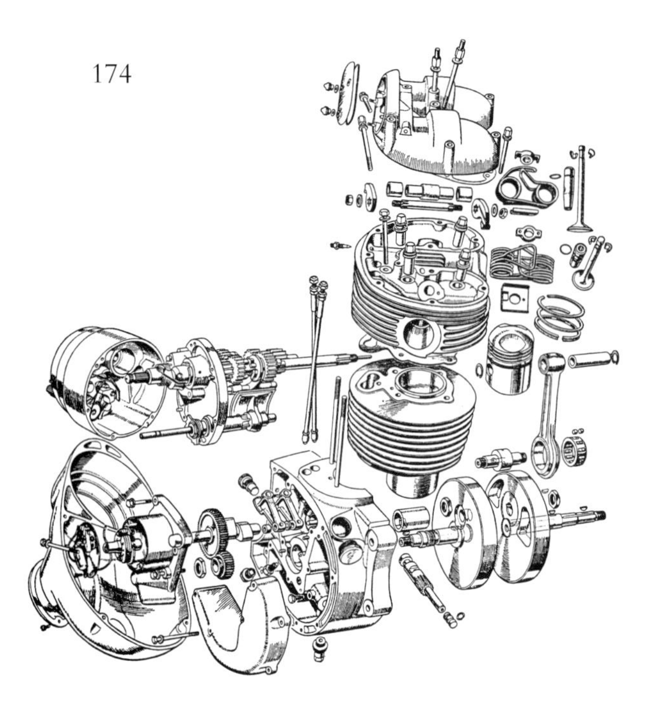

Exploded view of the AMC 248.5cc (69.85 × 64.85mm) engine that powered the Matchless G2 and AJS Model 14. Although it appeared to be of unit-construction design, the gearbox was actually separate. Note the hairpin valve springs.

the traditional AMC features. This also meant a single ohv layout instead of an ohc. The actual layout featured a single camshaft with a pair of trailing lever-type followers. This feature was also fundamental in the use of what amounted to a virtual copy of the existing G3-type cylinder head and valve-gear design. And by positioning the cylinder before and the camshaft behind the cylinder axis, there was increased space for the cam lobes and their followers.

Another design requirement, stated by AMC, was a minimum of side thrust on the followers, which meant that the pushrods had to be as near as possible vertical in front elevation. Rotation of the plane of the valves (through $21\frac{1}{4}$ degrees clockwise, seen from above) made this practical without the use of rocker spindles of differing lengths; in addition it had the advantage of bringing the exhaust port and spark plug more directly into the cooling airstream.

Manufactured in DTD24 aluminium alloy, the cylinder head featured a part-spherical combustion space with cast-in valve seats of austenitic cast iron. In addition there were diagonal vertical fins on the nearside (left) to direct air over the combustion chamber and spark-plug areas. The silicon-aluminium inlet valve was substantially larger than the exhaust valve, which was of Jessops G2 steel – valve head diameter being $1\frac{15}{32}$in (37mm) and $1\frac{3}{16}$in (29mm) respectively. Due to this significant difference, and the wish to avoid too sharp a bend in the exhaust tract, the valve-included angle of 75 degrees was split unequally: the inlet valve was at 35 degrees to the vertical, whilst the exhaust valve was set at 40 degrees.

The inlet tract was offset 10 degrees towards the right of the centreline of the head; the exhaust tract was also offset to the right, but this time by $11\frac{1}{2}$ degrees. This meant that, in effect, the cylinder head was skewed around 21.25 degrees, effectively bringing the exhaust to the right, and the carburettor to the left. The choke diameter of the latter was $1\frac{1}{16}$in (26mm), the carburettor type being an Amal Monobloc Type 376, with a downdraught angle of 12 degrees; there was a thick heat-insulating spacer between the carb and the head.

With an alloy cylinder head, the valve guides were manufactured in cast iron and were located axially by circlips and crossover hairpin valve springs. Four long thru-studs screwed into the crankcase held down the cylinder head and barrel; the separate die-cast rocker box was attached to the head by no fewer than nine bolts.

The rockers were of typical AMC built-up construction; on each, the arms were splined to the ends of what *The Motor Cycle* said was a 'live' spindle, and were separated by a hardened sleeve to which they were clamped by nuts on the spindle ends. Each rocker was supported by a pair of bronze bushes with an oil-retaining felt sleeve separating them. Owing to the unequal valve angles in the cylinder head, and the seen desirability of utilizing interchangeable pushrods, the exhaust rocker was mounted slightly lower in the box than the inlet component.

For both simplicity and quiet running, the single camshaft was driven directly by the crankshaft pinion. Both ends of the camshaft were supported in bronze bushes, one in the crankcase wall, the other in a light-alloy bolted-on case that surrounded the gears. On the outside of the case was the contact-breaker assembly (including the condenser), the points being operated by an extension of the camshaft and incorporating centrifugal automatic control of the ignition timing.

The cam followers featured curved operating faces and moved directly on a common spindle ahead of the camshaft. Of light-alloy tubing, the pushrods were equipped with steel ends, the upper of which embodied the valve-clearance adjusters. The pushrods were quite widely splayed and operated in a single tunnel of figure-eight cross-sections in the cylinder barrel; in the head each pushrod had its own tunnel.

Yet another feature that followed usual AMC design practice was the piston (with a 7.8:1 compression ratio). This was wire wound above the gudgeon pin and had a split skirt. It featured a single scraper ring and a pair of compression rings, the upper of these two being chromium plated and having a taper face for quick bedding in. The piston crown employed a shallow dome and flats, these providing valve-head clearance during the overlap period.

The connecting rod, of 1 per cent chromium steel, measured 5⅜in (136mm) between centres; within the ribbed big-end eye was a hardened-steel sleeve, which formed the roller track. The small-end bush was of aluminium alloy. As for the big-end bearing, this comprised two rows of ¼ × ¼in (6 × 6mm) rollers, ten in each, spaced by a Duralumin cage. Nominal crank-pin diameter was 1.2in (19mm), whilst En351 was employed for the hardened roller track sleeve, on a body of KE805. The crankpin was a parallel press fit in the cast-iron flywheels, the latter being 6½in (165mm) diameter by ⅞in (22mm) wide, and secured by nuts.

Manufactured of Ubas steel and with a journal diameter of ⅞in (22mm), the mainshafts featured flanged inner ends and were a parallel interference fit in the flywheels, each being located by a woodruff key. A pair of ball-race bearings supported the drive-shaft, their inner races spaced by the keyed-in sleeve of the timed crankcase breather, which discharged to the rear of the case. The timing-side bearing, in contrast, was a long phosphor-bronze bush, cut out on its underside to accommodate the oil-pump worm drive.

The engine sprocket was splined on to the drive-side mainshaft, and outboard of this was the rotor of the Wico Pacy AC generator; the stator being in the outer half of the primary chaincase, and both sides of the inner chaincase being dowelled to ensure accuracy of alignment.

The drive-side crankcase-half mated up with the primary chaincase, and the timing-side half blended into a domed cover which carried a circular plate providing access to the contact-breaker assembly.

Lubrication

A reciprocating plunger oil-pump worm, driven from the timing-side main, was similar in design and operation to the type already fitted to other Matchless (and AJS) singles, such as the G3L and G80. This drew oil from a 2½-pint (1.4ltr) oil tank (AMC referred to it as 'a container') which was bolted to the outside of the timing-side crankcase half, ahead of the timing case; the inboard wall of the tank was formed by the crankcase and the filler neck situated at the very front of the crankcase.

Part of the lubricating oil picked up by the supply side of the pump was fed to the worm chamber and thereafter passed through holes in the base of the worm thread into the mainshaft and then to the big-end bearing via drillways. The remainder of the lubricant travelled to the overhead rocker shafts via passages in the cylinder barrel and head. Grooves in the side of the valve-operating arms of the rockers led some of the oil to the valve stems ends – and there was also an adjustable bleed to the inlet valve guide.

Oil drained from the valve compartment down the pushrod tunnels to the timing gear. From the timing chest it overflowed into the crankcase to join the excess thrown out by the big end. The scavenge pump picked up the oil from the bottom of the crankcase and passed it across the rear of the engine to the felt cartridge oil filter, mounted longitudinally in the nearside (left) half of the crankcase and with access to this filter from the front. From the filter the oil returned across ahead of the cylinder and, with the oil filter cap removed, could be seen re-entering the tank.

The G2 two-fifty was launched in spring 1958 and was generally a tidy little machine, weighing in at 325lb (147kg) and able to top 70mph (113km/h).

The Transmission

To quote *The Motor Cycle*: 'The most ingenious single feature of the new models is the combination of the neatness of an integral gearbox with the ease of dismantling or unit replacement afforded by a separate box.'

Adjustment of the primary chain was done in the orthodox British way. The gearbox featured a cylindrical shell that matched up against a similar curvature at the rear of the crankcase; the offside (right) end cover of the gearbox fitted neatly within a hole in the engine side cover. Because the mainshaft lay considerably above the shell axis, rotation of the shell altered the position of the primary-chain centres. The mounting was identical in principle with that widely used for belt-driven dynamos on automobiles.

A pair of substantial steel straps attached under the rear of the crankcase were responsible for holding the gearbox in place. At the upper ends of these straps were eye bolts threaded to take tensioning bolts passing through a bar bridging the two steel plates that embraced the gearbox, and which bolted to the crankcase and frame-seat tube to form the rear mounting of the power unit. A draw bolt of conventional pattern rotated the gearbox after the straps had been loosened. Both the draw bolt and the strap bolts were readily accessible upon removal of a pressed-steel cover plate which was secured by two screws and, curving well round the rear of the gearbox, provided a very neat appearance, giving no indication of what lay beneath. This, of course, only added to the appearance of a full unit-construction design.

Standardization had been achieved by cleverly utilizing the four-speed gear cluster from the Piatti-designed, AMC two-fifty two-stroke single-cylinder machine. These provided internal ratios of 1, 1.30, 1.85 and 2.95:1. The gear change and selector mechanisms were also similar to the two-stroke components, whereas the clutch thrust operation followed that of the heavyweight ohv singles, with the floating cable arm pivoting on a thrust ball, and having on its other face a cam profile bearing on a fixed-centre roller.

Primary drive was by a ⅜ × 0.225in simplex chain running on sprockets with twenty-one and fifty teeth. The clutch employed four friction plates with bonded-on oil-resisting material, and in its centre a vane-type transmission shock absorber embodying rubber blocks.

In the outer half of the primary chaincase were two large holes, with screw-in plugs. The most forward of these holes served as a combined inspection, filling and level orifice, whilst the other provided access to an adjuster at the centre of the clutch pressure plate. Final drive was by a ½ × 0.305in chain running on nineteen (gearbox) and fifty-five (rearwheel) tooth sprockets, giving a top gear ratio of 6.9:1.

The Frame Design

The frame design is best described as the 'composite' type, being a mixture of steel tubing and a fabricated pressed-steel box section that ran under the engine and gearbox assemblies. Actually, had the engine been of true unit construction it could then (as on the Ducati ohc singles) have been used as a fully stressed member and thus dispensed with the entire box section under the engine/gearbox on the AMC design; this would have saved a considerable amount of weight.

The rear subframe was bolted on whilst the rear swinging arm had a pivot pin attached to the offside (right) leg and held by a collar on the nearside left; this spindle ran on bronze bushes. Suspension was provided by a pair of bought-in Girling (adjustable) hydraulically damped shock absorbers at the rear, with a pair of lightweight AMC hydraulically damped front forks raided from the groups' two-stroke spares bin (James and Francis-Barnett).

Wheel Size

In an era when the wheel size was almost universally 19 or 18in, the 17in used for the new AMC two-fifties was notable – although, as *The Motor Cycle* said, it was 'admirably suited to the proportions of the machine'. The 6in (183mm) full-width brake hubs were also taken from the James and Francis-Barnett stock, but were generally agreed to be fully capable of providing good braking performance for the 18bhp, 325lb (147kg), 70mph (113km/h) motorcycle.

Other Details

Other details of the newcomer's specification included a 6in (152mm) Wipac headlamp, in which was mounted a speedometer, ammeter and separate ignition and lighting switches; comprehensive mudguarding; and clutch and front brake controls welded to the handlebar. In standard guise the machine had a deep-section guard over the upper run of the final drive chain, but a fully enclosed chaincase was available as a cost option. This case was divided horizontally and embraced the swinging arm to which the upper and lower halves were bolted; the edges of the halves overlapped to prevent the ingress of road dirt and water. The front end of the case was shielded by a sheet-metal section bolted to the rear of the primary chaincase.

Finish and Prices

The frame, mudguards, stands, headlamp shell and such were finished in gloss black, whilst the 2¾gal (12.5ltr) fuel tank was in Cardinal red with silver lining. The main tank colour was repeated in a flash on each side of the engine outer casings, which also carried a small replica of the tank badge.

The 1959 G2

Engine:	Air-cooled, ohv single with vertical cylinder; alloy head; cast-iron barrel; vertically split aluminium crankcases; fully enclosed valve gear; hairpin valve springs; built-up crankshaft; single gear-driven camshaft; crossover enclosed pushrods; roller-bearing big end
Bore:	69.85mm
Stroke:	64.85mm
Displacement :	248.5cc
Compression ratio:	7.8:1
Lubrication:	Dry sump, plunger worm pump
Ignition:	Battery/coil 6-volt; alternator
Carburettor:	Amal Type 376 1⁄16in
Primary drive:	Duplex chain
Final drive:	Chain
Gearbox:	Four-speed, AMC, adjustable type
Frame:	All-steel construction, brazed and bolted; single main and front tubes; pressed steel under-channel
Front suspension:	AMC lightweight oil-damped telescopic forks
Rear suspension:	Two-piece swinging arm, with oil-damped adjustable twin shock absorbers
Front brake:	6in full-width drum, SLS
Rear brake:	6in full-width drum, SLS
Tyres:	3.25 × 17 front and rear

General Specifications

Wheelbase:	53in (1,346mm)
Ground clearance:	5.5in (140mm)
Seat height:	30in (762mm); 1961 onwards, 30.5in (775mm)
Fuel tank capacity:	2.75gal (12.5ltr); 1960 onwards, 3.25gal (15ltr)
Dry weight:	325lb (147kg)
Maximum power:	18bhp @ 7,200rpm
Top speed:	75mph (120km/h)

It was anticipated that production would begin in May 1958, but initially only for export. Then in mid-June it was announced that production of the G2 (and the AJS Model 14) was underway for the home market. The basic cost of either machine was £157 10s; with UK purchase tax added, this figure went up to £196 9s 8d; or with the optional, full enclosure of the rear chain, £199 12s (including purchase tax).

Performance Testing the G2

So what was the new Matchless G2 two-fifty like out on the road? Well, some indications of its abilities and weaknesses came by courtesy of an exercise carried out by *The Motor Cycle*'s George Wilson; his report appeared in the 26 February 1959 issue, albeit in AJS guise. He began his piece: 'since [the G2's] introduction in March last year, I have looked on it with mixed feelings. Technically the design is undoubtedly right out of the top drawer. But it has always seemed to me to be a modern machine in which the stylist had not gone far enough.' His first impressions were 'good – very good.' He considered that 'navigation was magnificent', and that both brakes were good (the back rather better than the front): they were smooth, and his feeling was that they would never lock the wheels. He also found that the 'engine is beautifully quiet mechanically', and that 'there is powerful punch low down on the rpm scale so that one can trickle in a highish gear.'

Other points that George Wilson found to his liking were, first, a lack of any vibration, and a smooth power delivery. The standard of comfort was 'high throughout' and he 'liked the relationship between the seat and handlebar.'

The G5

In early September 1959, AMC announced a new 348cc (72 × 85.5mm) version of the by now established G2 two-fifty. In the bulk of its details the engine followed its two-fifty ancestry with its *dé saxé* cylinder – the cylinder axis offset forward from the crankshaft axis – and a cylinder head in which the inlet and exhaust tract were oblique to the fore-and-aft line of the engine. The outward appearance of the new power unit was virtually the same as that of the two-fifty, although a distinguishing feature was an exhaust-valve lifter operating on the exhaust rocker.

A major internal difference lay in the crank flywheels which were flat faced and, viewed in side elevation, appeared as right-angled triangles, each with a rounded apex and a semicircular base. Cast iron was the material employed, and the thickness was 15⁄16in (24mm). The flywheel faces were recessed to receive the crankpin nuts. Crankpin diameter was 1½in (38mm), and a Duralumin cage spaced out the two rows of roller, their size and number being identical to the smaller engine size. The compression ratio was 7.5:1 instead of 7.8:1 on the two-fifty.

A larger valve was fitted – a 1⅝in (40mm) – whilst the inlet port size was 1⅛in (28mm); otherwise the two engines were essentially the same. Other changes included fresh gear ratios, 3.25 × 18 front and 3.25 × 18 rear tyres, and the more sturdy Teledraulic front forks from the heavyweight singles and twin-cylinder models. There was also a duplex, rather than a single primary chain, whilst the clutch had been given an extra plate.

Because of these changes the dry weight increased to 350lb (159kg); though this was still 32lb (14.5kg) lighter than the latest G3 single.

Testing the New G5

George Wilson was once again the lucky man amongst *The Motor Cycle*'s staff when he was elected to test the new G5: he took the very first G5 to leave the production line on a 500-mile-plus weekend trip to Llandrindod Wells in mid-Wales for the 25th British Experts Trial. These road impressions appeared in the 10 December 1959 issue.

Compared with the G2, the G5 not only had an extra 100cc, but was also a long-stroke format. This, suggested Wilson, 'contributes largely to the excellent power characteristics.' He then went on to explain what this low-speed punch meant: 'most important of all, you can change up early, and you can accelerate fairly hard without causing offence to drivers being overtaken, or to inhabitants in towns and villages on your route.'

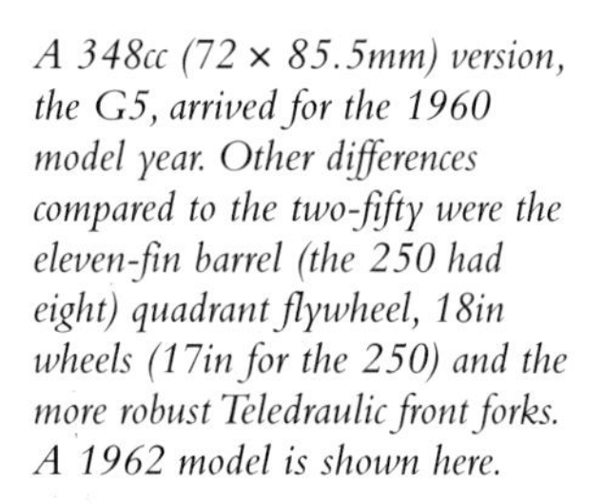

A 348cc (72 × 85.5mm) version, the G5, arrived for the 1960 model year. Other differences compared to the two-fifty were the eleven-fin barrel (the 250 had eight) quadrant flywheel, 18in wheels (17in for the 250) and the more robust Teledraulic front forks. A 1962 model is shown here.

Nevertheless he still found that 'when the whip was being used hard, the Matchless spoke with an over-loud tongue,' and that 'my feeling is that better muffling would be a good thing.' Once again he was impressed by the quietness of the engine:'Mechanical noise was virtually nil. Idling (which it did in true gas-engine style), the power unit is quiet to the point of being exemplary.'

When George Wilson had ridden the bike at first there had been a 'marked low-speed roll', and after a gauge showed there to be only 15lb pressure in the front tube, he concluded that was the answer. However, as he wrote:

> Putting up the pressure brought no improvement. A check revealed the steering head bearing adjustment to be apparently just right. But after the bearing was slackened off by half a flat on the adjusting nut, the handling was transformed. In Wales, and on the swervery on the way there and back, the model could be cranked over hard on wet or dry. The steering was just heavy enough to be truly positive, so that I knew exactly what the front wheel was doing. Even so, I think the handling could be improved even further if the suspension were softer. Under my 10 stone [63.5kg] load the front fork was hard and, at the rear, the suspension legs appeared reluctant also to react at speed below 50mph (80km/h).

With maximum speed in the region of 75mph (120km/h), and a mixture of good torque across the entire rev range and excellent handling, Wilson was able to tuck 200 miles (320km) into four hours with relative ease. He observed that 'in order to keep down exhaust noise, I generally notched top at about 45mph (72km/h)'; but he also found a 'light, impossible-to-beat gear change, and sweet transmission.'

Unfortunately for AMC, new learner laws restricting novices to machines of 250cc and below virtually killed off the traditional British 350cc four-stroke, and as the 1960s unfolded, this proved to be the case with the Matchless G5.

Detail Alterations: the 1961 Range

When the 1961 range was announced at the end of August 1960, it was very much a case of detail alterations, rather than major innovations, to the entire Matchless family, including the G2 and G5 singles.

One change concerned crankcase breathing arrangements. Previously the timed, rotary breather vented to the atmosphere via a hollow bolt in the nearside (left) crankcase half. This vent was now direct, and the hollow bolt replaced by a solid bolt repositioned to one side of the breather.

To improve top-gear engagement, the pin-type dogs on the sliding pinion, which mated with elongated holes in the fixed, output pinion, were exchanged for dogs with more normal segmental teeth. The side faces of the teeth had been given a slight reverse taper so there was less tendency for the dogs to slide out of engagement. In a further

The 1961 G5

Engine:	Air-cooled, ohv single with vertical cylinder; alloy head; cast-iron barrel; vertically split aluminium crankcases; fully enclosed valve gear; hairpin valve springs; built-up crankshaft; single gear-driven camshaft; crossover enclosed pushrods; roller-bearing big end
Bore:	72mm
Stroke:	85.5mm
Displacement:	348cc
Compression ratio:	7:1
Lubrication:	Dry sump, plunger worm pump
Ignition:	Battery/coil 6-volt; alternator
Carburettor:	Amal Monobloc 389/42 1⅛in
Primary drive:	Duplex chain
Final drive:	Chain
Gearbox:	Four-speed, AMC, adjustable type
Frame:	All-steel construction, brazed and bolted; single main and front tubes; pressed steel under-channel
Front suspension:	AMC Teledraulic forks; two-way oil-damped
Rear suspension:	Two-piece swinging arm, with oil-damped adjustable twin shock absorbers
Front brake:	6in; SLS; full-width drum
Rear brake:	6in; SLS; full-width drum
Tyres:	3.25 × 19 front and rear

General Specifications

Wheelbase:	54in (1,372mm)
Ground clearance:	6in (152mm)
Seat height:	29.5in (749mm); 1962, 30.5in (774mm)
Fuel tank capacity:	3.25 gal (15ltr)
Dry weight:	340lb (154kg)
Maximum power:	21bhp @ 7,200rpm
Top speed:	76mph (122km/h)

gearbox modification, a bronze bush was fitted to the layshaft bottom-gear pinion, thus obviating steel-to-steel contact.

But a potentially more worrying aspect of the G2 and G5-type gearbox design was never rectified. This was essentially due to the cylindrical nature of the shell itself and the location of the gears near the very top of this, which meant that anything less than the 3 full pints of lubricating oil could spell trouble. Another weakness was an appetite for gearchange springs. All this was a great pity, because when operating normally, the gearchange quality was excellent.

Previously only supplied as a cost option, the rear chaincase was now fitted as standard equipment. In addition, all AMC single-cylinder models had benefited from a modification intended to strengthen the drive to the rotary-reciprocating oil pump. Both the crankshaft worm and the pump-drive pinion featured a redesigned tooth, which brought them into closer engagement.

Prices, on 27 August 1960, were £203 17s 2d for the G2 248cc, and £221 19s for the G5 348cc; both of these included UK purchase tax.

Then in November 1960, on the eve of the London Earls Court Show, came a sports version of the G2, the G2S – although there were no real changes except for lower handlebars and what *The Motor Cycle* described as 'oceans of chromium plating'.

For 1962: Monitor and Matador

For the 1962 model year the two-fifty G2 became the Monitor, and the three-fifty G5 the Matador, though this was really just another ploy by AMC to generate more sales interest in a depressed market. The G2S was included in the Monitor tag.

To prevent the rider's foot from fouling the footrest when starting, a longer kickstart lever was used on the G2/G5 series. On the three-fifties there was an improved crankcase breather, and a change from ball- to roller-type bearing for the inner drive-side main bearing.

For the sports version of the two-fifty Monitor there was a redesigned handlebar, reducing the overall width to 24¾in (629mm); this was known as the 'ace-type', with long straight portions at the downward ends of the central curved section.

Prices (including UK taxes) at 14 September 1961 were £204 19s 2d for the G2 Monitor, £212 5s 7d for the G2S Monitor Sports, and £220 4s 2d for the G5 Matador.

A 1961 Matchless G2 S (Sport). In this case 'Sport' only meant extra chrome; this bike has touring handlebars.

Performance Testing the Matador

A report on the testing of the latest 348cc G5 Matador appeared in the 28 September 1961 issue of *The Motor Cycle*; the basic input of the tester's findings are related below:

> The G5 Matchless three-fifty offers a skilful blend of the most attractive qualities of both larger and smaller capacities. As against the larger it scores on lower initial cost, cheaper insurance and reduced fuel consumption. Compared with smaller models, it has the edge on performance – especially power in the medium-speed edge – particularly as it is not much heavier, and is generally more suited to sustained hard work. Although the Matador has an affinity with the G2 Monitor two-fifty and is, therefore, lighter than earlier Matchless three-fifties, it has a robust, comforting 'big-bike' feel. The riding position is not cramped and allows a relaxed, easy posture.

Unlike the two-fifty, the clutch and front brake levers (and the handlebar) were fully adjustable. There was again praise for the bike's handling and roadholding. During the test the Matador was ridden under a variety of weather conditions over many different sorts of surface, and at all times the steering and general stability were well above average. The tester again:

> At first there seemed a trace of heaviness in the steering at very low speeds, but it went unnoticed as one became more familiar with the machine which could, in fact, be ridden feet-up without difficulty at a walking pace. At the other end of the scale, the Matador could be laid into main-road curves and bends at really high speeds, yet it would hold its line without waver. Swift changes of direction could be achieved effortlessly, thanks to the lightish weight and excellent all-round handling characteristics.

As regards performance, a highest one-way speed of 76mph (122km/h) was achieved. But of far more importance was the bike's cruising abilities:

> Given average road conditions, the G5 would hustle along indefinitely at between 65 and 70mph [105 and 113km/h] as its cruising speed, without the engine showing signs of tiring. High-frequency vibration could be felt through the handlebar and footrests at speeds above about 60mph [96km/h] in top gear and at corresponding engine revolutions in the indirect gears, but the effect on the hands would, it was

> thought, be reduced almost completely by handlebar grips of a more resilient type than the smooth plastic ones fitted as standard.
>
> As regards starting, throughout the test the Matchless could be started easily whether the engine was cold or hot. An exhaust-valve lifter enabled the piston to be eased past compression, after which a single swinging kick sufficed on every occasion.

As when ridden earlier by George Wilson, 'mechanical quietness was markedly above average; even when the engine was cold there was no piston slap.' Gearchange quality, braking performance, lights, and a clutch that freed instantly all received positive comments.

On the debit side the tester observed: 'A more elaborate speedometer would be justified. The one fitted is of the non-trip type, and the total mileage recorder reads only to the nearest mile. Speed readings were approximately 5 per cent fast throughout the range.'

The test ended by saying: 'Finished in tartan red and black, and with its smooth, cranny-free engine-unit castings, the Matador is of attractive appearance. It offers lively, lusty performance, excellent brakes, steering and road holding. It is an excellent all-round proposition.'

The G2 CSR

Next in May 1962 came a new sports two-fifty, the 248cc G2 CSR. Compared to the existing but soon-to-be-axed G2S, this newcomer had more power, better braking, and the more robust Teledraulic front forks from the G5. There was also a larger carburettor (a 1⅛in 389 Monobloc), bigger inlet valve, longer induction tract, higher compression ratio (8:1), stronger valve springs, steel flywheels and stiffer connecting rod and crankpin.

As a result of the above changes it had been possible to raise the gear ratios. The front brake was on a British Hub Company light-alloy hub with a cast-iron drum shrunk in. The new 6in (152mm) front brake now sported a light-alloy shoe plate with cast-in air scoops. However, on the test machine the slots had not been opened, so air could not help in cooling. It was considered

The G2 CSR Super Sport two-fifty was introduced in May 1962. This featured a tuned engine, raised gearing, 17in wheels, Teledraulic forks, British Hub Co. alloy full-width hubs, chrome mudguards and abbreviated chainguard, and lower handlebars. This is a 1963 model.

that this was why the front brake 'suffered from fade during heavy applications'.

During the performance testing *The Motor Cycle* achieved a highest one-way speed of 75mph (120km/h); this was virtually the same as the G5 three-fifty. However, the bigger engine still scored on increased pulling power in the lower and mid-range.

Although a considerable improvement on the 'S' version, the G2 CSR was still no match for machines such as the Italian Aermacchi Ala Verde or Ducati Daytona, or the new Japanese invader, the Honda CB72 Super Sport. But compared with the majority of other British two-fifties of the period it was a decent performer – and a good-looking one, too. It was, as *The Motor Cycle* said:

> ...no cramped lightweight. First impression on straddling the Monitor Super Sports is of the 'man-size' dimensions of the riding position. The handlebar is virtually flat and slightly downswept at the grips – this was felt to be a good compromise between sporty styling and practicability, and results in a forward lean rather than a semi-crouch.

LEFT: May 1963, and pop singer Craig Douglas is seen here receiving instruction on how to ride a motorcycle (a G2 CSR) from AMC works motocross star Vic Eastwood (in the Barbour suit on pillion).

BELOW: A 1966 G2 CSR, with changes introduced for that season of alloy mudguards and swept-back exhaust pipe. In addition the cigar-shaped silencer had arrived for 1965, together with coil valve springs. Production of the G2 CSR, the last remaining Matchless 'Lightweight' model, ceased in July 1966.

The 1963 G2 CSR

Engine:	Air-cooled ohv single with vertical cylinder; alloy head; cast-iron barrel; vertically split aluminium crankcases; fully enclosed valve gear; hairpin valve springs; built-up crankshaft; single gear-driven camshaft; crossover enclosed pushrods; roller-bearing big end
Bore:	69.85mm
Stroke:	64.85mm
Displacement:	248.5cc
Compression ratio:	8:1; 1965 onwards, 9:1
Lubrication:	Dry sump, plunger worm pump
Ignition:	Battery/coil 6-volt; alternator
Carburettor:	Amal Monobloc 389 1⅛in
Primary drive:	Duplex chain
Final drive:	Chain
Gearbox:	Four-speed, AMC, adjustable type
Frame:	All-steel construction, brazed and bolted; single main and front tubes; pressed steel under-channel
Front suspension:	AMC Teledraulic forks; two-way oil-damped
Rear suspension:	Two-piece swinging arm, with oil-damped adjustable twin shock absorbers
Front brake:	British Hub full-width alloy drum, SLS
Rear brake:	British Hub full-width alloy drum, SLS
Tyres:	3.25 × 17 front and rear
General Specifications	
Wheelbase:	53in (1,346mm)
Ground clearance:	6.5in (165mm)
Seat height:	30in (762mm)
Fuel tank capacity:	3.25gal (14ltr)
Dry weight:	328lb (149kg)
Maximum power:	20bhp @ 7,400rpm
Top speed:	82mph (132km/h)

In other words, here was a machine that provided plenty of room and probably more comfort than could be expected of a lightweight sportster. *The Motor Cycle* tester ended by summing up in the following manner: 'The G2 CSR is not temperamental and is a lively, attractive mount. It will undoubtedly appeal to the rider who wants sporting lines plus useful performance.'

End of the Line

Several models in the Matchless/AJS range had been dropped when the 1963 models were announced at the end of September 1962. Chief amongst these were four lightweights: the AJS 14 Sapphire Sports, the Matchless G2S Monitor Sports, the AJS Model 8 Senator and the Matchless G5 Matador. The two-fifties were dropped in favour of the much improved CSR versions, whilst the three-fifties had become victims of a major drop in sales following the introduction of the new learner laws restricting new riders to a maximum of 250cc. A few months later, in July 1963, the axe fell too on the standard G2 two-fifty. This left only the sporting CSR.

In June 1964 came a class victory at Thruxton, albeit by an AJS 14CSR, rather than its Matchless brother. This unexpected victory in the teeth of serious foreign competition was gained by Peter Williams (son of the factory's chief development engineer, Jack) and Tony Wood. Visually, the only major change was the fitment of a 7R racing seat; internally, however, there were serious questions as to just how far from stock his engine was. It certainly had a fair turn of speed and lasted the distance.

Changes for the 1965 model year, with only the G2 CSR two-fifty remaining in the lightweight range, were as follows:

- compression ratio increased to 9.5:1;
- coil-valve springs replaced the hairpin type;
- closer ratio gears;
- cigar-shaped silencer, with no tailpipe.

A year later, when the 1966 range was announced, the G2 CSR was mechanically unchanged, but now came with alloy mudguards and a swept-back, 'Gold Star' pattern exhaust header pipe. Then in mid-July 1966 the last G2 CSR left the Plumstead production line, and its departure marked the end of the lightweight family.

13 Colin Jordan Seeley

The Seeley name will always be important in any story charting the fortunes of AMC (Associated Motor Cycles). Throughout his motorcycling career, C. J. Seeley was always closely connected to the Matchless marque, first as a competitor and dealer, and then as manufacturer when he took over the rights to build the Matchless G50 (and AJS 7R) when the Plumstead works finally went into receivership.

Colin Seeley was born on 2 January 1936 at Crayford, in Kent. From his early childhood, motorcycles were very much a way of life in the Seeley household. Colin learned to ride on his father Percy's Vincent Rapide V-twin sidecar outfit at fourteen in 1950; he passed his driving test to ride a bike a couple of years later, in 1952. As proof of how keen he was to become part of the motorcycle industry, the young Seeley, at fifteen years of age, gave up an engineering career to join Dartford dealers Schwieso Brothers, as a mechanic; Harold and Les Schwieso had been leading grass-track riders at their local Brands Hatch circuit.

In 1954, at eighteen years of age, Colin started his first motorcycle business venture, a repair shop in Belvedere, Kent; two years later he opened his

Colin Seeley, passengered by Wally Rawlings, with their Matchless G50 sidecar racing outfit at Oulton Park in the spring of 1963. With his close association with the AMC factory, it was perhaps inevitable that Colin should take over the racing side of the empire when it crashed in 1966.

LEFT: Colin Seeley's first 'works' rider was the experienced Derek Minter, seen here on a Seeley G50 Mark 1 at Snetterton in early spring 1966.

BELOW: 'Seeley 500' logo.

first motorcycle showroom, and was appointed main agent for Matchless and AJS. This began Seeley's long association with the AMC works in Plumstead Road, Woolwich, in south-east London. Other agencies soon followed, including at various times Francis-Barnett, Ariel, Velocette, Greeves and NSU, plus sidecars from Busmar, Canterbury, Watsonian and Wessex.

Competition Successes

The name 'Colin Seeley' first began to appear in many sporting motorcycle programmes in 1957. His first competition motorcycle was a Triumph T100C Trophy, with which he took part in scrambles, sprints, hill climbs and grass-track events. With 'Colin Seeley – The Rider Agent' proudly painted on his company's pick-up truck, he then turned to a Greeves two-stroke, riding at Canada Heights near Swanley, Kent, at that venue's inaugural meeting.

In 1961 he rode his first Matchless G50-engined machine with a Canterbury racing sidecar, and finished a brilliant sixth in his first Isle of Man TT, averaging 77.93mph (125.39km/h) for the four-lap, 150.92-mile (242.83km) race. This was a major turning point in his life; as he recalled to the author recently: 'What a proud moment for me, my passenger Wally Rawlings and the AMC factory.' Two more TT silver replicas were to follow on the Matchless, with third and sixth places in 1962 and 1963 respectively.

Colin Seeley's racing career then moved up a gear with the purchase of a BMW Rennsport outfit, and a leap on to the world stage. Seeley and Rawlings finished third overall in the 1964 World Championship series; their best placings

After Derek Minter, the next rider to receive official Seeley backing was John Blanchard. John is aboard a Seeley G50 at Brands Hatch, 24 March 1967.

were victory in the Dutch TT at Assen, and runner-up in the Isle of Man TT. Another third place in the championship table came in 1966, with runner-up position in France, and third places in both Belgium and West Germany.

Meanwhile on the commercial front, the first Seeley G50 Matchless and 7R AJS racing solos appeared in 1966; these were ridden by Derek Minter and John Blanchard that season on the British short circuits. The latter rode in the 1966 TT, finishing fourth on his Seeley G50 and sixth on the smaller-engined 7R-powered bike. John Cooper took over the original Seeley G50 in 1967, and rode it to considerable success over the next few seasons; he is still the owner of the same machine today.

Colin Seeley Manufacturer

When the AMC works went into liquidation later in 1966, all the racing assets of the group (Matchless, AJS and Norton) were bought out by Colin Seeley Racing Developments. The Norton side was later sold on to John Tickle in 1969. Based at Forge Works, Stapley Road, Belvedere, Colin Seeley Racing Developments soon built up an enviable reputation amongst racers not just in Britain, but all around the world, for its high standard of craftsmanship. In his first prototype Colin Seeley essentially followed a specification as outlined here:

- AMC G50 Matchless (or 7R AJS) engine;

John Blanchard; he also rode the four-cylinder German URS-engined Seeley. To produce the latter, Colin Seeley worked in collaboration with Helmut Fath, the designer of the engine.

Colin Seeley (left) and co-director Wally Rawlings, the latter Colin's former sidecar passenger; by 1967, when this picture was taken, Rawlings was responsible for G50 engine development.

Blanchard (Seeley G50) on his way to finishing runner-up in the 500cc class of the Irish North-West 200 race on 20 May 1967.

The Seeley stand at the London Earls Court Show in November 1967. At centre stage is a Seeley G50 Mark 3; at right, a four-cylinder URS-engined bike.

- AMC four-speed racing gearbox and clutch;
- Manx Norton Roadholder (racing) front forks;
- Manx Norton swinging arm;
- Robinson full-width front brake;
- Manx Norton conical rear brake;
- Dunlop 19in alloy rims;
- Dunlop triangular racing tyres;
- Girling rear shock absorbers;
- Seeley duplex full-cradle frame;
- Seeley fairing, tank and seat; aluminium mudguards;
- Smith racing tachometer;
- Seeley aluminium central oil tank;
- low-level exhaust system.

Important changes to specifications were made almost immediately; these included 18in rims and tyres, and a choice of four-, five- or six-speed gearboxes (thanks to an agreement with the Austrian Schafleitner concern). A hi-level exhaust system that exited on the nearside (left) of the bike was used at first, but this was soon abandoned.

Originally the price of either a G50 or 7R Seeley was £695 (February 1966), but by the time production of actual customer machines (as opposed to works development models for the likes of Minter and Blanchard) began in August 1966, a complete four-speed Seeley cost around £725 (depending upon the exact specification ordered by the customer). A six-speed Schafleitner gearbox was an additional £125. Even so, as Colin has revealed to the author, it was hard to make a profit, and in fact Seeley Racing Developments' first year of operations ended with a £5,000 loss. However, after a concerted effort, in the second year of operations a 'relatively modest' profit was recorded. In 1967, Colin Seeley also formed a connection with Helmet Fath, to build a Seeley-framed URS four-cylinder solo racer. This was ridden by John Blanchard, though he was later to say this had been a 'mistake'.

Developments in the Sixties

By the end of 1967, at the annual Earls Court Show in London, the Mark 2 Seeley was launched. This was different because its chassis, in Colin's own words, had been 'lightened, tidied up and made much neater in appearance; it remains my own favourite to this day.' The Mark 2 machines were built and sold from the beginning of 1968 until late 1969. The Mark 3 arrived during mid-1969, and production overlapped between Marks 2 and 3, depending upon customer preference.

This coincided with the decision by Colin and his co-director, Wally Rawlings, to drop the AJS 7R engine in favour of the newly released Japanese Yamaha TR2 engine in the 350cc class. This was simply a speed issue – even though the 1968 and 1969 500cc British Champion (on a Seeley G50) Dave Croxford described the Seeley 7R as the nicest machine he had ever ridden. But quite simply the 7R motor had become outpaced by the Yamaha twins. Colin Seeley, talking in December 1970, said: 'We had no alternative but to drop the 7R and cash in on the Yamaha by introducing the Yamsel design. The Mark 3 frame had been developed with the help of Seeley rider John Cooper.'

The Yamsel used the latest Mark 3-type frame, and although the Mark 3 was offered with both the Yamaha and G50 engines, Cooper still favoured the full loop Mark 2 chassis for his five-hundred mount.

By 1970 there were sixteen members of the Colin Seeley team, including himself and Wally Rawlings, plus general manager Ken Burnside (eighteen years with AMC), storeman Peter Engleton, and Colin's secretary Mrs Marie Bull. The two-man welding shop comprised Jack Wren, who had twelve years' welding experience with AMC, Jack being in charge of the Seeley frame department; and ex-AMC man Denny Barnes. They were geared up to produce 200 Seeley frames each year. Jack Wren, who was held in high regard by Colin Seeley, died on 6 January 2002, aged sixty-five.

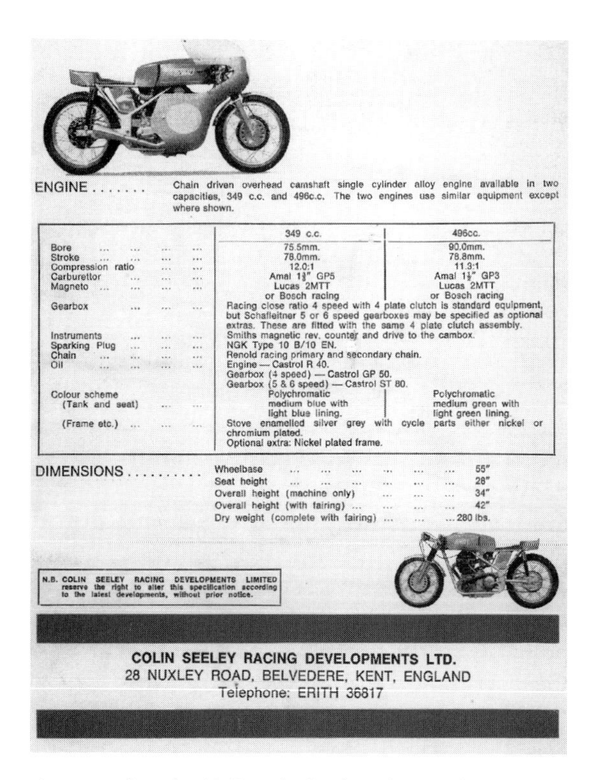

ENGINE .... Chain driven overhead camshaft single cylinder alloy engine available in two capacities, 349 c.c. and 496c.c. The two engines use similar equipment except where shown.

	349 c.c.	496cc.
Bore	75.5mm.	90.0mm.
Stroke	78.0mm.	78.8mm.
Compression ratio	12.0:1	11.3:1
Carburettor	Amal $1\frac{3}{8}''$ GP5	Amal $1\frac{1}{2}''$ GP3
Magneto	Lucas 2MTT or Bosch racing	Lucas 2MTT or Bosch racing
Gearbox	Racing close ratio 4 speed with 4 plate clutch is standard equipment, but Schafleitner 5 or 6 speed gearboxes may be specified as optional extras. These are fitted with the same 4 plate clutch assembly.	
Instruments	Smiths magnetic rev. counter and drive to the cambox.	
Sparking Plug	NGK Type 10 B/10 EN.	
Chain	Renold racing primary and secondary chain.	
Oil	Engine — Castrol R 40. Gearbox (4 speed) — Castrol GP 50. Gearbox (5 & 6 speed) — Castrol ST 80.	
Colour scheme (Tank and seat)	Polychromatic medium blue with light blue lining.	Polychromatic medium green with light green lining.
(Frame etc.)	Stove enamelled silver grey with cycle parts either nickel or chromium plated. Optional extra: Nickel plated frame.	

DIMENSIONS ....

Wheelbase	55"
Seat height	28"
Overall height (machine only)	34"
Overall height (with fairing)	42"
Dry weight (complete with fairing)	280 lbs.

N.B. COLIN SEELEY RACING DEVELOPMENTS LIMITED reserve the right to alter this specification according to the latest developments, without prior notice.

COLIN SEELEY RACING DEVELOPMENTS LTD.
28 NUXLEY ROAD, BELVEDERE, KENT, ENGLAND
Telephone: ERITH 36817

An extract from the 1968 Seeley brochure showing the Mark 2 (full cradle frame) models, with 350cc AJS 7R and 500cc Matchless G50 engines.

The Mark 3 Frame Design

The Mark 3 frames differed from the two earlier marks in having no cradles from the steering head downwards, and back under the engine and transmission. Instead there were rails going back horizontally from the steering head to the top rear suspension mountings, and also downwards at approximately 45 degrees from the top tank rails some halfway from the steering head to the beginning of the seat. The tubes ran either side to the swinging-arm pivot, so in effect the engine, gearbox and clutch assemblies were mounted in massive plates (which encircled the gearbox), the carburettor being placed between these tubes. The result was a lean and low motorcycle. By this time the swinging arm was also of Seeley design.

RIGHT: *By 1970 the Mark 3 Seeley had arrived, the main change being the deletion of the front down-tubes. Amazingly, the revised frame offered just as good handling, although weight was reduced by some 25 per cent.*

BELOW: *Crystal Palace, 30 March 1970: Seeley G50 riders Alan Barnett (10) and John Blanchard (2) battle it out for supremacy.*

New Ideas for the Seventies

Although the G50 Matchless-based Seeley engine continued in production into the 1970s, as the new decade dawned it was to come under increasing pressure. The first of these challenges had come from the Italian Linto machine in 1969; essentially this was a pair of Aermacchi ohv heads and cylinders in a common crankcase. But although fast, it was very expensive and, more worryingly, exceedingly unreliable.

Then at the beginning of the 1970s a new breed of five-hundred was introduced to challenge the long-running Matchless-based Seeley G50 engine. The first of these were the Kawasaki triple and the Suzuki twin – plus over-bored (usually 352cc) Yamaha TR2s. But all of these were very much stop-gap efforts, as from the middle of the decade both Suzuki and Yamaha came up with four-cylinder 500 two-strokes, which could be purchased by paying customers.

So in the 1970s the Seeley organization was forced to change direction and consider other power units. These included the Dr Gordon Blair QUB (Queens University Belfast) 500 single-cylinder two-stroke (1970), the Suzuki T500 Daytona (1972), and various big twins of 750cc from Norton, Triumph (and also the triple) and Weslake. Later still came a succession of Honda-powered bikes, including a 200cc ohc single (for

ABOVE: A newly manufactured Seeley G50 engine, c. 1971.
RIGHT: Slipper piston.

ABOVE: Crankshaft, cylinder barrel and double oil pumps.
RIGHT: Crankcase and timing cover.

ABOVE: Camshaft.
BELOW: Cambox assembly, with rocker arms.

Tony Osborne on a Seeley G50 Mark 2 at Brands Hatch in 1971.

Kevin Cowley cranks his Seeley over near the limit; 1971.

Seeley G50 rider John Taylor (2) takes the inside line at Thruxton from Ducati-mounted Alan Dunscombe (16); July 1971.

A Seeley rider about to bumpstart his machine into life during an early morning practice session for the 1971 Isle of Man TT races.

trials) and various across-the-frame, four-cylinder models for fast roadwork, the latter being produced in 750, 900 and 1,000cc engine sizes.

The End of an Era

In their 3 October 1972 issue, *Motor Cycle News* carried the headline 'Final death of the G50'. *MCN* went on to say: 'It's the end of an era. Colin Seeley has decided, quite sensibly as far as running a business is concerned, that the 500cc single-cylinder engine has reached the end of its useful life, and that it is not a financial proposition to make any more complete G50 machines.' In fact the last two genuine Seeley G50s (as compared to replica machines built by others more recently) had left the firm's Upper Belvedere, Kent, workshop in June 1972, some three years after Seeley had axed production of the 350cc 7R version of the legendary overhead camshaft engine.

By the time the last G50 Seeley was built, the design had reached the Mark 4 stage. Exact numbers have never been disclosed, even though Colin still has the original production ledgers. However, he says that even in his autobiography

A small number of Seeley G50 Condor roadsters were built and sold during the early 1970s; note the dynamo at the front of the crankcases.

Tony Rogers negotiates the hairpin section at Mallory Park in 1972. Note the non-standard, hi-level exhaust system.

he will not reveal this information. The marks and their production periods are as follows:

Mark 1: 1966–67;
Mark 2: 1968–69 (launched at the 1967 Earls Court Show);
Mark 3: 1969–71;
Mark 4: 1972–mid-1973.

There was also the Seeley G50 Condor road bike (*see* photograph on page 195).

It is also worth noting that the Seeley G50 racers built from late 1969 onwards used an exceptional long and tapered megaphone exhaust, designed by Dr Gordon Blair in Belfast.

At the time of the announcement in October 1972, Colin Seeley blamed the ACU (Auto Cycle Union) for 'a reluctance to make a stand on keeping the 500cc class for full five-hundreds.' This was in reference to the widespread use of what were essentially 350 Yamaha machines entered as 352cc. Seeley had continued by saying 'I have turned down orders for new G50s since deciding to give up production, but the real demand is not there any more.'

So from then on, frame kits, forks, disc brakes and other cycle parts were to form the full production capacity of the Seeley business for the remainder of the 1970s; complete bikes were usually powered by Japanese engines. Also during the mid- and late 1970s Colin Seeley was actively involved with the Brabham car concern.

Then came the worst recession in motorcycle history, and Colin Seeley bowed out altogether as a manufacturer.

ABOVE: The year is 1981, and the reunion is between John Blanchard and Colin Seeley (right) at Brands Hatch.

LEFT: Blanchard in action at Brands Hatch in 1981. The classic movement had arrived a couple of years earlier. Soon, many more Seeleys would take to the tracks again, both old and newly manufactured.

ABOVE: Stephen Whinn competing on his unfaired Seeley G50 Mark 4 at Carnaby Raceway, East Yorkshire, in 1982.

RIGHT: Motor Cycle News *'Man of the Year' John Cooper came out of retirement in July 1986 to parade his Seeley G50 Mark 2 at Donington Park.*

LEFT: A Seeley G50 Mark 4 with Gardner carburettor and Blair exhaust. This fairing-off view provides an excellent amount of detail.

BELOW: Former Suzuki world champion Hugh Anderson, with the Fred Walmsley Replica Seeley G50 ridden by Bill Swallow in classic racing events during the early 1990s.

Racing Team Manager

However, this was certainly not the end of Colin Seeley the man. With his vast experience and professionalism, his talent played a vital role in the Brabham Formula 1 car team. Then in the 1990s he was the man behind the 1989–95 Duckham's Oils/Crighton Norton Rotary racing team (which followed the John Player sponsored effort of the late 1980s and early 1990s). With riders of the calibre of Ian Simpson, Phil Borley, Mark Farmer and Jim Moodie, the squad made a big impact, including winning the 1994 national championship – officially known as the 'HEAT Supercup for TT Superbikes'.

During 1995 Simpson and Borley rode for what was then the official British Castrol Honda Superbike Team with Honda RC45 V-fours, managed by Colin Seeley. For the Isle of Man that year Colin rebuilt one of the RC45s for Joey Dunlop, on which the Ulsterman won the Senior TT. Of the official team riders for the 1995 TT, Philip McCullen won the Formula 1 race.

During 1997 Colin established the GSE Superbike Team with rider Sean Emmett, then in 1998–99 he helped the up-and-coming Australian rider Karl Muggeridge on his way into the World Super Sport championship series. Even as late as 2003 Colin was associated with Paul Smart's son Scott, at the BSB (British Super Bike) series. Today he runs Seeley Sport Management, and amongst his clients are Bonhams, the well-known auctioneers, for whom he acts as a consultant.

Without any doubt Colin Seeley has carved himself a special place in motorcycle history with a unique combination of hard work, enthusiasm and, most of all, an exceedingly high standard in everything he has attempted in his fifty-year involvement in the sport. But it was AMC and Matchless in particular who played a vital role in this unique story.

14 The Harris Rotax G80

In 1987, Harris formed Matchless Motorcycles Ltd at his works in Newton Abbot, Devon, to build the Rotax-powered G80 single.

During the mid-1980s Les Harris, owner of the Racing Spares Company – producers of components for British bikes – purchased a licence from the owner of the Triumph brand name, John Bloor, to produce the T140 Bonneville seven-fifty vertical twin. However, obviously knowing that it was Bloor's intention to launch an entirely new range of Triumph models, Harris realized that this venture only had a limited lifespan, and so formed a new company, Matchless Motorcycles. Production was based at facilities on the Decoy Industrial Estate in Newton Abbot, Devon, in fact from where Triumph Bonneville production had been undertaken from 1985. The Matchless operation began in mid-1987.

As with the re-launched Bonneville, the man in charge of design and production was Brian Jones. Other key personnel included Les Harris

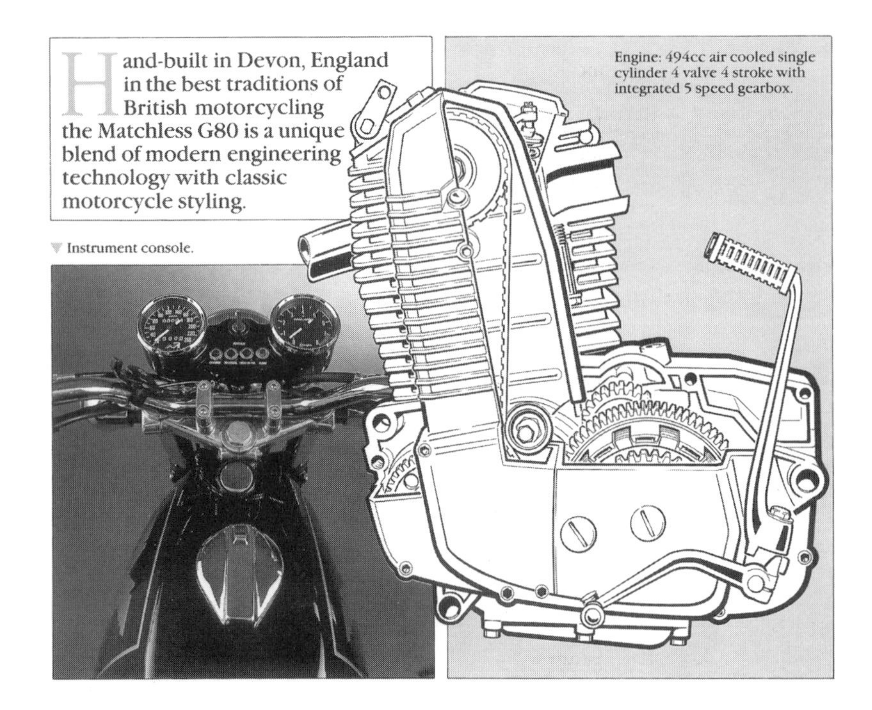

LEFT: *The Austrian-made, 494cc (89 × 79.4mm) sohc Rotax engine, with belt-driven cams, gear primary drive and five-speed gearbox in unit with the engine.*

BELOW: *Steeply angled rear shocks and 160mm drum rear brake.*

himself as managing director, his wife Shirley as a director, Keith Tiffin as company secretary and John Birch as purchase controller. In the new company's launch folder could be found the following statement: 'Matchless is the oldest motorcycle marque in Great Britain. With this in mind we have designed a classic-style motorcycle available in two versions, with or without electric start.'

The launch itself took place in Newton Abbot on 22 June 1987, and was attended by a collection of press and trade plus, as Frank Westworth described for *Motorcycle Enthusiast* magazine, 'sundry unidentifiable local dignitaries'. And Westworth continued:

> We had a good time, were treated to a very brief spin on a rather battered example of the revived Famous Name (the G80!) and were the recipients of a series of well-meaning but meaningless stream of platitudes from the assorted dignitaries, who were more concerned with being seen to be concerned about local unemployment than they were about the re-emergence of the Matchless name.

The 1987 G80 Matchless

But what about the motorcycle itself? As Frank Westworth said in the December 1987 issue of *Motorcycle Enthusiast*: 'The 1987 G80 Matchless is a new motorcycle. That is to say, it is not just an attempt at updating a one-million-year-old design sufficiently, on minute resources, to permit it to stagger through the morass of current legislation.'

There is no doubt that the reason to use the already existing Austrian Rotax engine was financial, because it costs far more to design this major component part of a motor vehicle than

Rotax

Rotax, makers of the Harris G80, began life as a small family engineering concern shortly after the beginning of the twentieth century in the German township of Dresden, manufacturing rear-wheel assemblies for pedal cycles. Then in 1920, it was reformed as a public company, as Rotax Werk. But there was still no hint of engine production until the 1930s, when the concern was acquired by Fichtel & Sachs.

Still located in Germany, but now residing at Schweinfurt, Rotax became involved in the manufacture of torpedo components for the military, leading up to the outbreak of World War II. During the conflict Rotax relocated to Austria due to heavy bombing; then at the end of the war it was registered as a German-controlled organization and placed under public administration in the American zone.

A move to its present location of Gunskirchen came in 1947 when the original owners of the factory were allowed to return. But it was not to be for another eight years that Rotax became an Austrian company as part of a compensation agreement between the major powers involved in the war.

Following this agreement, the Austrian government returned Rotax to the private sector by selling it to the Vienna-based Lohnerwerke organization – and this was how things remained until 1970 when the Canadian-based Bombardier Group took control of Lohnerwerke and thus Rotax.

The merger created Bombardier-Rotax Gmbh, with the Gunskirchen plant building a truly vast range of engines not only for motorcycles, but also for snowmobiles and agricultural uses, whilst the Vienna production facilities were used to manufacture tramcar parts and exhaust systems. Production at Rotax's Gunskirchen plant in 1970 reached 267,300 engines, with just over 1,000 workers being employed. But since then the workforce has decreased due to automation and new machine tools by Bombardier-Rotax.

Strangely, Rotax has never sold complete motorcycles; instead it has become Europe's leading proprietary engine supplier to the two-wheel industry; its clients include Aprilia BMW, Colton, MZ and, of course, the Harris Matchless concern. In addition, Rotax supplies both four- and two-stroke engines for all forms of motorcycle sport, as well as the world of karting.

anything else. There was also a large slice of Italian sourced parts, including the brakes, wheels, suspension and carburettor. So what was actually British? The answer was the frame. And here, Westworth considered that 'Brian Jones has produced a chassis that matches the characteristics of the power unit to perfection. The Matchless steers superbly, even when carting my ample self and rather less ample wife along!'

Interestingly, the frame of the Harris G80 contained the engine's lubricating oil in the box-section top and front down-tubes. It unbolted forward of the engine and below the swinging arm to permit engine removal. The frame also carried the box-section swinging arm, which itself featured a pair of steeply canted shocks. Strangely the frame, including the box-section top frame tube carrying oil, was very similar to the Italian Harley-Davidson two-strokes of the mid-1970s.

The improvements in the new bike were obvious; and as Frank Westworth pointed out, 'Those who wonder what progress has been made in the twenty years or so since the last G80 Matchless was bolted together, should swallow the prejudice and take a look.' First and foremost was the four-valve single overhead cam engine that was smooth, torquey and refined – 'civilized' describes it well. It was also considerably quieter, both mechanically and in its exhaust, than the pushrod engines that powered the original Plumstead-built G80s.

The 'new' G80's electrical system was another area that was hugely improved over the old: it was now a 12-volt system with electronic ignition, which meant decent lights (featuring a 60/45 watt headlamp) and reliability. Electric start was also a cost option – something that owners of Plumstead models could only dream of!

Yet another cost option was the fitment of a second front disc. A period road tester had this to say of the original set-up: 'Braking is another area where competence, rather than brilliance, is the

Italian Paioli front forks, Brembo two-piston brake caliper and four-bolt solid disc.

order of the day. The single disc was quite adequate for the speeds attained, and the rear 160mm drum complemented the set-up admirably, permitting fuss-free retardation when required.'

The 35mm Italian-made, Paioli front forks had an adjustable anti-dive mechanism that Frank Westworth described as 'One odd piece of techno-junk.' And the general opinion is that, as with Japanese bikes of the period, the Paioli anti-dive was more of a gimmick than a feature that actually did much. This was corroborated by a 1987 test where the report said: 'I have ridden a bike with it, and a bike without it, and honestly could not tell them apart.'

More of a problem was the price, which at £2,700 at its launch was considered high. Also the Harris G80 came at a time when sensible, everyday bikes were going out of fashion, to be replaced by 'niche' marketing in the motorcycle industry, where buyers were being tempted by race replicas or Paris–Dakar off-roaders, with only MZ and BMW offering bikes similar to the newly reborn Matchless.

The 1987 Harris G80

Engine:	Air-cooled, Rotax sohc four-valve single, with twin exhaust ports, unit construction, belt-driven camshaft
Bore:	89mm
Stroke:	79.4mm
Displacement:	494cc
Compression ratio:	9.2:1
Lubrication:	Dry sump
Ignition:	Electronic, 12-volt
Carburettor:	Dell'Orto 36mm
Primary drive:	Gear
Final drive:	Chain
Gearbox:	Five-speed, foot-change
Frame:	Tubular, full cradle; square-section swinging arm
Front suspension:	Paioli 35mm with anti-dive
Rear suspension:	Swinging arm with twin Paioli shock absorbers
Front brake:	Single Brembo 260mm hydraulically operated disc, Brembo two-piston caliper
Rear brake:	Drum, 160mm; conical hub
Tyres:	Front 100/90H/19; rear 110/90H/18

General Specification

Wheelbase:	54in (1,372mm)
Ground clearance:	6½in (165mm)
Seat height:	31in (787mm)
Fuel tank capacity:	3.3gal (15ltr)
Dry weight:	330lb (150kg)
Maximum power:	N/A
Top speed:	95mph (153km/h)

Matchless Versus Yamaha

In October 1988, *Motorcycle Enthusiast* ran a road-test comparison in which the Harris G80 was pitted against Yamaha's SRX-600 single. The test was headlined 'Near Neighbours', and in many ways this was true: both were large-displacement

One of the Harris machines outside the south Devon factory.

four-stroke singles, and both featured a single overhead camshaft and four valves. They also shared five-speed gearboxes and gear primary drive. But one difference was that the Matchless cost £500 more than the Yamaha and had 114cc less (494 compared to 608cc).

Both the test bikes were privately owned, and not factory-supplied 'test specials'. Furthermore both had worked in their first year of life, spending most of their miles carrying their owners to work in central London. To quote their owners: '[neither] machine is mollycoddled, cleaning being regarded as secondary to maintenance, and polishing being largely ignored.'

One glitch that showed up in the London traffic was that despite its having been freshly serviced, the G80 had a 'notable tendency to stall. Rapid stops and attendant pedal-bashing could result in an impressive spit from the carb and the cessation of mechanical activity.' The tester found this annoying, saying that it 'spoiled the bike's otherwise excellent city manners.' However, it should be noted that the standard air cleaner had been removed during an earlier service and replaced with a K&N filter, and the tester reasoned that this could have caused the stalling. The owner found that if he 'rolled the throttle closed, rather than snapping it shut, then it didn't happen.' And the test G80's tickover was perfect, *Motorcycle Enthusiast* reporting that 'It just chuff-chuffed away happily to itself.'

Both the G80 and the SRX600 were not the best of starters (both test bikes being kickstart only), and on the Harris Matchless the kickstart was on the nearside (left).

One area where the British bike scored heavily was comfort, the tester saying: 'Where the G80 had a big soft seat and upright bars, the SRX had a narrow, short and hard seat, allied to a set of fab-looking, but wrist-straining clip-ons. The two bikes, so similar on paper, are poles apart when ridden.' And although the Yamaha's engine was bigger, it was the Matchless that pulled away from lower engine revs the best.

LEFT: 'Matchless Devon' badge.

BELOW: One of the Harris G80s fitted with a Suzuki GS500 twin-cylinder engine, a very neat conversion snapped by the author at the VMCC Founders Day, Stanford Hall, in July 2002.

The test bike had twin front discs that the *Motorcycle Enthusiast* tester described as 'superb: the bike wears a single disc as standard, but Mark (the owner) prefers the greater confidence provided by the addition of a second. They were very good indeed, and were totally unaffected by the greasy spray from wet streets.'

Actually the biggest difference between the British and Japanese singles was their marketing priorities:

> The Yamaha is styled to appeal in a svelte street racer way, with its grey-painted frame highly visible as it wraps around the big silver engine and smart silver tank and panels. The Matchless is aimed at the rider who is concerned more with his comfort than his street cred – and it succeeds, the big comfortable seat and high bars making for a luxurious riding position.

The same priorities could be seen in the design of the two bikes' exhaust systems. 'The SRX had one of the neatest exhausts around; twin headers empty into a stubby silencer which blats away merrily below and behind the rider's right trotter.' Whereas the G80:

> ...also carried twin headers: these vent into a huge chrome trumpet which looks more like a refugee from the MZ style guide than a British silencer. In keeping with its practical identity, the Matchless exhaust permits the fitting of a sturdy centre stand, while Yamaha riders must be content with just a side stand.

In the summing up of that October 1988 road test comparison, *Motorcycle Enthusiast* found:

> ...Two motorcycles that are designed to use almost identical features in almost completely opposite ways. The Yamaha SRX-600 uses its trial bike-derived big single motor to power a fine scratcher's tool, while the Matchless G80 uses the competition-proved Rotax engine to drive a totally modern bike that has a trad British riding position. Both do their jobs well, and it is up to the buyer to decide where his priorities lie. If you want a sporty posture and flash styling, go for the Yamaha; if you prefer to sit perched above the traffic in comfort aboard a bike with very understated styling, ride a Matchless.

The Harris Matchless G80 was offered with a choice of silver, black or metallic burgundy for the fuel tank and side panels. Chassis components such as frame, swinging arm, stands and chainguard were in black. The mudguards were stainless steel, the headlamp, exhaust and wheel rims chrome-plated.

Harris G80 UK Dealers

Castle Street, Brighton
Bryants, Biggleswade
SRM, South Glamorgan
MD Motorcycles, Wellington, Somerset
Camelford Bike Bits, Camelford, Cornwall
Terry Hobbs Motorcycles, Plymouth
Devimead, Tamworth
Roebuck Motorcycles, Pinner, Middlesex
DD Motorcycles, Maidenhead
Jack Lilley, Shepperton, Middlesex

The End of the Line

Somehow the Harris G80 never quite made it. Even though the bike was fortunate to carry a famous marque name and model number, it was not exciting enough to attract enough customers away from the opposition, which was mainly Japanese, and it was too expensive to worry the likes of MZ or Jawa/CZ. Then again for £2,700 (virtually £6,000 at 2004 values) prospective classic bike owners thought they would rather have an original Plumstead model in their garage. So ultimately the entire project has to be judged a failure – even though in many ways the Harris G80 is a good motorcycle. Even so, it does have the honour of being the last production motorcycle to carry the famous Matchless 'M' badge on its tank sides, thus retaining a special place for itself in motorcycling history.

Index